"LE FRANÇAIS SANS FRONTIÈRES"
Collection dirigée par Christian Baylon
Maître assistant de linguistique à l'université de Montpell..

MICHÈLE VERDELHAN
Assistante en linguistique générale
à l'université de Montpellier.

MICHEL VERDELHAN
Professeur à l'École Normale
de Montpellier.

PHILIPPE DOMINIQUE
Agrégé de l'université
Maître assistant à l'université d'Aix-en-Provence.

A Contemporary Program for
Communicating in French

Illustrations Gérard BOUYSSE

NATIONAL TEXTBOOK COMPANY • *Lincolnwood, Illinois U.S.A.*

Documents—Written language.
You will be introduced to many types and forms of written language (letters, notes, ads, passports, tickets, instructions, menus, recipes, and more). These authentic documents reflecting the character of daily life in France were chosen to relate to the theme of the lesson in which they appear.

Vocabulaire, grammaire—The meanings of words and how to use them.
Here you will learn the vocabulary and grammar necessary for the written and oral exercises in each lesson.

Exercices écrits—Writing exercises.
You will start at the beginning of the book by filling in blanks with appropriate words and phrases. Then you will restructure sentences or create new sentences based on a given model. Finally, you will make use of previously learned material to write your own sentences.

Structures orales—Spoken French.
The grammatical structures presented orally in the lesson are presented in chart form. Repeating the sequences recorded on the cassettes will help you master these structures.

Prise de parole—Your turn to speak.
These exercises are designed to help you acquire fluency and spontaneity in French conversation through oral activities that range from simple questions and answers to role-playing and free speaking. Communication may take place as conversations among students, between students and teacher, or in the form of commentaries by individual students on the documents, photos, or humorous drawings in the text.

With its integrated approach to language learning, *Sans Frontières 1* will help you develop a sound foundation in the French language. It promotes skills that will allow you to communicate naturally *and* effectively throughout the French-speaking world.

1 1.1 Jacques Martineau, pianiste

* Je m'appelle Jacques Martineau.
  J'ai vingt-cinq ans.
* Je suis pianiste.

* Je suis français.
  Je suis né à Marseille.
* J'habite à Paris, place de la Contrescarpe.

Je m'appelle Jacques Martineau.

J'habite à Paris, place de la Contrescarpe.

[a]

Je suis né à Marseille.

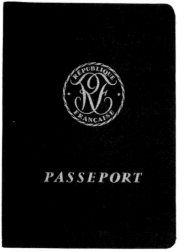

NOM *Surname*	MARTINEAU
PRÉNOM *Christian Name*	Jacques François Pierre
NÉ LE *Date of birth*	12 février 1957
A *Place of birth*	Marseille
Nationalité	française
PROFESSION	Pianiste / musicien
DOMICILE *Address*	2 place de la Contrescarpe, Paris

PASSEPORT

②
Henri DUVAL ①
Journaliste
③
④ 15 rue de la Liberté
75015 PARIS

1	nom	Il s'appelle Henri Duval.
2	prénom	
3	profession	Il est journaliste.
4	adresse/ domicile	Il habite à Paris, 15 rue de la Liberté.

VOCABULAIRE

les professions :

journaliste
pianiste
médecin
infirmièr(e)
dentiste
secrétaire
architecte
étudiant(e)

les nombres :

1 un	8 huit	14 quatorze	20 vingt	27 vingt-sept
2 deux	9 neuf	15 quinze	21 vingt et un	28 vingt-huit
3 trois	10 dix	16 seize	22 vingt-deux	29 vingt-neuf
4 quatre			23 vingt-trois	
5 cinq		17 dix-sept	24 vingt-quatre	30 trente
6 six	11 onze	18 dix-huit	25 vingt-cinq	31 trente et un
7 sept	12 douze	19 dix-neuf	26 vingt-six	40 quarante
	13 treize			50 cinquante

(voir tableau complet en bilan p. 33)

GRAMMAIRE

1. le genre :

féminin   masculin

Elle est chinoise

Il est mexicain

NOM	(en) FRANCE	(au) JAPON	(en) CHINE	(au) MEXIQUE	(en) ALLEMAGNE	(en) TUNISIE
ADJECTIF Masculin	français	japonais	chinois	mexicain	allemand	tunisien
Féminin	française	japonaise	chinoise	mexicaine	allemande	tunisienne

2. Les verbes

sujet	verbe	
je	suis	allemand
	m'appelle	Kurt
j'	ai	28 ans
	habite	à Bonn

première personne

sujet	verbe	
il	est	américain
	s'appelle	Dan
elle	a	30 ans
	habite	à Tokyo

troisième personne

Marie CAMARAT
Infirmière

7 avenue Bosquet
75007 PARIS

1. *Recopiez et complétez :* (*)

Elle s'appelle . . . .

Elle est . . . .

Elle . . . . *à Paris* . . . .

Henri-Alexandre FABRE
· Architecte

2 boulevard de Toulon
13100 AIX-EN-PROVENCE

Il . . . .

. . . . *est* . . . .

. . . . *2* . . . .

(*) *Attention !* Tous les exercices écrits doivent être faits sur un cahier. *N'écrivez pas sur le livre !*

FICHE D'INSCRIPTION

NOM ... GORETTA

Prénom ... Angela

Né(e) le ... 16 - 3 - 58

A ... Napoli

Nationalité ... italienne

Profession ... Secrétaire

Domicile 18 via Cavour
... TORINO -

Sans Frontières

2. Recopiez et complétez :

Elle s'appelle . . . .

. . . .

Elle est née

à . . . .

Elle est . . . .

Elle est . . . .

Elle habite . . . .

3. Recopiez et complétez votre fiche :

NOM . . . .

Prénom . . . .

Né(e) le . . . .

A . . . .

Nationalité . . . .

Profession . . . .

Domicile . . . .

4. Recopiez et complétez

Je m'appelle . . . .

. . . .

Je suis né (e) . . . .

. . . .

. . . .

. . . .

5. Recopiez et remplissez selon le modèle en utilisant : *acteur, actrice, président, américain (e), français (e)*

Nom :   Charlie Chaplin   acteur   américain

Nom :   . . . .

Nom :   . . . .

Nom :   . . . .

6

Nom :			Profession :			Domicile :	
je	m'	appelle **Anna**	je	suis	**infirmière**	j'	habite à **Paris**
il	s'	appelle **Hans**	il	est	**médecin**	il	habite à **Oslo**
elle	s'	appelle **Carmen**	elle	est	**étudiante**	elle	habite à **Londres**

● *Présentez-les :*

Jean
LEBOURGEOIS
Canadien
Architecte
Montréal

Helmut KRANTZ
Allemand
Acteur
Stuttgart

Yoko OZAWA
Japonaise
Étudiante
Kyoto

Carmen RIVERA
Mexicaine
Journaliste
Acapulco

*Présentez-votre voisin
ou votre voisine :*

Il/ Elle s'appelle . . . .
. . . .

Présentez-vous :

Je m'appelle . . . .

. . . .

● **Mimez des professions.**

La classe essaie de deviner :

il est . . .

elle est . .

1.2 Bonjour, Monsieur Martineau

(dix heures)

✳ Jacques : Bonjour, madame Lenoir, bonjour, monsieur Lenoir. Ça va ?

Le concierge : Ça va. Et vous, monsieur Martineau ?

Jacques : Ça va. S'il vous plaît monsieur Lenoir, quelle heure est-il ?

Le concierge : Il est dix heures !

Jacques : Merci !

✳ Jacques : Bonjour, monsieur l'agent.

L'agent : Bonjour, monsieur Martineau.

✳ Jacques : Salut, François. Comment ça va ?

François : Salut, Jacques. Ça va. Et toi ?
(le coiffeur)

Jacques : Ça va !

(Dix-sept heures)

✳ Jacques : Au revoir, Joseph. A demain.

Joseph Lorentz : Au revoir, Jacques.
(Le chef d'orchestre) A demain.

✳ Jacques : Bonsoir, madame Lenoir.

La concierge : Bonsoir, monsieur Martineau.

(vingt-trois heures trente)

✳ Le présentateur : Il est vingt-trois heures trente. Bonne nuit, madame, bonne nuit, mademoiselle, bonne nuit, monsieur.

[wa]

Jacques dit bonsoir à François, le coiffeur.

Salut, François, ça va? Ça va, et toi?

Au revoir, madame Lenoir.

7.00	Bonjour la France
8.00	**INFORMATIONS**
10.00	Il s'appelle Don Juan
11.15	Un, deux, trois...
12.00	Midi magazine
13.00	**INFORMATIONS**
14.30	Profession : architecte
16.00	Mexico, Mexico
17.00	Salut !
19.00	**INFORMATIONS**
20.00	A l'Opéra
21.30	Bonsoir, Paris
22.45	Ça va ? et vous ?
23.30	Bonne nuit

PLAN 1
10 heures - Dans l'escalier
Jacques et le concierge :
Il dit bonjour au concierge

PLAN 2
10 heures 05 - Devant la maison
Jacques et l'agent de police :
Il dit bonjour à l'agent

PLAN 3
10 heures 10 - Dans la rue
Jacques et le coiffeur :
Il dit bonjour au coiffeur

VOCABULAIRE

● **le lieu :**

Il est **dans** la rue, **devant** la maison.
Elle est dans la maison.

la rue - l'escalier - la maison...

● **l'heure :**

Quelle heure est-il ? Il est ...

a) neuf heures

b) onze heures et quart
(quinze)

c) sept heures et demie
(trente).

d) deux heures moins le quart
(une heure quarante-cinq)

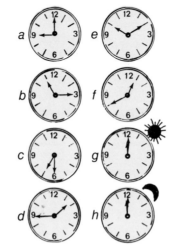

e) dix heures dix

f) une heure moins vingt
(midi quarante)

g) midi
(douze heures)

h) minuit...
(zéro heure)

● **les salutations :**

Bonjour
Bonsoir
Salut
Ça va ?
Ça va, et toi ?
Ça va, et vous ?

Au revoir
A demain
A bientôt
Salut
Bonsoir
Bonne nuit

GRAMMAIRE

1. les articles (définis)

	masculin	féminin	masculin ou féminin
	le coiffeur domicile	**la** concierge maison	**l'** agent - étudiante escalier - adresse
Il dit bonjour...	...**au** coiffeur	...**à la** concierge	...**à l'** agent - étudiante

a) invariable : le pianiste - le concierge - le secrétaire - le journaliste
la pianiste - la concierge - la secrétaire - la journaliste

b) variable : l'étudiant - le musicien - l'acteur - le coiffeur
l'étudiante - la musicienne - l'actrice - la coiffeuse

c) attention ! le médecin - l'ingénieur - le professeur - le chef d'orchestre
(la femme médecin - la femme ingénieur...)

3. la coordination : ET

Monsieur **et** madame Lenoir - Jacques **et** François - Le nom **et** le prénom.

1. *Écrivez l'heure selon le modèle :*

8 h 40 = a) huit heures quarante b) neuf heures moins vingt
10 h 30 - 6 h 45 - 13 h 15 - 0 h 10 - 21 h 25 - 23 h 50

2. *Choisissez : le - la - l'*

président	journaliste	architecte	rue	profession
agent de police	coiffeuse	étudiant	opéra	nom
acteur	secrétaire	médecin	maison	domicile
infirmière	concierge	coiffeur	escalier	prénom

3. *Recopiez et reliez :*

à l' •   • concierge
                               • coiffeur
Jacques dit bonjour   au •   • étudiant
                               • agent
                               • journaliste
à la •   • étudiante

4. *Regardez la bande dessinée p. 8 et complétez :*

Plan 3 ...... dix ...... rue.
Jacques et ...... coiffeur.
(Il dit ...... coiffeur.)

Plan 4 ...... heures. ...... l'opéra.
Jacques ...... chef d'orchestre.
(Il .... au revoir ...... chef d'orchestre.)

Plan 5 ...... escalier ...... et ...... concierge.
(Il dit ...... concierge.)

Je	suis		
Il		dans	l'escalier
Elle	est	devant	la maison

Je	dis	bonjour	au	médecin
Il		bonsoir	à l'	infirmière
Elle	dit	au revoir	à la	concierge
Jacques		bonne nuit	à	François
				monsieur Lenoir

- **Décrivez les dessins ou les photos**

  en employant *il est ... (+ profession)*
  et il est ... devant, à côté, dans ... (+ lieu)

- **Décrivez et faites parler les personnages**

  en employant *il est ...... heures. Il/Elle dit ...... bonjour/bonsoir ......*

- **Saluez votre voisin ou votre voisine**

  Demandez/Donnez l'heure à votre voisin ou votre voisine

1.3   Le rendez-vous

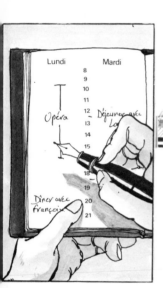 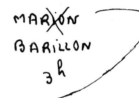

La journaliste :	Allô ? 707.54.15 ? Jacques Martineau ?
Jacques :	Oui.
La journaliste :	Bonjour, monsieur Martineau. Je suis journaliste. Est-ce que vous êtes libre lundi pour une interview ?
Jacques :	Non, lundi je ne suis pas libre. Je travaille.
La journaliste :	Et mardi ?
Jacques :	Oui, mardi je vais à l'Opéra à 5 heures et demie, mais je suis libre de 3 h à 5 h. Vous pouvez venir à 3 h ?
* La journaliste :	D'accord. Rendez-vous à 3 h. Je m'appelle Vivienne Barillon.
Jacques :	Marion ?
La journaliste :	Non, Barillon.
Jacques :	Vous pouvez épeler, s'il vous plaît ?
La journaliste :	B-A-R-I-L-L-O-N.
Jacques :	D'accord : Barillon.
La journaliste :	Au revoir, monsieur Martineau et merci beaucoup.
Jacques :	Au revoir, mademoiselle

[i]

Vivienne Barillon est journaliste.

Jacques est libre mardi après-midi.

Vous êtes libre lundi ?

INTONATION : Vous êtes libre ?

Oui, mardi je suis libre

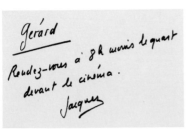

Gérard
Rendez-vous à 8 h moins le quart
devant le cinéma.
Jacques

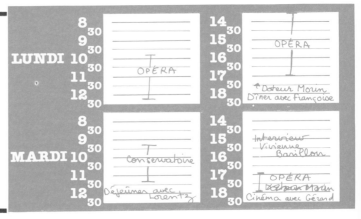

	8:30			14:30	
LUNDI	9:30			15:30	OPÉRA
	10:30	OPÉRA		16:30	
	11:30			17:30	Docteur Morin
	12:30			18:30	Dîner avec Françoise

	8:30			14:30	
MARDI	9:30			15:30	Interview Vivienne Barillon
	10:30	Conservatoire		16:30	
	11:30			17:30	OPÉRA Docteur Morin
	12:30	Déjeuner avec Lorentz		18:30	Cinéma avec Gérard

VOCABULAIRE

- **les jours :**

lundi, mardi, mercredi, jeudi, vendredi, samedi, dimanche.

- **les moments de la journée :**

matin, après-midi, soir.

- **les activités de la journée :**

travailler, déjeuner, dîner, aller au cinéma, à l'opéra...

- **le lieu :**

chez le docteur, chez la journaliste, chez l'architecte..., au cinéma, à la radio, à l'aéroport, à l'opéra

au restaurant,   **chez** le coiffeur.

GRAMMAIRE

1. les verbes

		DÉJEUNER	DINER	TRAVAILLER
1re personne	je	déjeune	dîne	travaille
2e personne	tu	déjeunes	dînes	travailles
	vous	déjeunez	dînez	travaillez
3e personne	il/elle	déjeune	dîne	travaille

	ÊTRE	ALLER	POUVOIR	DIRE	VENIR
je	suis	vais	peux	dis	viens
tu	es	vas	peux	dis	viens
vous	êtes	allez	pouvez	dites	venez
il/elle	est	va	peut	dit	vient

2. la négation : NE...PAS

Je **ne** suis **pas** libre.
Je **ne** travaille **pas**.
Je **n'**ai **pas** vingt ans.

3. l'interrogation (la question) : EST-CE QUE ?

(Est-ce que) tu déjeunes chez Pierre **?**
— Oui, je déjeune chez Pierre.
— Non, je ne déjeune pas chez Pierre.

4. verbe + verbe (à l'infinitif)

Est-ce que tu peux venir ?   Vous pouvez épeler ?   Il peut venir dîner mardi.

1. *Répondez aux questions*

Est-ce que Jacques est pianiste ?   — *Oui, il est pianiste.*
Est-ce que Vivienne est étudiante ?   — *Non, elle n'est pas étudiante, elle est journaliste.*

Est-ce que Vivienne travaille à l'Opéra ? . . . .

Est-ce que Jacques habite à Paris ? . . . .

Est-ce que Vivienne s'appelle MARION ? . . . .

2. *Mettez les verbes à la forme qui convient*

*Est-ce que vous (**aller**) à l'Opéra ? Je ne (**aller**) pas chez le dentiste le samedi.*
*Vous (**pouvoir**) venir mardi. Comment ça (**aller**) ? Est-ce que tu (**pouvoir**) venir dîner lundi ?*
*Vous (**être**) infirmière ?*

3. *Mettez en ordre*

est Jacques lundi libre est-ce que ?   libre n'est Vivienne pas lundi matin
ne pas le je mardi travaille   cinéma pouvez au venir vous ?

4. Recopiez et complétez les questions

Jacques ne travaille pas le mardi.

— *Est-ce* .... *lundi ?*

Il n'est pas libre le matin.

— .... *l'après-midi ?*

Vivienne ne peut pas aller chez Jacques.

— .... *Jacques* .... *Vivienne ?*

Il ne peut pas venir à 3 heures.

— .... *3 heures et demie ?*

5. Sur le modèle : *« Rendez-vous à 8 h devant le cinéma. »*
donnez des rendez-vous (par écrit) à votre voisin ou à votre voisine.

Est-ce que	tu vous	es êtes	architecte médecin		Oui	je	(ne)	suis	...
Est-ce qu'	il elle	est	étudiant(e) journaliste	?	Non	il elle	(n')	est	pas ... ...

Est-ce que	tu vous	viens venez	à l'opéra au cinéma		Oui, ...
Est-ce qu'	il elle	vient	chez le coiffeur au restaurant	?	Non, ...

Est-ce que	je tu	peux peux		déjeuner	au restaurant		Oui...
Est-ce qu'	il elle	peut	venir	habiter travailler	à la maison chez Jacques	?	Non...

● **Regardez l'emploi du temps de Françoise Lebourg, étudiante**

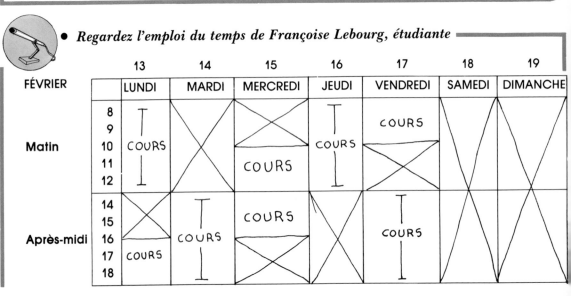

FÉVRIER		13 LUNDI	14 MARDI	15 MERCREDI	16 JEUDI	17 VENDREDI	18 SAMEDI	19 DIMANCHE
Matin	8 9 10 11 12	COURS		COURS	COURS	COURS		
Après-midi	14 15 16 17 18	COURS	COURS	COURS		COURS		

16

Dialoguez

Est-ce que Françoise est libre le lundi matin ?
— Non, elle n'est pas libre.

Est-ce que Françoise travaille le lundi après-midi ?
— Elle ne travaille pas de 14 h à 16 h. Elle travaille de 16 h à 18 h.

Mardi ? Mercredi ? ...

● **Regardez l'agenda de Jacques p. 14. Posez des questions** *(avec ou sans « Est-ce que... »).*

Est-ce que Jacques travaille à 8 h ?
Jacques déjeune avec Vivienne ?

. . . .

● **Épelez** *(cf. tableau bilan p. 33)* SNCF USA URSS SOS

    votre nom
    le nom de votre rue... et les noms de ces rues de Paris.

● **Jeu du téléphone**

Françoise Lebourg, étudiante, téléphone au Dᴿ Morin (nº 954.13.23)
pour un rendez-vous.

Imaginez le dialogue en employant :

. . . . . . *épelez* . . . . . . *rendez-vous* . . . . . . *ne travaille pas* . . . . . .
Le docteur donne un rendez-vous mercredi à 17 h.

● **Posez des questions à votre voisin ou à votre voisine :**

Est-ce que { *tu es* / *vous êtes* } *libre, jeudi à six heures ?*

Est-ce que { *tu travailles* . . . . ?
vous travaillez . . . . ?

1.4 L'interview

* *Jacques :* Bonjour, mademoiselle.

Vivienne : Bonjour, monsieur Martineau.

Jacques : Par ici...

* Est-ce que vous voulez un café ?

Vivienne : Volontiers.

* *Jacques :* Voulez-vous une cigarette ?

Vivienne : Non merci. Je ne fume pas.

* Je peux commencer ?

Jacques : D'accord.

Vivienne : Vous êtes musicien, vous aimez Bach, Mozart, Beethoven.

Jacques : Bien sûr. Et aussi Gerschwin, Bartok, ...

Vivienne : Aimez-vous aussi le jazz ?

Jacques : Oui, beaucoup.

* *Vivienne :* Et le folk ?

Jacques : Un peu.

* *Vivienne :* Le disco ?

Jacques : Pas du tout.

* *Vivienne :* Qu'est-ce que vous faites le week-end?

Jacques : Je joue un peu au tennis et au football, mais je préfère lire et écouter la radio.

Vivienne : Vous écoutez... France-Musique ?

Jacques : Bien sûr !

Bonjour. Voulez-vous un café ?

Oh ! oui. J'aime beaucoup le café.

Aimez-vous le jazz ? Oui, beaucoup.

Le week-end, je joue au tennis et j'écoute la radio.

VACANCES 3 000

questionnaire :

Nom .... DUPRÉ ....
Prénom .... François ....
Adresse 13 Rue de Paris (EVRY) ...
Date de naissance . 6 mars 1946 ....

Vous aimez voyager un peu .... ☐
        beaucoup .... ☒
        pas beaucoup .... ☐

Vous préférez la mer .... ☒
     la montagne .... ☐
     la campagne .... ☐

Vous aimez sortir un peu .... ☐
        beaucoup .... ☐
Vous détestez « sortir » .... ☐
Vous préférez :
le théâtre .... ☐
le cinéma .... ☒

Chère Maman,

François est photographe. Il adore voyager. Il parle anglais, espagnol et italien. Il adore la musique et le cinéma. Il aime beaucoup la montagne. Il déteste la campagne, il adore la mer.

les promenades .... ☐
les visites .... ☐
les week-ends à la campagne .... ☐
les concerts .... ☒
les conférences .... ☐
les expositions et musées .... ☐
les spectacles sportifs .... ☐
le sport (pratiqué) .... ☐
le restaurant .... ☐
la danse .... ☐
les réceptions .... ☐
ou : .... ☐

VOCABULAIRE

● **les sentiments :**
aimer, adorer, préférer, détester...

● **les degrés :**
un peu; beaucoup, pas du tout

● **les activités :**
manger, boire, dormir, lire, fumer...
écouter la radio, regarder la télé,
jouer au football...

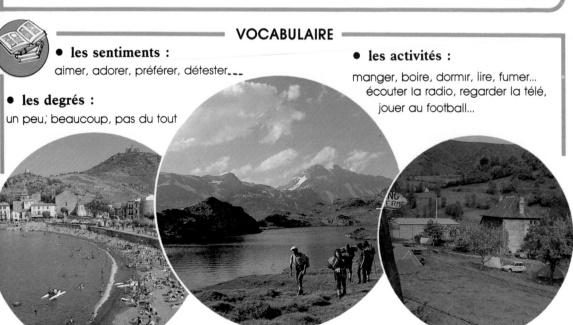

● **lieux (de vacances) :** la mer, la montagne, la campagne.

GRAMMAIRE

1. les articles (indéfinis)

masculin	féminin
un café étudiant	**une** cigarette étudiante

2. les verbes

	FAIRE	VOULOIR	DORMIR
je	fais	veux	dors
tu	fais	veux	dors
vous	faites	voulez	dormez
il/elle	fait	veut	dort

3. le nom complément d'objet

Il veut **un café**.
Elle aime **un photographe**.

4. l'interrogation

a) **Est-ce que** vous voulez une cigarette ?
b) Vous voulez une cigarette **?** *(intonation)*
c) Voulez-**vous** une cigarette ? *(inversion)*

Qu'est-ce que...? Quel...? Quelle...?
Qu'est-ce que vous faites le week-end ?
Qu'est-ce qu'il fait ?
Quel jour es-tu libre ?
Quelle heure est-il ?

1. *Répondez par écrit aux questions*

— *Aimez-vous lire ? voyager ? boire ? manger ? dormir ? jouer au football ? jouer au tennis ?*

— *Préférez-vous la mer, la campagne ou la montagne ?*

— *Préférez-vous aller au cinéma, au théâtre ou au concert ?*

— *Préférez-vous regarder la télévision, écouter la radio, ou lire ?*

2. *Transformez en vous aidant du tableau*

aime un peu	+		n'aime pas beaucoup	–	
beaucoup	++		pas du tout	– –	
adore	+++		déteste	– – –	

Joseph Lorentz, chef d'orchestre :
lire (+), Beethoven (+++), le football (−), la radio (++) = Joseph Lorentz aime lire,
il adore Beethoven...

Mme Lenoir, concierge :
écouter la radio (++), regarder la télévision (+ ++), aller au cinéma (+++), jazz (− −),
l'opéra (++), dormir (+), le café (+++)

3. *Et vous, qu'est-ce que vous aimez, qu'est-ce que vous n'aimez pas ?*

tu vous il	veux voulez veut	une cigarette un café dormir	?	Est-ce que... Est-ce qu'...	?

elle il vous tu	(n')	aime aime aimez aimes	un peu beaucoup pas pas du tout	le café, la télé... boire, fumer... écouter la radio aller au cinéma	?	**Oui,** . . . . . **Non,** . . . . .

- ***Qu'est-ce qu'il fait le week-end? Décrivez.***

Interrogez votre voisin ou votre voisine
sur son week-end.

Qu'est-ce que vous faites/tu fais le week-end?

- ***Jeu de mime***

Interrogez votre voisin ou votre voisine sur ses goûts.
Traduisez ses mimiques :

Vous aimez l'Opéra?
il (elle) n'aime pas l'Opéra
il (elle) déteste...
il (elle) adore...

- **Faites parler les personnages en employant**

  il aime, n'aime pas, adore, déteste...

  Donnez votre avis : *J'aime un peu, beaucoup..., je déteste...*

1.5 La répétition

SALLE PLEYEL

Vendredi 4 Novembre à 20h30

MOZART
concerto en mi pour piano
o
BERLIOZ
symphonie fantastique

Orchestre : LORENTZ
Direction : Josef LORENTZ
Piano : Jacques MARTINEAU

Ici Vivienne Barillon. Je suis à la salle Pleyel pour une répétition de l'orchestre Josef Lorentz.
Au programme, il y a des œuvres de Berlioz et Mozart.
Les musiciens arrivent. Ils disent bonjour au chef d'orchestre. Josef Lorentz est grand, brun, mince. Je ne vois pas le pianiste !

✶ Ah, il arrive ! Jacques Martineau est souriant, sympathique...

✶ Et voici deux jeunes violonistes. Elles sont en retard ! Josef Lorentz n'est pas content !

✶ « — Mesdemoiselles, vous êtes prêtes ?

✶ Mesdames messieurs, s'il vous plaît, nous pouvons commencer ? »

LES LIAISONS

Elle est à la salle Pleyel pour une répétition.

Les deux violonistes sont en retard. Elles arrivent.

Mesdemoiselles, vous êtes prêtes ?

CHORALE SAINT-THOMAS D'AQUIN
Dir. : NICOLE POMMERET

22 - 24
OCTOBRE
à 21 heures

SALLE
PLEYEL

RECITAL DU PIANISTE

MIGUEL ANGEL
ESTRELLA

SAMEDI
24
OCTOBRE
à 20 h 30

HAENDEL - BEETHOVEN - DEBUSSY - CHOPIN

EGLISE
SAINT-MERRI

SEXTUOR Jeanne LORIOD

CAVEAU DE LA BOLEE
LE DIMANCHE à 22 heures
THE SESSION
JAZZ MUSIC
25, r. de l'Hirondelle (pl. St-Michel) 354-62-20

JAZZ UNITÉ

| du 3 juin au 5 juin | CHRIS MAC GREGOR |
| du 6 juin au 9 juin | SAM RIVERS QUARTET |

«LES QUATRE TEMPS»
LA DEFENSE TEL. 776 44 26
Restaurant ouvert jusqu'à 2h du matin

VENDREDI 25 SEPTEMBRE

Th. des Champs-Elysées, 15, av. Montaigne. 563-07-96. - 20h30 : ORCHESTRE DE PARIS, direct. D. Barenboïm. Beethoven : symphonies n° 3 et 4. Pl. 40 à 90 F.
Institut Polonais, 31, rue Jean-Goujon. - 20h30 : Récital de piano par Jolanta BRACHEL. Œuvres de Chopin, Allain, Szymanowski, Liszt, Rachmaninov, Scriabine.

LUNDI 28 SEPTEMBRE

Gaveau, 25, rue La Boétie, 563-20-30. - 21h : Récital de piano par Daniel VARSANO. Sonates de Beethoven. Pl. 40 à 80 F, réd. 35 et 50 F, étud. 30 F.

MERCREDI 23 SEPTEMBRE

Sainte Chapelle, bd du Palais, loc. 260-31-84. - 21h : Récital de guitare par Ichiro SUZUKI. Œuvres de Mozart, Turina, Bach. Pl. 30 à 65 F, réd. 30 et 45 F.

VOCABULAIRE

● **la description physique**

grand - petit   gros - mince
grande - petite   grosse - mince
jeune - vieux   brun - blond - roux
jeune - vieille   brune - blonde - rousse...

● **la description psychologique**

gai/souriant - triste   content - mécontent
gaie/souriante - triste   contente - mécontente
sympathique - antipathique   gentil - méchant
sympathique - antipathique   gentille - méchante...

● **la musique (instruments et musiciens)**

piano - pianiste
flûte - flûtiste
violoncelle - violoncelliste
violon - violoniste
trompette - trompettiste
guitare - guitariste
harpe - harpiste...

GRAMMAIRE

1. les verbes

$$\overline{\text{VOIR}}$$

singulier	1ʳᵉ personne	je vois	nous voyons	1ʳᵉ personne	*pluriel*
	2ᵉ personne	tu vois	vous voyez	2ᵉ personne	
	3ᵉ personne	il/elle voit	ils/elles voient	3ᵉ personne	

	ÊTRE	POUVOIR	VOULOIR	ALLER	VENIR
nous	sommes	pouvons	voulons	allons	venons
vous	êtes	pouvez	voulez	allez	venez
ils/elles	sont	peuvent	veulent	vont	viennent

2. le pluriel des articles (définis et indéfinis)

le - la - **les**
un - une - **des**

les musiciens de l'orchestre Lorentz

un musicien

le musicien Jacques Martineau

des musiciens

		masculin	féminin
article défini	singulier	le musicien l'infirmier	la musicienne l'infirmière
	pluriel	les musiciens les infirmiers	les musiciennes les infirmières

ATTENTION	**Il dit bonjour...**	au musicien à l'infirmier aux musiciens aux infirmiers	à la musicienne à l'infirmière aux musiciennes aux infirmières

article indéfini	singulier	un musicien	une musicienne
	pluriel	des musiciens	des musiciennes

3. les adjectifs qualificatifs

	masculin	féminin
singulier	content gai jeune	contente gaie jeune
pluriel	contents gais jeunes	contentes gaies jeunes

sujet	verbe	attribut
Il	est	souriant
Elle	est	souriante
Ils	sont	souriants
Elles	sont	souriantes

nom	épithète
un homme	brun
une femme	brune
des hommes	bruns
des femmes	brunes

4. les présentatifs

Voici Jacques Martineau
Voilà le chef d'orchestre
Au programme, **Il y a** des œuvres de Bach

5. le complément du nom

des œuvres	**de Mozart**
une répétition	**de l'orchestre**

1. Regardez les documents p. 24. Recopiez et complétez

Lundi 28 septembre . . . . un récital de . . . . . . à la salle . . . . . . à . . . . . . heures. Au programme . . . . œuvres de Beethoven. . . . . . . 23 . . . . . . à la Sainte Chapelle . . . . . . heures. Au programme . . . . . . Mozart, Turina, Bach. Vendredi 25 . . . . . . à l'institut polonais . . . . . .

2. Transformez

Elle s'appelle . . . . . . Elle est . . . . . . Elle a . . . . . .
Elle aime . . . . . . Elle cherche . . . . . .

> Anne Laure, 25 ans, brune, gaie, infirmière, aime tennis et musique. Cherche homme, 40 ans, blond, grand et gentil, pour mariage.

3. Décrivez-vous *Je m'appelle . . . . . . Je suis . . . . . . J'ai . . . . . . J'aime . . . . . .*

4. Présentez-vous dans un texte d'annonce

Est-ce que	Vivienne Jacques est le chef les étudiants les musiciens sont	content(s) contente(s) sympathique(s) gai(s) gaie(s)	? Oui, ... Non, ...

Est-ce que	je suis tu es il/elle est nous sommes vous êtes ils/elles sont	blond[s] blonde[s] petit(s) petite(s) mince(s) jeune(s)	? **Non, ...**

● **Regardez les programmes page 24 et faites parler les personnages**

a. — *Qu'est-ce que vous faites lundi ?*
— *Nous allons à* . . . .
— *Qu'est-ce que vous allez écouter ?*
— *Nous allons écouter* . . . .
— *Qu'est-ce qu'il y a au programme ?*
— *Il y a des œuvres de* . . . .
b. . . . . . . *tu* . . . . . . *mercredi ?*
c. . . . . . . *elles* . . . . . . *vendredi ?*
d. . . . . . . *ils* . . . . . . *dimanche ?*

(Lundi ? — salle gaveau. — Ste chapelle — Mercredi ? — vendredi ? — Institut polonais — dimanche ? — caveau de la bolée)

● **Vous invitez votre voisin ou votre voisine à venir à un concert.**

Vous :   *Il y a un concert samedi soir à* . . . .
        Tu viens ?   *Vous venez* . . . . ?
        Tu veux venir . . . . ?   *Vous voulez* . . . . ?
        Est-ce que tu peux . . . . ?   *Est-ce que vous* . . . . ?

Lui/Elle : *D'accord, je suis libre. Qu'est-ce qu'il y a au programme ?* . . . .

ou :   *Non, je ne peux pas. Je ne suis pas libre.*
        (Non, nous ne pouvons pas. Nous ne sommes . . . . *)*
        Je vais au cinéma/ théâtre/ restaurant avec . . . .
        (Nous allons . . . . *)*

● **Décrivez les personnages** *(en utilisant grand-petit, jeune-vieux, gai-triste* . . . . *)*

● **Décrivez votre voisin ou votre voisine**

27

BILAN

A. Tests

1. Recopiez et complétez

Miloud habite . . . Tunisie ; il est . . . .
Jack habite . . . Amérique ; il est . . . .
Klaus habite . . . Allemagne ; il est . . . .
Dolores habite ; Mexique ; elle est . . . .
Lin Chan Ping habite . . . Chine ; elle est . . . .

Exemple :
*Maria Beatriz habite **au** Portugal ; elle est **portugaise**.*

2. Présentez-les

Jean, 24 ans, étudiant, né à Lyon ; 5, rue Auguste-Blanqui, Lyon.
Sandra, 30 ans, dentiste, née à Rome ; 21, via Torino, Milan.
Manuel, 41 ans, architecte, né à Madrid ; 3 Calle San Fernando, Madrid.
Ursula, 35 ans, secrétaire, née à Bonn ; 58, Alexanderstrasse, Stuttgart.
Éva, 45 ans, médecin, née à Upsala ; Kungsgatan 37, Bergen.

Exemple : François a 28 ans, il est photographe, il est né à Marseille.
Il habite : 27, boulevard de l'Hôpital à Paris.

3. Qu'est-ce qu'ils disent ? Choisissez

9 h 15 — *Salut, madame.*
        — *Bonjour, madame.*
        — *Bonne nuit, madame.*
22 h   — *Ça va ?*
        — *Salut.*
        — *Bonne nuit.*
20 h   — *Bonjour.*
        — *Au revoir.*
        — *Bonsoir.*
10 h   — *Bonjour, monsieur.*
        — *Au revoir, Pierre.*
        — *Ça va, Pierre.*
23 h   — *Salut.*
        — *Bonne nuit.*
        — *Ça va ?*

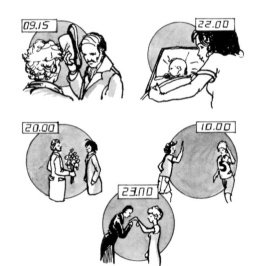

4. Emploi de LE, LA, L', LES : Recopiez et complétez

Elle adore . . . . . . campagne.
Je dîne avec . . . . . . architecte.
. . . . . . infirmière est en retard.
Vous aimez . . . . . . café ?
. . . . . . musiciens aiment . . . . . . musique.
. . . . . . hôtels sont vides.
La concierge est dans . . . . . . escaliers.
Jacques aime . . . . . . jazz.
Il n'est pas content : . . . . . . musiciens ne sont pas prêts.

5. Emploi de AU, A LA, A L', AUX : Recopiez et complétez

Josef Lorentz habite ...... hôtel.
Elle ne va pas beaucoup ...... cinéma.
Tu viens ...... aéroport ?
Les musiciens vont ...... répétitions.
J'aime beaucoup aller ...... montagne.

6. Emploi de UN/UNE, LE/LA : Recopiez et complétez

Veux-tu ...... cigarette ?
...... présentateur dit bonsoir.
Vous ne regardez pas ...... télévision ?
Jacques a ...... répétition à 17 heures.
Au revoir, je vais chez ...... coiffeur.

7. Emploi de A, AU, CHEZ : Recopiez et complétez

Je n'aime pas aller ...... l'hôtel.
Le président du Venezuela arrive à 17 heures ...... l'aéroport de Roissy.
Le week-end, ils adorent aller ...... la campagne.
Vous pouvez venir ...... Pierre à 10 heures ?
Est-ce que vous voulez venir ...... théâtre ?
Je ne suis pas libre samedi matin, je vais ...... le coiffeur.
Elle a un rendez-vous ...... le dentiste à 5 heures.
Est-ce que vous aimer aller ...... cinéma ?
Elle n'aime pas aller ...... restaurant.
Il est ...... le médecin.

8. Mettez le verbe à la forme qui convient

— *Qu'est-ce qu'elles (**faire**) le week-end ? — Elles (**aller**) à la campagne.*
— *Est-ce que tu (**pouvoir**) venir ? — Non, je ne (**être**) pas libre.*
— *Est-ce qu'elles (**lire**) beaucoup ? — Oh, oui. Elles (**adorer**) lire.*
— *Vous (**travailler**) à Paris ? — Oh oui, nous (**être**) étudiantes ici.*
— *Est-ce que Paul et Martine (**venir**) avec nous ? — Non, ils ne sont pas libres : ils (**travailler**).*

9. Trouvez la bonne réponse

— **Vous habitez à Paris ?**
— *Volontiers / D'accord / Non.*
— **Vous voulez venir au cinéma ?**
— *Oui ça va / Oui, volontiers / Oui, je comprends.*
— **Au revoir ; je vais travailler chez moi.**
— *Bonjour / Salut / Merci.*
— **Je peux fumer ?**
— *S'il vous plaît / Merci beaucoup / Oui bien sûr.*
— **Vous aimez la montagne ?**
— *Pas du tout / Volontiers / D'accord.*

10. Mettez l'adjectif à la forme qui convient

*Elles sont (**petit-vieux**).*
*Elle est (**souriant-gai-sympathique**).*
*Ils sont (**grand-mince**).*
*Elles sont (**petit-jeune-blond**).*
*Ils sont (**méchant-antipathique**).*

B) Images pour...

"J'habite à Paris, place de la Contrescarpe."

la place de la Contrescarpe

Dans le Quartier latin, le rendez-vous des étudiants, des musiciens, des chansonniers

la rue Mouffetard

Près de la place de la Contrescarpe, le marché de la « Mouffe »

un café parisien

A la terrasse, une bière, un jus de fruit, un petit « crème » ou un « noir »

"Mardi, je vais à l'opéra."

l'Opéra de Paris ou Palais garnier

Construit en 1874, architecte Charles Garnier (style Napoléon III), 2 200 places, peinture de Chagall

la Répétition

Le chef d'orchestre, les violonistes et les violoncellistes

le concert

L'orchestre national :
Au programme, des musiciens français du début du siècle, Debussy, Fauré, Ravel

C. Texte complémentaire

(Un samedi rue Mouffetard à Paris)

Lui :   — *La place est libre, s'il vous plaît ?*
Elle :   — *Oui.*
Lui :   — *Je peux m'asseoir ?*
Elle :   — *Bien sûr.*
Lui :   — *Vous êtes française ?*
Elle :   — *Non. Je suis canadienne.*
Lui :   — *... vous habitez à Paris ?*
Elle :   — *Non. J'habite à Lyon.*
Lui :   — *Vous aimez Lyon ?*
Elle :   — *Oui, beaucoup.*
Lui :   — *Qu'est-cè que vous aimez à Lyon ?*
Elle :   — *Les restaurants... et les Lyonnais aussi. Ils aiment bien boire et manger. Ils sont gentils, souriants.*
Lui :   — *Vous aimez les Parisiens.*

Elle :   — *Les Parisiens sympathiques, oui !*
Lui :   — *Je m'appelle Frédéric. Et vous ?*
Elle :   — *Francine.*
Lui :   — *Vous êtes à Paris pour le week-end, Francine ?*
Elle :   — *Oui.*
Lui :   — *Et qu'est-ce que vous faites à Paris le week-end ?*
Elle :   — *Je vais au théâtre, à l'opéra, au concert.*
Lui :   — *Vous aimez le jazz ?*
Elle :   — *J'adore.*
Lui :   — *Je vais à un concert de jazz à 9 heures au New Morning. Il y a un pianiste sud-africain. Vous voulez venir ?*
Elle :   — *Volontiers.*

D. Aide-mémoire

1. Les nombres

0	zéro	20	VINGT	30	TRENTE	80	QUATRE-VINGTS
1	un	21	vingt et un	31	trente et un	81	quatre-vingt-un
2	deux	22	vingt-deux	32	trente-deux	82	quatre-vingt-deux
3	trois	23	vingt-trois	33	trente-trois...	83	quatre-vingt-trois
4	quatre	24	vingt-quatre			84	quatre-vingt-quatre
5	cinq	25	vingt-cinq	40	QUARANTE...	85	quatre-vingt-cinq
6	six	26	vingt-six	50	CINQUANTE...	86	quatre-vingt-six
7	sept	27	vingt-sept	60	SOIXANTE...	87	quatre-vingt-sept
8	huit	28	vingt-huit			88	quatre-vingt-huit
9	neuf	29	vingt-neuf			89	quatre-vingt-neuf
10	DIX			70	SOIXANTE-DIX	90	QUATRE-VINGT-DIX
11	onze			71	soixante et onze	91	quatre-vingt-onze
12	douze			72	soixante-douze	92	quatre-vingt-douze
13	treize			73	soixante-treize	93	quatre-vingt-treize
14	quatorze			74	soixante-quatorze	94	quatre-vingt-quatorze
15	quinze			75	soixante-quinze	95	quatre-vingt-quinze
16	seize			76	soixante-seize	96	quatre-vingt-seize
17	dix-sept			77	soixante-dix-sept	97	quatre-vingt-dix-sept
18	dix-huit			78	soixante-dix-huit	98	quatre-vingt-dix-huit
19	dix-neuf			79	soixante-dix-neuf	99	quatre-vingt-dix-neuf

100 cent, **200** deux cents..., **1 000** mille, **1 000 000** un million

2. L'alphabet

A	a	[a]	comme Adèle	N	n	[ɛn]	comme Nicolas
B	b	[be]	comme Berthe	O	o	[o]	comme Oscar
C	c	[se]	comme Célestin	P	p	[pe]	comme Pierre
D	d	[de]	comme Désiré	Q	q	[ky]	comme Quentin
E	e	[ø]	comme Eugène	R	r	[ɛr]	comme Raoul
F	f	[ɛf]	comme François	S	s	[ɛs]	comme Suzanne
G	g	[ʒe]	comme Gaston	T	t	[te]	comme Thérèse
H	h	[aʃ]	comme Henri	U	u	[y]	comme Ursule
I	i	[i]	comme Irma	V	v	[ve]	comme Victor
J	j	[ʒi]	comme Joseph	W	w	[dubløve]	comme William
K	k	[ka]	comme Kléber	X	x	[iks]	comme Xavier
L	l	[ɛl]	comme Louis	Y	y	[igrɛk]	comme Yvonne
M	m	[ɛm]	comme Marcel	Z	z	[zɛd]	comme Zoé

3. Le calendrier

Les jours de la semaine
lundi, mardi, mercredi, jeudi, vendredi, samedi, dimanche.

Les mois de l'année
janvier, février, mars, avril, mai, juin, juillet, août, septembre, octobre, novembre, décembre.

E. Conjugaison

Le présent de l'indicatif

	ÊTRE	AVOIR	TRAVAILLER	ARRIVER	AIMER
je/j'	suis	ai	travaille	arrive	aime
tu	es	as	travailles	arrives	aimes
il/elle	est	a	travaille	arrive	aime
nous	sommes	avons	travaillons	arrivons	aimons
vous	êtes	avez	travaillez	arrivez	aimez
ils/elles	sont	ont	travaillent	arrivent	aiment

	MANGER	COMMENCER	APPELER	S'APPELER
je/j'	mange	commence	appelle	m'appelle
tu	manges	commences	appelles	t'appelles
il/elle	mange	commence	appelle	s'appelle
nous	mangeons	commençons	appelons	nous appelons
vous	mangez	commencez	appelez	vous appelez
ils/elles	mangent	commencent	appellent	s'appellent

	ALLER	FAIRE	VENIR	LIRE	DORMIR
je	vais	fais	viens	lis	dors
tu	vas	fais	viens	lis	dors
il/elle	va	fait	vient	lit	dort
nous	allons	faisons	venons	lisons	dormons
vous	allez	faites	venez	lisez	dormez
ils/elles	vont	font	viennent	lisent	dorment

	DIRE	VOULOIR	POUVOIR	BOIRE	VOIR
je	dis	veux	peux	bois	vois
tu	dis	veux	peux	bois	vois
il/elle	dit	veut	peut	boit	voit
nous	disons	voulons	pouvons	buvons	voyons
vous	dites	voulez	pouvez	buvez	voyez
ils/elles	disent	veulent	peuvent	boivent	voient

Mme Delort : — S'il vous plaît, madame Richaud, qui est-ce ?

Une secrétaire : — C'est la dame, là-bas.

Mme Delort : — Bonjour madame, je suis Sophie Delort, je suis...

Mme Richaud : — Ah ! Vous êtes la nouvelle secrétaire ! Enchantée. Nous travaillons ensemble. Le bureau devant la fenêtre est libre. Ça va ?

Mme Delort : — Oui, oui.

Mme Richaud : — Il y a un travail urgent.

Mme Delort : — Oui, qu'est-ce que c'est ?

Mme Richaud : — Ce sont des lettres pour monsieur Arnaud.

Mme Delort : — Qui est monsieur Arnaud ?

Mme Richaud : — C'est le Chef des Ventes. Le papier et le carbone sont dans le tiroir. La machine marche bien mais ce n'est pas un modèle électrique.

Mme Delort : — Bon. Je commence...

Mme Delort : — Qu'est-ce que c'est ?

Mme Richaud : — C'est la sonnerie de midi. Je déjeune dans un restaurant derrière la mairie. Vous voulez venir ?

Mme Delort : — Oui, volontiers.

Madame Delort travaille avec madame Richaud.

Le carbone est dans le bureau.

(•)

(*) *Attention ! voir page 158*

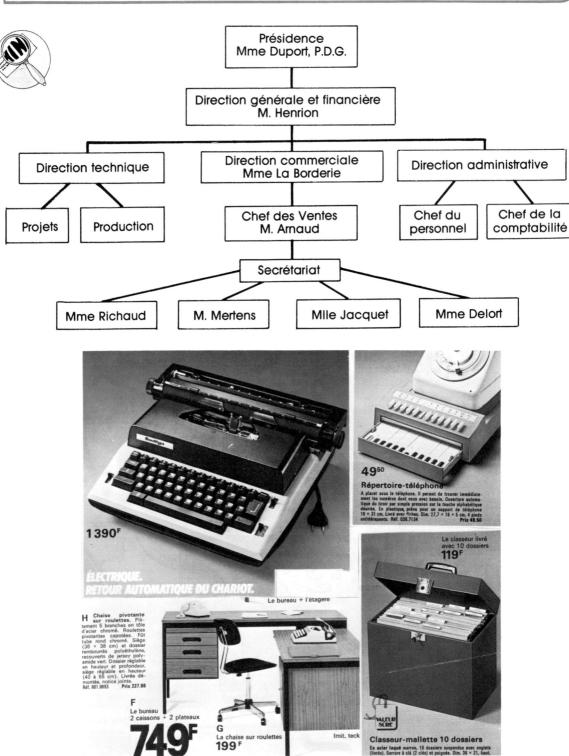

Présidence
Mme Duport, P.D.G.

Direction générale et financière
M. Henrion

Direction technique

Direction commerciale
Mme La Borderie

Direction administrative

Projets

Production

Chef des Ventes
M. Arnaud

Chef du
personnel

Chef de la
comptabilité

Secrétariat

Mme Richaud

M. Mertens

Mlle Jacquet

Mme Delort

1390F

**ÉLECTRIQUE.
RETOUR AUTOMATIQUE DU CHARIOT.**

49⁵⁰
Répertoire-téléphone
À placer sous le téléphone. Il permet de trouver immédiatement les numéros dont vous avez besoin. Ouverture automatique du tiroir par simple pression sur la touche alphabétique désirée. En plastique, prévu pour un support de téléphone 18 × 31 cm. Livré avec fiches. Dim. 27,7 × 18 × 5 cm. 4 pieds antidérapants. Réf. 038.7134. **Prix 49.50**

Le bureau + l'étagère

Le classeur livré
avec 10 dossiers
119F

H Chaise pivotante sur roulettes. Piètement 5 branches en tôle d'acier chromé. Roulettes pivotantes capotées. Fût tube rond chromé. Siège (38 × 38 cm) et dossier rembourrés polyéthylène, recouverts de jersey polyamide vert. Dossier réglable en hauteur et profondeur, siège réglable en hauteur (40 à 55 cm). Livrée démontée, notice jointe.
Réf. 001.0693 **Prix 227.00**

F
Le bureau
2 caissons + 2 plateaux
749F

G
La chaise sur roulettes
199F

Imit. teck

Classeur-mallette 10 dossiers
En acier laqué marron, 10 dossiers suspendus avec onglets (livrés). Serrure à clé (2 clés) et poignée. Dim. 36 × 21, haut.

• le matériel de bureau

le bureau, le siège *(la chaise, le fauteuil)*
le téléphone, la lampe, la machine à écrire... .

le tiroir, le classeur, le fichier, la corbeille à papier
les stylos, les crayons, la règle, la gomme...

• le lieu

devant - derrière, sur - sous

dans, à côté de

• les repas

le matin - le petit déjeuner
(déjeuner - prendre le petit déjeuner)
à midi - le déjeuner *(déjeuner)*
le soir - le dîner *(dîner)*
à minuit - le souper *(souper)*

GRAMMAIRE

1. l'interrogation sur l'objet

Questions	Réponses
Qu'est-ce que c'est... ?	c'est... ce n'est pas... + singulier ce sont... ce ne sont pas... + pluriel
Est-ce que c'est... ?	oui, c'est... non, ce n'est pas + singulier
Est-ce que ce sont... ?	oui, ce sont... non, ce ne sont pas... + pluriel (+ je ne sais pas)

2. l'interrogation sur la personne

Qui est M. Arnaud ?   c'est...
Qui est-ce ?   c'est... ce sont...
Qui es-tu ?   je suis...
Qui êtes-vous ?   je suis... nous sommes

(+ je ne sais pas)

3. le féminin des adjectifs   ATTENTION

masculin		nouveau	beau	vieux
masculin avant voyelle		nouvel	bel	vieil
féminin		nouvelle	belle	vieille

37

1. Faites des phrases en commençant par c'est... ce n'est pas...

   ce sont... ce ne sont pas...

le chef des ventes	des concierges sympathiques
un petit bureau	un nouveau modèle
des lettres urgentes	une machine électrique
un travail urgent	la sonnerie de midi
des vieilles machines	des étudiants

2. Recopiez et complétez avec le verbe être

Le bureau ...... devant la fenêtre. Le papier et le carbone ...... dans le tiroir.

Madame Delort ...... la nouvelle secrétaire. Qui ...... monsieur Arnaud ?

Qui ...... vous ? Je ...... le nouveau Chef des Ventes.

3. Nouveau - nouvelle - nouvel ? Choisissez et écrivez

c'est une nouvelle machine

c'est un nouveau sport

c'est un nouvel hôtel

programme - aéroport - restaurant - école - adresse - étudiant - docteur - infirmière - acteur

4. Regardez l'organigramme de la page 36. Recopiez et complétez

Le PDG de la société, qui est-ce ?

C'est ....

Qui ...... Directeur Général et Financier ?

....

Est-...... M. Arnaud est le Directeur Commercial ?

....

Qui est dans le secrétariat de M. Arnaud ?

Il y a ....

5. Qu'est-ce que c'est ?

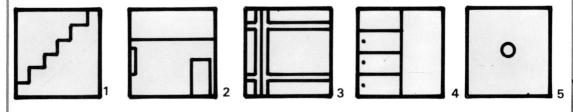

C'est un escalier ....

Réponses : 2. une maison 3. une fenêtre 4. un bureau 5. un tiroir

1.

Madame Richaud, Le Chef des Ventes, Monsieur Mertens, Jacques Martineau, Madame Duport,	**qui est-ce ?**	**C'est**	une secrétaire. M. Arnaud. un secrétaire. un pianiste. le PDG.

2.

Est-ce que

c'est...	le directeur ? la secrétaire ? un dentiste ? une vieille machine ? une nouvelle lampe ?	**Oui, c'est...** **Non, ce n'est pas...**	le directeur la secrétaire un dentiste une vieille machine une nouvelle lampe
ce sont...	des secrétaires ? les directeurs ? les nouveaux bureaux ?	**Oui, ce sont...** **Non, ce ne sont pas...**	des secrétaires les directeurs les nouveaux bureaux

● ***Qu'est-ce que c'est ? Répondez sur le modèle*** *C'est...* (personnage ou animal)
+ dans... sur... devant...

C'est un homme dans...

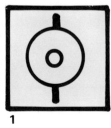

1

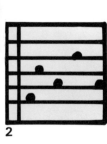

2

3

4

5

Réponses :

5. Un cochon derrière une maison.
4. Un rhinocéros dans un sac.
3. Une girafe devant une fenêtre.
2. Des oiseaux sur des fils électriques.
1. Un Mexicain sur un vélo.

Sur ces modèles, faites un dessin
Interrogez votre voisin(e)

Vous : *qu'est-ce que c'est ?*
Lui/Elle : *c'est...*
Vous : *oui, c'est.../non, ce n'est pas...*

● *Est-ce que vous les reconnaissez?*

  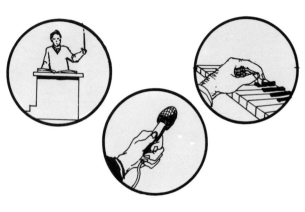

C'est une concierge.
C'est la concierge de Jacques Martineau.
Elle s'appelle...

● **Qui est-ce? Jeu du portrait**

votre voisin(e) : *c'est un homme?*   **vous :** *oui.../non...*   **lui/elle :** *il est français?...*

● **Qu'est-ce que c'est? (Trouvez le pays, la ville, le lieu)**

Qu'est-ce que c'est?

Dialoguez avec votre voisin(e).

Donnez votre avis.

Mme Richaud : — C'est un petit restaurant. Il y a une carte, un menu, et un plat du jour. C'est bon et pas cher.

(Dans le restaurant)

Mme Richaud : — Qu'est-ce qu'il y a aujourd'hui ?

Le garçon : — Le plat du jour, c'est du poulet au riz.

Mme Delort : — Pour moi, un plat du jour.

Le garçon : — Et pour vous ?

Mme Richaud : — Je voudrais un steak-frites.

Le garçon : — Bien, madame. Et comme boisson ? Du vin ?

Mme Delort : — Non, pas de vin pour moi.

Mme Richaud : — Alors de l'eau, s'il vous plaît. Une carafe.

Le garçon : — Et comme dessert, mesdames ? Crème caramel, fruit, glace ?

Mme Delort : — Pour moi, une crème caramel.

Mme Richaud : — Pas de dessert pour moi. Vous prenez du café ?

Mme Delort : — Oui.

Mme Richaud : — Alors deux cafés et l'addition, s'il vous plaît.

(Dans la rue)

Mme Richaud : — On se dit « tu » ?

Mme Delort : — D'accord.

Mme Richaut : — Tu habites ici à Évry ?

Mme Delort : — Oui, à côté de l'« Agora »

Mme Richaud : — Tu es mariée ?

Mme Delort : — Divorcée.

Mme Richaud : — Et tu vis seule ?

Mme Delort : — Oui.

Mme Richaud : — Tu es libre samedi soir ? Tu veux dîner chez nous ?

Mme Delort : — Je veux bien, c'est sympa.

41

[i]
[e]

— Sophie, veux-tu dîner chez nous ?

— Oui, merci.

— Alors rendez-vous samedi à huit heures et demie.

MENUS DE LA SEMAINE :

menu minceur

pour la famille

Petit déjeuner : une biscotte
thé au citron

Déjeuner : salade verte
poulet
une pomme

Dîner : potage de légumes
fromage (yaourt)

salade de tomates,
charcuterie,
lapin aux champignons,
fromage,
glace,
bordeaux

pour les copains

salade niçoise, pizza, jambon cru,
fromage, tarte aux pommes, beaujolais

en tête à tête

huîtres
steak au poivre,
gâteau au chocolat, champagne

PLATS RÉGIONAUX FRANÇAIS :

**Le cassoulet
(Aquitaine)**
haricots blancs, charcu-
terie

**La bouillabaisse
(Provence)**
poissons, pommes de
terre, pain, ail, épices

**La fondue savoyarde
(Savoie et Dauphiné)**
fromage, ail, vin blanc
pain

VOCABULAIRE

● **les repas en France**

Au petit déjeuner, **on mange** : des biscottes, des croissants, du pain, du beurre, de la confiture.

on boit : du café, du thé, du lait, du chocolat.

Au déjeuner ou au dîner, **on mange** : hors-d'œuvre (ou entrée), plat (viande ou poisson), légume, fromage, dessert.

on boit : de l'eau, du vin, de la bière.

● **État civil :** célibataire   marié(e)   divorcé(e)   veuf (veuve)

GRAMMAIRE

1. l'article partitif : du, de la, de l', des

C'est **un** veau

C'est **du** veau
(article partitif)

		devant une consonne	devant une voyelle
Singulier	*Masculin*	**du** poulet	**de** l'eau
	Féminin	**de la** viande	
Pluriel	*Masculin Féminin*	**des** frites	

2. la négation et l'article partitif :

Il prend...
{ du vin
de la viande
des haricots
du dessert
de la salade
de l'eau

Il ne prend pas de...

pas d'...
{ vin
viande
haricots
dessert
salade
eau

3. ON = NOUS

On déjeune ensemble ? = nous déjeunons ensemble ?   On se dit « tu » ? = nous nous disons « tu » ?

4. conjugaison :

PRENDRE
je prends
tu prends
il/elle/on prend
nous prenons
vous prenez
ils/elles prennent

VIVRE
je vis
tu vis
il/elle/on vit
nous vivons
vous vivez
ils/elles vivent

5. le pronom personnel complément (après préposition)

pour } moi - nous
chez } toi - vous

1. *Du, de la, de l', des. Choisissez :*

Est-ce que vous voulez . . . . . . cafés ?

— Non, nous ne prenons pas . . . . . . café, nous buvons . . . . . . chocolat.

Est-ce que vous buvez . . . . . . bière ?

— Non, je préfère . . . . . . eau.

Vous voulez . . . . . . frites ?

— Non, je veux . . . . . . salade.

Voulez-vous . . . . . . confiture ?

— Non, je préfère . . . . . . beurre.

2. *prendre — vouloir — vivre*

Choisissez et complétez en mettant le verbe à la forme qui convient :

Madame Richaud ne . . . . . . pas seule.

Nous . . . . . . du travail.

Je ne . . . . . . pas travailler le samedi.

On . . . . . . du vin ?

Ils préfèrent . . . . . . à la campagne.

Est-ce que vous . . . . . . l'addition ?

Au petit déjeuner, elles . . . . . . du thé.

3. **Complétez avec un article défini ou partitif :**

— *J'aime beaucoup . . . . . . musique.*

— *Est-ce qu'il y a . . . . . . musique chez toi ?*

— *Est-ce que vous faites . . . . . . sport ?*

— *Oui, j'aime beaucoup . . . . . . sport.*

— *Je n'ai pas . . . . . . travail aujourd'hui.*

— *. . . . . . travail pour M. Arnaud est urgent.*

— *. . . . . . papier est dans le tiroir.*

— *Je veux . . . . . . papier pour machine.*

4. **Yves et Martine sont au restaurant. Qu'est-ce qu'ils prennent ?**

il/elle/on	prend	de l'eau de la viande du poulet un dessert des frites
ils/elles	prennent	

il/elle/on	ne	prend	pas	d'eau
ils/elles		prennent		de viande de café de frites

Jacques déjeune au self-service. Qu'est-ce qu'il prend ?

● *Interrogez votre voisin ou votre voisine*

— *Qu'est-ce que vous prenez*
au petit déjeuner ?

— *Que prend un Allemand,*
un Anglais, un Américain...
au petit déjeuner, au déjeuner, au dîner ?

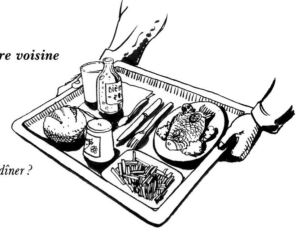

● *Dites ce que vous aimez et ce que vous n'aimez pas. Demandez à votre voisin(e) ce qu'il aime. Choisissez votre menu et passez votre commande*

Les Salades

SALADE DE TOMATES.		8.00
Tomatoes salad		Tomaten Salat
SALADE DE SAISON.		8.00
Salad according to season		Salat nach Jahrezeit
SALADE MIXTE.		12.00
Mixed salad		Gemischte Salat
SALADE MAITRE D'HOTEL.		20.00
Laitue, gruyère, jambon, tomates		
Lettuce, Swiss cheese, ham, tomato		
Salat, Schweizerischer Käse, Schinken, Tomaten		
SALADE SPÉCIALE		24.00
Laitue, tomate, gruyère, œuf dur, thon		
Lettuce tomato, Swiss cheese, hard boiled egg, tunny fish		
Salat, Tomaten, Schweizerischer Käse, Hart gekochtes Ei, Tunfisch		
SALADE DU CHEF		17.00
Laitue, tomate, haricots verts, cervelas, oignon		
Lettuce, tomato, french beans, saveloy, onions		
Salat, Tomaten, grüne Bohnen, Schlackwurst, Zwiebeln		
SALADE " MISTRAL ".		22.00
Salade, crudités, gruyère, pommes fruits		
Salade, raw vegetables, Swiss cheese, apples		
Salat, Rohkost, Schweizerischer Käse, Äpfeln		
SALADE AUVERGNATE		28.00
Salade, jambon de Pays, Cantal, pommes à l'huile		
Salade, country ham, Cantal cheese, potatoes salad		
Salat, Landschinken, Cantal Käse, Kartoffeln Salat		

Glaces et Desserts

Toutes les tartes sont fabrication " MAISON "
Our tarts are home made – Unsere Torte sind Heingemacht

TARTE AUX POMMES		12.00
Apple tart		Apfel Torte
TARTE AUX FRUITS		12.00
Fruit tart		Obst Torte
TARTE TATIN		15.00
Tatin tart		Tatin Torte
TARTE A L'ORANGE		15.00
Orange tart		Orange Torte
TARTE AUX CITRONS		15.00
Lemon tart		Zitrone Torte
PATISSERIES, AMANDINES		4.50
Pastries		Klein Kuchen
FRUITS DE SAISON		4.50
Fruits		Obst
CONFITURE		4.50
Jam		Konfitüre
CREME CARAMEL.		8.50
Caramel cream		Karamel Kreme
MOUSSE AU CHOCOLAT		8.50
Chocolate foam		Schokolade Schaum

Plats garnis

STEAK (Bavette).		23.00
Steak		Steak
HAMBURGER		22.00
Hamburger		Hamburger
FAUX-FILET ÉCHALOTES		30.00
Sirloin with shallots		Ochsenstück mit Schallotte
ESCALOPE PANÉE.		28.00
Veal scallop		Wiener Schnitzel
COTE DE PORC		22.00
Pork chop		Schwein Kotelette
FILET DE BŒUF AU POIVRE		41.00
Beef fillet with pepper sauce		Ochsen Filete mit Pfeffer Sosse
CHOUCROUTE		24.00
Sauerkraut		Sauerkraut

EN SAISON

FRAISES AU SUCRE.		
Strawberries with sugar		Erdbeeren mit Zucker
FRAISES CHANTILLY.		
Strawberry with whipped cream		Erdbeeren mit Schlagsahne
ANANAS FRAIS AU KIRSCH		
Pineapple with Kirsch		Ananas mit Kirschwasser

— — —

ANANAS SPLIT	20.00
BANANA SPLIT	20.00
PECHE MELBA.	16.00

● *Est-ce que vous aimez ?*

La choucroute *(Alsace)*
chou, charcuterie, pommes de terre

● *Jeu de rôle : le garçon et le client*

le client : *la choucroute qu'est-ce que c'est ?*
le garçon : *c'est du chou avec de la...*

● **Décrivez un plat de votre pays. Invitez votre voisin(e) à goûter un plat de votre pays.**

Tu es libre...? (lundi, mardi...) oui..., non...
Tu veux venir... (déjeûner, dîner...)
Tu aimes le/la...?

Interrogez-le (la)... (sans être indiscret !)

— *Tu es... (célibataire, marié) ?*

2.3 Chez le boucher

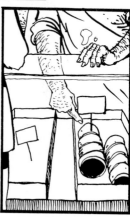

*Elle :   — Tu viens avec moi à la boucherie ?

Lui :   — D'accord.

*Le boucher :   — A vous, madame Richaud. Vous désirez ?

Elle :   — Combien coûtent les côtelettes d'agneau ?

Le boucher :   — 50 francs le kilo.

Elle :   — Bon, alors je voudrais quatre côtelettes.

*Le boucher :   — Voilà — 600 grammes... 30 francs.

Lui :   — On achète un rôti pour le dîner de samedi ?

Elle :   — Bonne idée — Vous avez du rôti de veau ?

*Le boucher :   — Non, je n'ai plus de veau, mais j'ai encore un rôti de porc.

Elle :   — Bon, d'accord.

Le boucher :   — Pour combien de personnes ?

Elle :   — Cinq.

Le boucher :   — Voilà un beau rôti. Il pèse 1,200 kg — Et avec ça ?

Elle :   — C'est tout. Ça fait combien ?

Le boucher :   — 30 et 66, ça fait 96 francs.

*Elle :   — Tu payes, chéri ?

*Lui :   — Une seconde... Zut ! Je n'ai plus d'argent !

*Elle :   — Alors je fais un chèque. Tu peux prendre ça ? Merci.

— Qu'est-ce que vous désirez ?

[ɛ]

— Quatre belles côtelettes
    (•)

[e]

— Tu peux payer, chéri ?

— Oui, je peux faire un chèque.

(*) cf. page 158

Mémoire

Pour Samedi

Vin – Bière
Rôti de porc – Steak
jambon
Carottes – oignons
poireaux – haricots verts
Lait – yaourts – fromages
Pommes – poires – oranges
Huile – vinaigre
Café – thé – sucre

ROGER

Rien que des
viandes fraiches
NI CONGELÉES, NI SURGELÉES

PRIX DE VENTE
HABITUELS
Garantis jusqu'au 20/12/1981

	le kg
Faux-filet	45,00 F
Rumsteck	43,00 F
Entrecôte	43,00 F
Noix de veau	46,00 F
Escalope	50,00 F
Epaule d'agneau	28,00 F
Côtes 1ère agneau	38,00 F
Côtes 1ère porc	25,00 F
Saucisson ail	15,00 F
Pintade	16,00 F

VOCABULAIRE

- **l'argent**

les billets :

500 F

100 F

50 F

20 F

la monnaie (les pièces de monnaie) :
10 F, 5 F, 2 F, 1 F, 0,50 F (francs).
50 c, 20 c, 10 c, 5 c (centimes).

carte bleue

les autres moyens de paiement :
les chèques, les cartes de crédit.

4976123456789   VISA
EXPIRE A FIN
MONSIEUR CHRISTIAN DUVAL

48

• commerces (magasins), commerçants et articles

la boucherie	la boulangerie	la charcuterie	l'épicerie	la crèmerie
le boucher la bouchère	le boulanger la boulangère	le charcutier la charcutière	l'épicier l'épicière	le crémier la crémière
viande, volaille	pain, pâtisserie, confiserie	charcuterie, conserves	alimentation générale, conserves, fruits-légumes, boissons	beurre, œufs, fromage, lait, produits laitiers

la pharmacie	la droguerie	le bureau de tabac	la librairie
le pharmacien la pharmacienne	le/la droguiste	le/la buraliste	le/la libraire
médicaments, produits de beauté	produits d'entretien	tabac, cigarettes, timbres, articles pour fumeurs, cartes postales	livres, journaux, article de papete- rie, cartes postales

• acheter - vendre

le client, la cliente
l'acheteur, l'acheteuse

le marchand, la marchande
le vendeur, la vendeuse
le commerçant, la commerçante

GRAMMAIRE

1. conjugaison

VENDRE	ACHETER	PAYER
je vends	j' achète	je paie/paye
tu vends	tu achètes	tu paies/payes
il/elle/on vend	il/elle/on achète	il/elle/on paie/paye
nous vendons	nous achetons	nous payons
vous vendez	vous achetez	vous payez
ils/elles vendent	ils/elles achètent	ils/elles paient/payent

2. encore - ne...plus

il y a encore du pain
j'ai encore de l'argent
le boucher a encore du bœuf

il n'y a plus de pain
je n'ai plus d'argent
il n'a plus de veau

3. au - chez

au à la } + nom du commerce à l'	chez le chez la } + nom du commerçant chez l'
au bureau de tabac à la pharmacie à l'épicerie	chez le boulanger chez la droguiste chez l'épicier

4. interrogation sur le poids et le prix

	question	réponse
prix	Ca coûte combien ? Combien (est-ce que) ça coûte ?	Ca coute... 25 F Ça fait... 10,50 F
poids	Combien pèse le rôti ? Il pèse combien, le rôti ?	Il pèse... 500 g Il fait... 1,6 kg

1. *Qu'est-ce qu'on achète ? Recopiez et complétez.*

1. Chez l'épicier, on achète du sucre, ...

2. A la . . . ., ... de l'aspirine . . . .

3. . . . . . . la boulangère, ...

4. . . . ., ... des cigarettes . . . .

5. . . . . boucher, ...

6. . . . . . . crémerie, ...

2. *Écrivez ces prix selon le modèle :*

23,50 F = 23 francs et 50 centimes.

18,25 F - 130 F - 47,80 F - 1 630 F - 123,50 F - 3 812 F

3. Aidez-le à faire les courses !

*Le café, c'est à l'épicerie (chez l'épicier...),
les cigarettes...*

**4. Faites votre liste de courses
   pour la semaine**

café
cigarettes
pain
aspirine
4 tranches
de jambon
1 rôti de
veau

5. Beau - belle - bel ? Choisissez et écrivez

c'est une belle machine

c'est un beau rôti

c'est un bel hôtel

bureau - machine - magasin - librairie - aéroport - escalier - maison - acteur - programme.

	vous voulez...	vous demandez le prix...
je voudrais	du fromage	C'est combien les 100 g ?
	de la viande	C'est combien le kilo ?
	de l'huile	C'est combien la bouteille ?
	des cigarettes	C'est combien le paquet ?

Faites parler le client et le marchand

— *Je voudrais du vin s'il vous plaît.*
— *Vous voulez du vin ! Je ne vends pas de vin, ici c'est une crémerie, ce n'est pas une épicerie.*

● *Qu'est-ce que vous achetez ? Passez votre commande :* Je voudrais...
vous avez 100 F, vous avez 200 F, vous avez 300 F

PETITS POIS LEBRETON
extra fins, le lot de 2 boîtes 4/4 .. **9,95**

**HARICOTS VERTS
DOMAINE DE LA BORDE**
extra fins, la boîte 4/4 .... **8,45**

**CŒURS DE PALMIER
MADREITA**
importé du Brésil,
la boîte 500 g net égoutté **9,95**

**CŒURS D'ARTICHAUTS
LES DELECTABLES**
importé d'Espagne, le lot
de 2 boîtes 200 g net égoutté **7,90**

**FONDS D'ARTICHAUTS
LES DELECTABLES**
importé d'Espagne, le lot
de 2 boîtes 200 g net égoutté **9,55**

**CHAMPIGNONS DE PARIS
LA MAISON 1ᵉʳ choix**
le lot de 3 boîtes 1/4 .... **8,60**

**FLAGEOLETS
VAL DE LOIRE**
la boîte 4/4 .... **4,85**

ASPERGES HOLCO
importées de Hollande, le bocal
72 cl 425 g net égoutté **14,70**

ASPERGES PIC NIC PIQUIO
importées de Formose,
le lot de 3 boîtes 1/4 .... **12,95**

OLIVES VERTES GRODYN
dénoyautées, le sachet
320 g net égoutté **4,50**

SAUMON PINK SOCRA
au naturel, importé d'URSS
la boîte 185 g net égoutté **6,50**

CRABE KING KILDA
importé d'URSS, la boîte
185 g net égoutté **18,95**

MIETTES DE CRABES
au naturel grade B, importées de
Thaïlande, la boîte 127 g
net égoutté, le lot de 2 .... **11,25**

CREVETTES PIQUIO
décortiquées cocktail, importées
de Thaïlande, la boîte 127 g,
net égoutté, le lot de 2 .... **9,65**

**COQUILLES ST JACQUES
AROK**
préparées, la boîte 1/4
+ 3 coquilles vides **12,40**

FOIE DE MORUE COOK
le lot de 2 boîtes 1/6 .... **6,30**

**DÉLICE DE FOIE DE
VOLAILLE RECAPET**
au madère, le rouleau 320 g **3,95**

**PARFAIT DE FOIE
LAFOREST PÉRIGORD**
à l'oie, le rouleau 320 g **6,75**

CACAHUÈTES SPLIT
le lot de 2 sachets de 250 g **10,80**

**SPÉCIALITÉS
APÉRITIVES SOUFFLÉS
SPLIT** au fromage, à la tomate,
à la cacahuète ou fumé au choix,
le lot de 3 sachets de 60 g **3,90**

**SAUCISSES COCKTAIL
TULIP**
le lot de 2 boîtes 125 g **6,25**

VIN ROUGE BORDEAUX
Appellation contrôlée,
la bouteille 75 cl............. **7,2**

**VIN ROUGE
SAINT EMILION**
Appellation contrôlée,
Château la Croizille 1979,
la bouteille 75 cl............. **21,5**

**VIN ROUGE
CÔTES DU RHÔNE**
Appellation contrôlée,
la bouteille 75 cl............. **6,5**

**VIN ROUGE BEAUJOLAIS
VILLAGES**
Appellation contrôlée,
la bouteille 75 cl............. **10,7**

VIN BLANC MUSCADET
Sèvres et Maine sur lie,
appellation contrôlée Domaine
de Viaud, la bouteille 75 cl..... **9,2**

**VIN BLANC
GROS PLANT**
vin délimité de qualité
supérieure BEAUQUIN,
la bouteille 75 cl............. **6,4**

VIN BLANC
d'Alsace Sylvaner appellation
contrôlée, la bouteille 70 cl **9,9**

● *Faites-les parler : demandez les articles, les prix...*

— *Je voudrais 2 kg de pommes de terre s'il vous plaît.*
— *Et avec ça ? ... 1 salade... 1 litre d'huile...*
— *Je n'ai plus d'huile...*
— *Ça fait combien ? etc.*

● *Allez faire des courses avec votre voisin(e) :*

Vous : *Tu viens avec moi à la .... chez le ....?*
Lui : *Oui, qu'est-ce que tu veux acheter ?*
Vous : *Je voudrais .... Tu peux payer ?*
Lui : *Oui, j'ai de l'argent. Non ....*

*La mère : — Qu'est-ce que tu fais, Didier ?

Le fils : — Je travaille.

*La mère : — Il faut ranger ces affaires. Nous attendons une invitée ce soir.

Le fils : — Qui est-ce ?

La mère : — C'est une collègue de bureau.

*La mère : — A qui est ce pull ? A ta sœur ?

Le fils : — Non, il n'est pas à elle. Il est à son amie Brigitte.

La mère : — Et cet appareil photo, il est à qui ?

Le fils : — A mon copain Gilles.

*La mère : — C'est ton blouson de cuir ça ?

Le fils : — Oui.

La mère : — Tu fumes Didier ?

Le fils : — Non maman.

La mère : — Et ces cigarettes, à qui elles sont ? A toi ?

Le fils : — Non. Elles sont à papa.

La mère : — Ton père ne fume pas de blondes.

Le fils : — Alors elles sont à Brigitte... ou à Gilles.

*La mère : — Et ces allumettes dans la poche de ton blouson, elles sont à Brigitte ou à Gilles !

Ce pull est à son amie. C'est une collègue.

liaisons : Cet appareil photo n'est pas à moi.

Et ces allumettes, elles sont à toi ?

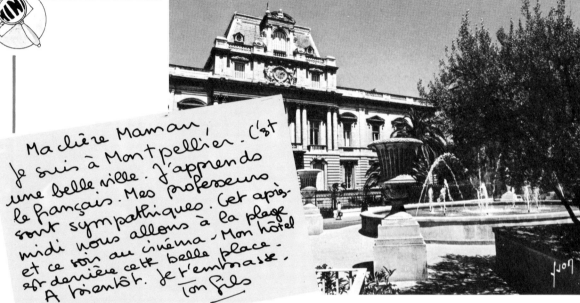

Ma chère Maman,
Je suis à Montpellier. C'est
une belle ville. J'apprends
le français. Mes professeurs
sont sympathiques. Cet après-
midi nous allons à la plage
et ce soir au cinéma. Mon hôtel
est derrière cette belle place.
A bientôt. Je t'embrasse.
Ton fils

VOCABULAIRE

• 1 blouson
• 1 jean
• 1 débardeur
• 1 chemise

total : 361 F

• 1 sweat-shirt
• 1 jupe

total : 168 F

• 1 gilet
• 1 chemisier
• 1 jean

total : 237,50 F

54

• les vêtements

pantalon - pull-over - chandail - gilet - short - jean - robe - jupe - chemise - chemisier - veste - blouson - manteau - imperméable - bas - chaussettes - slip - tee-shirt - soutien-gorge - collant - souliers - chaussures - bottes - écharpe...

• les matériaux

un blouson **de** cuir - un blouson **en** cuir
en cuir - en laine - en coton - en nylon...

une table **en** bois - une table **de** bois -
en bois - en verre - en fer - en pierre...

• la famille et les amis

a) les parents

la mère (Colette Richaud)
(la femme de Pierre)

le père (Pierre Richaud)
(le mari de Colette)

b) les enfants

le fils (Didier Richaud)
(le frère d'Isabelle)

la fille (Isabelle Richaud)
(la sœur de Didier)

c) les amis

Gilles

Brigitte

(le copain/l'ami de Didier Richaud).

Sophie Delort
la collègue de Mme Richaud
— elles travaillent ensemble —
et sa nouvelle amie .

(la copine/l'amie d'Isabelle).

• Être (1 mot - 3 sens)

1. Mme Delort est la nouvelle secrétaire. *(C'est la nouvelle secrétaire)*.
2. Le bureau est devant la fenêtre. *(Il se trouve devant la fenêtre)*.
3. Le pull est à Brigitte. *(C'est le pull de Brigitte. Il appartient à Brigitte)*.

1. adjectifs démonstratifs

singulier	masculin	**ce**	ce blouson
		cet	cet appareil
	féminin	**cette**	cette carte postale
pluriel	masculin	**ces**	ces blousons
	féminin		ces cigarettes

2. adjectifs possessifs

(à moi) (à toi) (à lui/à elle)

singulier	masculin	**mon**	**ton**	**son**	mon/ton/son copain
	féminin	**ma**	**ta**	**sa**	ma/ta/sa copine
	avant voyelle	**mon**	**ton**	**son**	mon/ton/son ami mon/ton/son amie
pluriel		**mes**	**tes**	**ses**	mes/tes/ses cigarettes

3. pronoms personnels compléments (après préposition)

	singulier	
1re personne	**moi**	Elle travaille *avec* moi.
2e personne	**toi**	Je vais *chez* toi.
3e personne	**lui/elle**	Il marche *devant* elle. Elle marche *derrière* lui.

4. l'interrogation sur l'appartenance

A qui est ce blouson ? Il est à lui.
A qui sont ces cigarettes ? Elles sont à lui.

5. l'obligation

Il faut + infinitif { Il faut travailler.
Il faut payer.
Il faut venir chez nous.

1. Ce, cette... Mon, ton, son... Choisissez et écrivez :

Ex. : Ces cigarettes, ce sont mes cigarettes

cigarettes (à moi) - hôtel (à lui) - magasin (à moi) - appareil (à toi) - robe (à elle) - allumettes (à toi) - chaussures (à lui) - adresse (à elle) -

2. Mon-ton-son/ma-ta-sa. Quels sont les possessifs qui peuvent convenir :

frère - sœur - copine - père - mère - ami - amie - étudiante - professeur.

3. *Écrivez au singulier et faites une phrase selon le modèle :*

mes amies   → (souriant) : *mon amie est souriante.*   mes frères   → (grand) : . . . .

ses invitées   → (content) : . . . .   tes voisines   → (petit) : . . . .

ses appareils → (vieux) : . . . .   ses photos   → (vieux) : . . . .

4. *Recopiez et complétez avec l'adjectif démonstratif qui convient :*

Qui est . . . . . . dame ? . . . . . . appareil est japonais . . . . . . vêtements ne sont pas chers.

Elles sont à qui, ... cigarettes ? Tu aimes . . . . . . musique ? J'habite dans . . . . . . hôtel.

5. *Recopiez et complétez avec l'adjectif possessif qui convient :*

— Brigitte, c'est l'amie d'Isabelle ?   — Oui, elle habite chez . . . . . . parents.

— Oui, c'est . . . . . . amie.   — Quelle est . . . . . . adresse ?

— Elle habite Évry ?

6. *A qui est-ce ? Écrivez :*

Ce pull est à ....

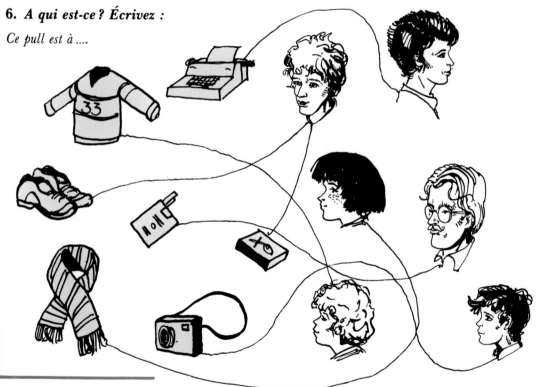

A qui	est	ce pull ? cet appareil ? cette veste ?	A moi. A Gilles. A lui.	A toi ? A Gilles ? A lui ?	Oui, c'est mon pull. Oui, c'est son appareil. Oui, c'est sa veste.
	sont	ces allumettes ? ces chaussures ?	A elle. A mon père.	A elle ? A ton père ?	Oui, ce sont ses allu- mettes. Oui, ce sont ses chaus- sures.

● *Qui est-ce ?* *C'est M. Richaud et son fils...*

 *Continuez*

● **Au voleur !**

Jouez la scène

le voleur :	*Ce violon est à moi.*
la victime :	*Non, ce n'est pas ...... violon, c'est ...... violon !*
un témoin :	*C'est vrai ! ce violon n'est pas à lui, il est ...... violoniste.*

« Volez » un objet à votre voisin(e) et dialoguez :

vous :	*Ce stylo, ce manteau ...... est à moi !*
lui :	*Non, ...*
un autre ·	*C'est vrai ! ......*

Brétécher : « Les Gnan Gnan » © Ed. GLENAT

2.5 L'apéritif

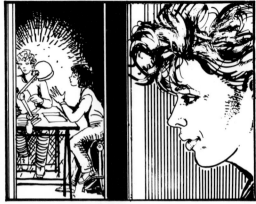

JUS D'OR

M. Richaud : — Alors vous aimez notre ville madame Delort ?

Sophie : — Vous pouvez m'appeler Sophie.

M. Richaud : — Alors vous pouvez m'appeler Pierre.

Sophie : — Oui, j'aime beaucoup Évry. C'est une ville agréable et j'aime bien l'architecture moderne.

M. Richaud : — Et votre travail, ça marche ?

Sophie : — Oui, je suis contente, ça marche bien.

Colette : — Et ses collègues sont sympa.

Pierre : — Vous avez des enfants, Sophie ?

Sophie : — J'ai un fils. Il vit chez mes parents à Reims. Et vos enfants, ils ne sont pas là ?

Colette : — Ils sont dans leur chambre. Ils font leurs devoirs.

Pierre : — Bon. On prend un apéritif !

Pierre : — Qu'est-ce que vous prenez ? Du jus d'orange, du jus de raisin, du jus d'abricot, du jus de pomme, du whisky ? Ah non, il n'y a plus de whisky. La bouteille est vide.

Sophie : — Alors, du jus de pomme.

Sophie : — Qu'est-ce que vous faites dans la vie, Pierre ?

Pierre : — Je suis représentant. Je vends des jus de fruit.

Sophie : — Ah, je comprends...

[ã]

Les enfants sont dans leur chambre.

On prend un jus d'orange ?

Pierre est représentant.

FICHE FAMILIALE D'ÉTAT CIVIL
et de nationalité française (1)

dressée en application du décret du 26 septembre 1953 modifié par le décret du 22 mars 1972 (J.O. du 23 mars) et l'arrêté du 22 mars 1972 (J.O. du 23 mars 1972) modifié par l'arrêté du 16 mai 1974 (J.O. du 18 mai 1974).

NOM (2) : **LECLERC**
(Nom de jeune fille pour les femmes mariées, veuves ou divorcées)

Prénom (s) : **Colette - Françoise - Marie**
(au complet dans l'ordre de l'état civil)

Né (e) le : **6 MARS 1946**
(Le mois doit être inscrit en toutes lettres)

à : **Paris (2e)**
(Commune et département. Pour Paris et Lyon, indiquer l'arrondissement)

de **LECLERC Charles - Edmond**
(Nom et prénoms du père)

et de **LECLERC Thérèse née MARTIN** (3)
(Nom et prénoms de la mère)

Marié (e) le : **4 Juillet 1966**

à : **Paris (13e)**
(Commune et département. Pour Paris et Lyon, indiquer l'arrondissement)

Conjoint : **RICHAUD Pierre - Henri**
(Nom (2) et prénom (s).)

Né (e) le : **9 Juin 1941**

à : **Chartres (Eure et Loir)**

Observations (4) :

LE MALADE IMAGINAIRE.

PERSONNAGES

ARGAN, malade imaginaire. . . . . . .
BÉLINE, seconde femme d'Argan . . . .
ANGÉLIQUE, fille d'Argan et amante de
    Cléante. . . . .
LOUISON, petite fille[1] d'Argan et sœur
    d'Angélique. . . . .
BÉRALDE, frère d'Argan. . . . .
CLÉANTE, amant d'Angélique . . . . . .
MONSIEUR DIAFOIRUS, médecin . . . .
THOMAS DIAFOIRUS, son fils et amant
    d'Angélique. . . . .
MONSIEUR PURGON, médecin d'Argan .
MONSIEUR FLEURANT, apothicaire. . .
MONSIEUR BONNEFOY, notaire . . . .
TOINETTE, servante . . . .

La scène est à Paris.

1. *Petite fille* signifie ici *fillette.*

VOCABULAIRE

● **la famille** (suite)

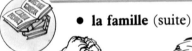

Les grands-parents

Auguste Richaud
le grand-père
(de Didier/Isabelle)
le beau-père
(de Colette)

Élise Richaud
la grand-mère
la belle-mère

Thérèse Leclerc   Charles Leclerc

Les parents

Pierre

Colette

Isabelle   **Les petits enfants**   Didier

l'oncle - la tante - le cousin - la cousine...   le beau-frère - la belle-sœur - le beau-père - la belle-mère.

- **qu'est-ce que vous prenez ?**

jus de fruit, alcool (apéritif, digestif),
eau minérale (eau « plate », eau gazeuse)...

12 h, 19 h, l'apéritif
Après le repas, les « digestifs »

- **1 verbe - 3 sens**

« MARCHER »
Sens 1 : Il marche dans la rue.
Sens 2 : La machine marche bien.
Sens 3 : Et le travail, ça marche ?

« FAIRE »
Sens 1 : Qu'est-ce qu'ils font ? Ils font leurs devoirs.
Sens 2 : Qu'est-ce qu'il fait (dans la vie) ? Il est représentant.
Sens 3 : Combien ça fait ? Ça fait 100 F.

GRAMMAIRE

1. adjectifs possessifs

singulier	*masculin*	notre	votre	leur	C'est notre votre leur	bureau
	féminin					
pluriel	*masculin*	nos	vos	leurs	Ce sont nos vos leurs	amis - amies
	féminin					

2. pronoms personnels compléments (après préposition)

	pluriel	
1re *personne*	**nous**	Ils habitent chez nous.
2e *personne*	**vous**	C'est à vous ?
3e *personne*	**eux/elles**	Vous êtes avec eux/elles ?

3. conjugaison

COMPRENDRE

je comprends
tu comprends
il/elle/on comprend
nous comprenons
vous comprenez
ils/elles comprennent

1. Recopiez et complétez en employant : son, sa, ses, leur, leurs.

Voici Didier et ...... sœur.   Voici Didier et ...... mère.

Voici Didier, Isabelle, et ...... copains,   Voici Brigitte et ...... ami Gilles.

Brigitte et Gilles.   Voici Isabelle et ...... parents.

2. Recopiez et complétez la lettre de Sophie Delort à sa mère :

... chère Maman,

Je suis contente à Évry. ...... travail marche bien. ...... amis Colette et Pierre sont sympa .....

enfants s'appellent Isabelle et Didier. Comment va ...... petit Jérôme. Est-ce qu'il est gentil

avec ...... grand-mère ?

A dimanche. Je t'embrasse.

                                        ...... fille Sophie.

3. Choisissez la bonne réponse :

                                                                    leurs
a) Sophie demande à M. et Mme Richaud : « Comment s'appellent tes   enfants »
                                                                    vos

               Ma   sa
b) Colette répond : «Nos fils s'appelle Didier et leur sœur Isabelle. »
               Notre   ma

                                 mon
c) Pierre demande à Sophie : « Il a quel âge, votre fils ? »
                                 son

                                             vos
d) Pierre demande à Colette et Sophie : « Elles sont sympa, nos   collègues ? »
                                             leurs

4. Votre famille :

Présentez votre famille en indiquant les noms et prénoms de vos grands-parents ; les prénoms de vos
parents, frères, sœurs (et enfants) ; leurs professions, leurs adresses...

Ce	blouson		ton frère ?	Oui c'est	**son** blouson.
Cette	veste	est à	Jacques ?		**sa** veste.
Cet	imperméable		maman ?	Non, ce n'est pas	**son** imperméable.

	chaussures		toi ?		**mes** chaussures.
	cigarettes		moi ?	Oui, ce sont	**tes** cigarettes.
	affaires		elle ?		**ses** affaires.
Ces		sont à			
	allumettes		vous ?		**nos** allumettes.
	chaussettes		nous ?	Non, ce ne sont pas	**vos** chaussettes.
	enfants		eux ?		**leurs** enfants.

● *Au café*

Faites-les parler. *Pour moi une bière...*

(le garçon s'est trompé) Corrigez.
Pour lui ce n'est pas un sandwich, c'est une bière...

● **Une grande famille**

Donnez des noms à chaque personnage et imaginez des liens de parenté.
X est le... frère/cousin/père, etc. de Y

Interrogez votre voisin ou votre voisine sur sa famille...
(liens de parenté, noms, prénoms, âges, professions, etc.)

... sur sa profession, ses goûts :

Vous :	*Qu'est-ce que vous faites ?*		*Vos collègues sont sympa ? ...*
Lui/Elle	*Je suis...*	**Lui/Elle**	*Oui..., non...*
Vous :	*Votre travail, ça marche ?...*	**Vous :**	*Vous aimez cette ville ?...*

BILAN

A. Tests

1. *Recopiez et complétez avec* **UN, UNE, DES, CE, CET, CETTE, CES :**

J'ai ...... ami aux États-Unis. ...... ami habite New York.
Qui est ...... dame ? C'est ...... vendeuse du magasin.
Je ne fume pas ...... cigarettes. Je préfère ...... blondes.
J'ai ...... travail urgent ...... matin.
Je n'aime pas ...... musique. Il est à toi, ... disque ?
Nous attendons ...... invités ...... soir.
Garçon ! ...... côtelettes ne sont pas bonnes. Nous voulons ...... steaks.
Qui c'est, ... garçon ? C'est ...... copain.
Vous avez ...... petits classeurs ? Oui. Vous voulez ...... modèle ?
...... épicier a ...... magasin moderne.

2. *Recopiez et complétez avec* **PAS DE, PAS D', PAS DES :**

Il n'y a ...... fruits.
Les Dumont n'ont ...... enfants.
Il ne fume ...... blondes.
Elles n'ont ...... amies.
Je ne mange ...... conserves.

Ce ne sont ...... amis.
Nous n'avons ...... timbres.
Ce ne sont ...... cigarettes américaines.
Je n'ai ...... cigarettes blondes.
Ils n'achètent ...... vêtements.

3. *Au restaurant, vous demandez :*

« Garçon, je voudrais ...... un-une, du - de la - de l' ...... ?
pomme, vin, sel, poivre, yaourt, vinaigre, veau, croissant, eau, confiture, beurre, fruit, huile, pain, riz,

4. *Transformez et complétez avec* **DU, DE LA, DE L', DES, DE, D',** *comme dans le modèle :*

crémerie : produits laitiers mais pas fruits .
Un crémier vend des produits laitiers mais ne vend pas de fruits .

boulangerie : ...... pâtisserie mais pas ...... lait
boucherie : ...... viande mais pas ...... boissons
librairie : ...... cartes postales mais pas ...... articles pour fumeurs
crémerie : ...... fromage mais pas ...... huile
épicerie : ...... huile mais pas ...... huîtres

5. *Qui dit quoi ? Employez je n'ai plus de/je ne vends pas de... :*

exemple : droguiste/conserves : « Je ne vends pas de conserves. »
épicier/jambon : « Je n'ai plus de jambon. »

buraliste/timbres
boucher/pain
crémier/vin
épicier/légumes
droguiste/médicaments

libraire/cartes postales
charcutier/veau
boulanger/croissants
pharmacien/aspirine
buraliste/allumettes

6. Que fait...? Qui sont...? Qui est...? Comment s'appelle...?

Posez des questions sur le groupe souligné :

M. Arnaud, c'est le chef des ventes.
La Directrice Commerciale s'appelle Mme La Borderie.
Gilles et Brigitte sont les amis de Didier et Isabelle.
Le fils de Sophie s'appelle Jérôme.
Pierre Richaud est réprésentant.

7. Posez les questions qui donnent les réponses suivantes :

Je m'appelle Henri Dumas.
Pour moi, un steak-frites.
Des côtelettes et un beau rôti de veau.
40 et 27, ça fait 67 F.
Ce stylo ? Il est à moi.
Elles font leurs devoirs.
Je suis secrétaire.
Non, elles ne prennent pas de dessert.

8. Faites des phrases selon le modèle.

Exemple :
Paul / jouer / frère Alain
a) Paul joue avec son frère Alain.
b) Il joue avec lui.

1. Sophie / travailler / amie Colette.
2. Jérôme / habiter / grands parents
3. Est-ce que vous / dîner / frère ?
4. Didier et Isabelle / regarder la télévision / parents
5. Gilles / aller au cinéma / amies Brigitte et Isabelle

9. Complétez et répondez selon le modèle :

A qui ...... pull ? A la sœur de Pierre.
A qui est ce pull ? Il est à sa sœur.

1. A qui ...... vêtements ? Aux parents de Didier et Isabelle.
2. A qui ...... maison ? Aux amis de Pierre.
3. A qui ...... imperméable ? A la fille de Colette.
4. A qui ...... cigarettes ? A la copine de Didier.
5. A qui ...... pantalon ? A Brigitte.
6. A qui ...... journal ? A la femme de Pierre.
7. A qui ...... paquets ? A M. et Mme Richaud.
8. A qui ...... article ? A la cliente.
9. A qui ...... boucherie ? A M. Dumas.
10. A qui ...... écharpe ? A la mère d'Isabelle.

10. Mettez l'adjectif à sa place et faites l'accord :

M. et Mme Durand sont les concierges. (**nouveau**)
Voici des lettres. (**urgent**)
Nous avons des machines. (**électrique**)
Près de la place il y a des restaurants. (**petit**)
Voilà une choucroute. (**beau**)
Vous avez un imperméable. (**beau**)
Quelle est votre adresse ? (**nouveau**)
Pierre et François sont nos collègues. (**nouveau**)
Il y a un hôtel. (**nouveau**)
Il habite une chambre. (**petit**)
Dans notre ville, il y a des restaurants. (**sympathique**)
Elle porte des vêtements. (**moderne**)

B. Images pour...

« Tu habites ici à Évry ? »

Évry ville nouvelle

Évry est près de Paris dans le département de l'Essonne. La ville nouvelle est prévue pour 200 000 habitants. A côté de la préfecture, on trouve un centre commercial, un ensemble culturel «l'Agora» avec piscine, bibliothèque, théâtre, patinoire... L'architecture d'Évry est originale.

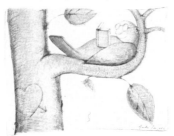

VIVRE A EVRY 1

Une terrasse pour chaque appartement.
Des écoles ouvertes sur des jardins.
Des transports rapides, des pistes cyclables...

Evry 1. Le quartier des Pyramides.

Marne-la-Vallée   (Val-de-Marne)   «La Ferme du Buisson»

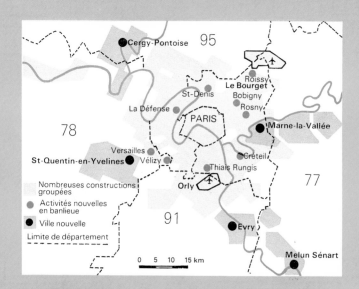

«J'aime bien l'architecture moderne»

Les architectes et les urbanistes des villes nouvelles veulent inventer une nouvelle architecture et un nouvel «art de vivre» pour l'an 2000. Ils veulent aussi réunir les logements, les lieux de travail et les équipements sociaux (commerces, administrations, centres de loisirs).

Il y a 5 villes nouvelles à côté de Paris : Cergy-Pontoise, Saint-Quentin-en-Yvelines, Évry, Melun-Sénart et Marne-la-Vallée.

Saint-Quentin-en-Yvelines. Le quartier des 7 mares.

Sculpture de Klaus Schultze.

La ville nouvelle d'Évry (Essonne).

C. Texte complémentaire

Le garçon :	— *Qu'est-ce que vous prenez, monsieur ?*
Frédéric :	— *Je voudrais un diabolo, s'il vous plaît.*
Francine :	— *Qu'est-ce que c'est, un diabolo ?*
Frédéric :	— *C'est de la limonade avec de la menthe.* *Vous voulez essayer ?*
Francine :	— *Non, merci. Je préfère ma glace.*
Frédéric :	— *Alors, on se retrouve devant la porte du club, ce soir ?*
Francine :	— *D'accord. C'est à quelle adresse ?*
Frédéric :	— *C'est 9 rue des Petites-Écuries. Qu'est-ce que vous faites dans la vie, Francine ?*
Francine :	— *Je suis secrétaire. Je travaille dans . . . .*

Francine, la Canadienne est secrétaire de direction dans une banque. Elle parle français, anglais et allemand. Elle a vingt-sept ans, n'est pas mariée et vit à Lyon avec sa sœur Diana. Leurs parents sont au Canada.

Le week-end, Francine aime bien aller à Paris chez ses amis canadiens. Diana préfère le sport : elle est libre le vendredi à midi et va faire du ski dans les Alpes.

Frédéric est savoyard. Sa famille est de Chamonix. Ses grands-parents ont un petit hôtel de dix chambres à Chamonix et ses parents un restaurant à Paris. Leur spécialité ? La fondue, bien sûr. Et Frédéric, qu'est-ce qu'il fait dans la vie ? Il travaille à l'aéroport de Roissy. Il est à Air-France. Air-France, c'est son travail, mais sa vie, c'est la guitare. Le week-end, Frédéric joue de la guitare électrique dans un club de jazz.

D. Aide-mémoire

1. *Orthographe : Les pluriels en X*

- **les noms :**
  — les noms en **au, eau, eu** prennent un X au pluriel :
  un bureau, des bureaux ;
  un neveu, des neveux
  — les noms en **al** font **aux** au pluriel :
  un cheval, des chevaux
  — quelques noms en **ail** et **ou** font **aux** et **oux** au pluriel :
  travail - travaux, chou - choux
- **les adjectifs :**
  — les adjectifs en **eau** font **eaux** au masculin pluriel :
  nouveau - nouveaux, beau - beaux

2. *Unités de mesure*

- le poids :

un gramme	1 g
un kilo(gramme)	1 kg
une livre	500 g
une tonne	1 000 kilos

- la longueur

un centimètre	1 cm
un mètre	1 m
un kilomètre	1 km

- le volume

un centimètre cube	1 cm^3
un mètre cube	1 m^3
un litre	1 l

- le temps

une seconde	1 s
une minute	1 mn
une heure	1 h
un jour	24 h

E. Conjugaisons

EMBRASSER	DÉSIRER	CÔUTER	MARCHER
j embrasse	je désire	je coûte	je marche
tu embrasses	tu désires	tu coûtes	tu marches
il/elle/on embrasse	il/elle/on désire	il/elle/on coûte	il/elle/on marche
nous embrassons	nous désirons	nous coûtons	nous marchons
vous embrassez	vous désirez	vous coûtez	vous marchez
ils/elles embrassent	ils/elles désirent	ils/elles coûtent	ils/elles marchent

PESER	ACHETER	RANGER	PAYER
je pèse	j' achète	je range	je paie/paye
tu pèses	tu achètes	tu ranges	tu paies/payes
il/elle/on pèse	il/elle/on achète	il/elle/on range	il/elle/on paie/paye
nous pesons	nous achetons	nous rangeons	nous payons
vous pesez	vous achetez	vous rangez	vous payez
ils/elles pèsent	ils/elles achètent	ils/elles rangent	ils/elles paient/payent

PRENDRE	APPRENDRE	COMPRENDRE
je prends	j' apprends	je comprends
tu prends	tu apprends	tu comprends
il/elle/on prend	il/elle/on apprend	il/elle/on comprend
nous prenons	nous apprenons	nous comprenons
vous prenez	vous apprenez	vous comprenez
ils/elles prennent	ils/elles apprennent	ils/elles comprennent

ATTENDRE	VENDRE	VIVRE
j' attends	je vends	je vis
tu attends	tu vends	tu vis
il/elle/on attend	il/elle/on vend	il/elle/on vit
nous attendons	nous vendons	nous vivons
vous attendez	vous vendez	vous vivez
ils/elles attendent	ils/elles vendent	ils/elles vivent

gris   blanc   bleu   vert   jaune

violet/mauve   noir   orange   rouge

rose   brun/marron

✳ *Alain :*	— On s'arrête ici ? Moi, j'aime bien cet endroit. Et vous ?
Luc :	— Tu es fou ! On ne peut pas camper dans un champ, près d'une ferme ! C'est défendu !
Anne :	— Les fermiers sont là. On peut leur demander.
✳ *Anne :*	— Pardon monsieur, je peux vous demander un renseignement ?
Le fermier :	— Bien sûr !
✳ *Anne :*	— Est-ce qu'il y a un terrain de camping près d'ici ?
Le fermier :	— Ah non ! il faut aller à St-Pol.
Anne :	— C'est loin ?
Le fermier :	— C'est à 10 km.
La fermière :	— Vous n'êtes pas français ?
Luc :	— Non.
La fermière :	— Vous venez d'où ?
Luc :	— De Lausanne, en Suisse.
Marie-Claude :	— On vient visiter votre belle région.

✳ *La fermière (à son mari) :*	— Ils sont sympathiques, ces jeunes !
Le fermier :	— Vous voulez rester combien de temps ?
Alain :	— Deux ou trois jours !
Le fermier :	— Bon ça va ! Vous pouvez camper ici !
Anne :	— Vous nous donnez l'autorisation ? Oh, merci beaucoup.
Luc :	— C'est très gentil, merci.
✳ *Alain :*	— Où est-ce qu'on peut monter la tente ?
Le fermier :	— Là-bas, sous les arbres.
Luc :	— Excusez-nous, est-ce qu'on peut faire du feu ?
Le fermier :	— Oui, mais je vous demande de faire attention aux artichauts. Bon. On vous laisse. On a du travail. A bientôt.
Tous :	— A bientôt... A tout à l'heure... et merci encore.

On ne peut pas camper dans un champ.

Les fermiers sont là! On peut leur demander.

[ø]

Est-ce qu'on peut faire du feu?

[œ]

A tout à l'heure.

REGLEMENT DU CAMPING

Il est interdit de faire du bruit le soir après 10 h.

Prière de jeter les ordures dans les poubelles.

Il est interdit de laver la vaisselle dans les lavabos.

Les transistors ne doivent pas gêner vos voisins.

Il est interdit de laisser les chiens se promener librement.

Les barbecues sont interdits.

Nous vous demandons d'avoir une tenue correcte.

Après 10 h interdiction de rouler en voiture dans le camping.

VOCABULAIRE

• le camping

Le terrain de camping, la tente, la caravane, un sac à dos, un matelas pneumatique, un sac de couchage, une chaise pliante, une table pliante, un camping-gaz, une glacière, une lampe de poche...

- **autoriser, interdire**

— Demander une autorisation (une permission)

Est-ce que je peux...   vous demander un renseignement.
Est-ce que vous me permettez de...   camper ici.
Est-ce que vous m'autorisez à...   faire du feu.

— Donner une autorisation (autoriser, permettre)

Oui, vous pouvez...   Je vous donne l'autorisation, la permission, le droit de...
Je vous permets de...   Je vous autorise à...

— Refuser une autorisation (défendre, interdire)

Non, vous ne pouvez pas...   C'est défendu ! c'est interdit !
Je vous défends, je vous interdis de...

- **verbes, adjectifs et noms**

Autoriser   C'est autorisé   une autorisation
Interdire   C'est interdit   une interdiction
Permettre   C'est permis   une permission
Défendre   C'est défendu   « défense de... »

- **formules de politesse**

Pour remercier :
Merci, merci beaucoup, merci encore. C'est très gentil...

Pour s'excuser :
Pardon, excusez-moi.

Pour dire au revoir :
Au revoir, à bientôt, à tout à l'heure, à demain, à lundi (mardi...)

GRAMMAIRE

1. Les pronoms personnels compléments indirects

(A qui est-ce qu'il parle ?)

— A moi   Il **me** parle
— A toi   Il **te** parle
— A lui
      elle   Il **lui** parle

— A nous   Il **nous** parle
— A vous   Il **vous** parle
— A eux
      elles   Il **leur** parle

- ATTENTION !

Anne parle **à la fermière.** Elle **lui** parle.
Anne parle **au fermier.** Elle **lui** parle.

Le fermier parle **à Anne et Marie-Claude.** Il **leur** parle.
Le fermier parle **à Luc et Alain.** Il **leur** parle.

2. Interrogation sur le lieu

— *Où est-ce qu'*on peut camper ?   **Ici, là, là-bas...**
   Où peut-on camper ?   **Sous** les arbres. **Près** de la ferme.
                                          A côté du champ...

— *Où est* le terrain de camping ?   **A** 10 km, à 50 km..., **loin,** tout
                                          près, à côté...

— Vous venez *d'où ? D'où* venez-vous ? **De** Suisse, **de** Paris... **de** loin.
— *Où* allez-vous ?   **A** Londres, **en** Bretagne.

73

3. Pronoms personnels d'insistance

Moi,	je	_fais_	du football.
Toi,	tu		
Nous,	nous	faisons	du tennis.
Vous,	vous	faites	du camping.
Lui,	il	fait	de la peinture.
Elle,	elle		
Nous,	on		
Eux,	ils	font	de la musique.
Elles,	elles		

4. Un verbe - 2 constructions : demander

— **Demander quelque chose** *(à quelqu'un)* :

Anne demande un renseignement aux fermiers.
Elle demande aux fermiers l'autorisation de camper.

— **Demander** *(à quelqu'un)* **de faire quelque chose.**

Je vous demande de sortir.
Il leur demande de faire attention aux artichauts.

---

1. D'où viennent-ils ? Où vont-ils ?

2. Remplacez les noms soulignés par des pronoms :

ex. : Le *fermier* permet aux *Suisses* de camper chez lui.
— *Il leur permet de camper chez lui.*

La *fermière* donne un renseignement aux *jeunes Suisses.*
Anne demande *à la fermière* l'autorisation de camper.
Pierre parle *à Sophie.*
Les *étudiants* demandent un renseignement au *professeur.*
Sophie parle *aux enfants de Pierre et Colette.*

Le *fermier et sa femme* demandent aux *campeurs* de faire attention aux pommes.
Mme *Richaud* demande des côtelettes au *boucher.*
M. *Richaud* donne un jus de fruits *aux enfants.*
La *secrétaire* demande un renseignement au *chef des ventes.*
Le *directeur* parle *à ses secrétaires.*

3. Trouvez les questions :

ex. : Il vient d'Angleterre.
(Question :) D'où vient-il ?

1. Vous pouvez mettre votre voiture devant la maison.
2. Non, il n'y a pas de cinéma près d'ici.
3. Du pain ? Il y a une boulangerie à 3 km.
4. Non, on ne peut pas camper dans un champ.
5. Elles viennent du Venezuela.

4. Remettez dans l'ordre :

1. Un/vous/je/renseignement/demander/peux.
2. Leur/de/il/faire attention/demande.
3. Ici/camper/permet/de/nous/il.
4. Lui/vous/l'autorisation/pouvez/demander.
5. Est-ce qu'/où/tente/monter/leur/ils/peuvent.

5. *Que dit le personnage* **a** *? Trouvez la bonne réponse :*

Ils ne me parlent pas !
Je ne lui parle pas !

Je te parle   Tu lui parles ?
Je leur parle   Tu me parles ?

6. *Regardez tous ces panneaux :*
cette forêt est « protégée ».

Donnez le règlement correspondant
aux panneaux en embloyant :

il est défendu, interdit de...,

il faut faire attention à...

---

1. **Anne** demande un renseignement **à la fermière ?**
Oui, **elle lui** demande un renseignement.
le boucher vend un rôti à **M. et Mme Richaud ?**
Oui, **il leur** vend un rôti.

2. A qui est-ce que **tu** parles ?   A **moi ?**   Oui **je te** parle.
A qui est-ce qu'**il** parle ?   A **eux ?**   Oui, **il leur** parle.
A qui est-ce qu'**il** téléphone ?   A **elle ?**   Oui, **il lui** téléphone.

• *Il va à Rome. Elle aussi peut-être ?*
Il lui pose beaucoup de questions :
sa nationalité, sa profession, sa destination...
Il veut fumer, ouvrir la fenêtre.
Imaginez le dialogue :

Lui :   *Je peux vous demander quelque chose ?*
Elle :   *Bien sûr.*
Lui :   *Vous allez à Rome ?*
Elle :   *Non,...*
Elle :   *Oui, ...*

- **Ils participent à une conférence internationale.**
Ils se présentent.
Continuez le dialogue.

M. Freitag :	*Moi, je m'appelle Klaus Freitag.*
	Je suis allemand, je viens de...
M. Y :	*Moi, je suis belge, je m'appelle...*
	Je viens de...
M. Freitag :	*Et M. Andretti ?*
M. Y :	*Lui, il est...*
	Et Anne Garcia ?...

- **Jeu : le « chef ».**
Vous demandez une autorisation.
Le « chef » accepte ou refuse.
Dialoguez.

Vous :	*S'il vous plaît, est-ce que je peux,*
	est-ce que vous me permettez de
	(téléphoner, fumer, lire le journal...) ?
Lui :	*Oui, je vous permets de, ...*
	Je vous autorise à...
Vous :	*Merci, merci beaucoup, c'est très gentil...*
Ou bien :	*Non, je ne vous permets pas...*
	Je vous défends de...
	C'est défendu, c'est interdit !

- **Interrogez votre voisin :**

Vous êtes français ? Vous habitez où ?
Vous venez d'où ? Où allez-vous cet été ?
Vous restez ici combien de temps ?

- **Qu'est-ce qu'ils font**
pendant leurs vacances ?
Faites-le(s) parler :
Moi, je... Eux, ils...

- **Et vous qu'est-ce que vous faites pendant vos vacances ? Et votre voisin(e).**
Moi, je fais du tennis. Moi, je... Lui, il...

- **Demandez un renseignement à votre voisin(e).**
vous voulez jouer au tennis, aller à la plage,
faire des courses, aller au cinéma...

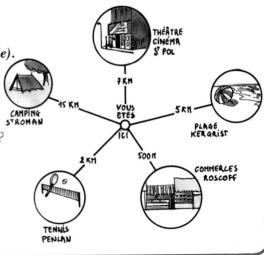

Ex. :

Vous :	*Je peux vous demander un renseignement ?*
Lui-Elle :	*Bien sûr !*
Vous :	*Est-ce qu'il y a un tennis près d'ici ?*
Lui-Elle :	*Oui, à...*
	Non, il faut aller à...
Vous :	*C'est loin ?*
Lui-Elle :	*C'est à...*
	Non, c'est à...

∗ Luc :	— Oh, zut ! Regardez ! La roue arrière est à plat !
Alain :	— Bon. Luc, prends la tente dans le coffre. Marie-Claude, gonfle les matelas pneumatiques. Moi, je change la roue, Luc, tu peux sortir le cric et la manivelle, s'il te plaît.
Luc :	— Voilà. N'oublie pas de mettre le frein à main.
∗ Alain :	— Je n'arrive pas à desserrer cette roue. Tu veux bien m'aider ?
Luc :	— Bien sûr. Ouf ! ça y est !
∗ Alain :	— Qui a des cigarettes ?
Marie-Claude :	— Moi, j'en ai.
Luc :	— Il y a encore de la bière ?
Anne :	— Non, il n'y en a plus !
∗ La fermière :	— Alors, les jeunes, ça va ?
Tous :	— Oui, oui. Très bien.
La fermière :	— Je vais à St-Pol au supermarché. Est-ce que vous avez besoin de quelque chose ?
Anne :	— Oui, il nous faut de la viande, des fruits, du pain...
Luc :	— Et de la bière !
La fermière :	— Eh bien, venez avec moi.
Anne :	— On y va, Marie-Claude ?
Marie-Claude :	— D'accord. Allons-y.

77

Anne :	— Attends! Je prends de l'argent!
Alain :	— Pensez au pain!
Marie-Claude :	— Oui, on y pense.
Luc :	— Et n'oubliez pas la bière!
✳ Alain :	— Dites, Madame, qu'est-ce qu'on peut visiter dans la région?
La fermière :	— Eh bien, il y a la mer, la plage. Et puis il faut voir Morlaix, St-Pol et Roscoff. Il y a une fête à Roscoff ce soir. Allez-y!
Luc :	— Le guide conseille de visiter Brasparts. Où est-ce Brasparts?
La fermière :	— Ah, c'est dans la montagne.
Alain :	— Il y a des montagnes ici?
La fermière :	— Oui, les Monts d'Arrée. Ça fait 400 m d'altitude.
Luc :	— 400 m! Une montagne!

[ã]
[ɛ̃]

Prends la tente dans le coffre!
● ● ● ● (●) ●

Moi, je change la roue.
● ● ● ● ●

Mets le frein à main. !
● ● ● ● ●

Pensez à la viande et au pain.!
● ● ● ● ● ● ● ●

VENEZ EN BRETAGNE!
Prenez la route de la mer!

Allez à Roscoff!

ROSCOFF 5 000 habitants *(les Roscovites)*

Par la route	Paris	540 km
	Rennes	215 km
	Brest	62 km
	Morlaix	28 km
Par le train	Gare S.N.C.F. à Morlaix	

HÔTELS (avec restaurant)

Hôtel Talabardon	*50 chambres*
Hôtel d'Angleterre	*40 chambres*
Hôtel Régina	*60 chambres*
Hôtel des Bains	*50 chambres*
Hôtel Bellevue	*25 chambres*
Hôtel de la Plage	*27 chambres*
Hôtel du Centre	*21 chambres*

SYNDICAT D'INITIATIVE dans la chapelle Sainte-Anne

- **Il faut voir**
  — l'église de Notre-Dame (1550, style Renaissance).
  — **les maisons du XVIᵉ et du XVIIᵉ siècles** près du port (n° 25 maison de « Marie Stuart »).
- **Arrêtez-vous**
  — **à la petite chapelle Sainte-Barbe** et regardez l'entrée de la rivière de Morlaix, le château du Taureau.
  — **au couvent des Capucins** : le grand figuier, un arbre géant de 362 ans (1621, 600 m² de surface).

ROSCOFF, *son port international (liaisons avec la Grande-Bretagne et l'Irlande), ses plages, sa vieille ville, son centre de thalassothérapie et de biologie marine.*

- *Nous vous conseillons de :*
  — manger des crêpes et des coquillages,
  — prendre un bain d'algues,
  — visiter l'aquarium.
- *Dans la région on peut visiter :*
  — **l'île de Batz** (*prononcez BA*) : Belles plages de sable fin, phare de 68 m (prenez le bateau sur le port, 15 minutes de traversée).
  — **St-Pol-de-Léon**, ville commerçante. Chapelle du Kreisker et cathédrale (XVᵉ siècle).

• dans le guide

conseiller *(un conseil)*, visiter *(une visite)*, s'arrêter *(un arrêt)*...

† une église   ⩽ un point de vue - un panorama

⌂ un château   ⥾ un phare

M un musée   ⩕ une côte rocheuse

⨄ un port (de plaisance)   ⁓ une plage...

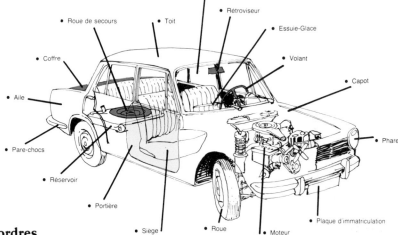

• la voiture (l'auto) : des « pannes »

La roue est à plat
Le réservoir est vide
Le phare est cassé

il faut changer la roue.
il faut faire le plein.
il faut réparer le phare.

Labels on diagram: Pare-Brise, Rétroviseur, Roue de secours, Toit, Essuie-Glace, Coffre, Volant, Capot, Aile, Phare, Pare-chocs, Réservoir, Portière, Siège, Roue, Moteur, Plaque d'immatriculation

• les demandes - les ordres

(en classe)

Regardez ! Écoutez ! Répétez ! Apprenez !
Parlez ! Lisez ! Écrivez ! Faites attention ! ......
N'oubliez pas ! Ne parlez pas !
Entrez ! Sortez ! Asseyez-vous ! Levez-vous ! ......

Tu veux bien m'aider ?   Oui, je veux bien
Tu veux venir avec moi ?   D'accord, Bien sûr !
Tu peux m'aider ?   Non ! Je ne veux pas !
Tu peux venir avec moi ?   Non ! Je ne peux pas !
Aide-moi ! Viens avec moi !   Oui, d'accord. Ah non !

GRAMMAIRE

1. L'impératif

a) formation.

Vous visitez la Bretagne ⟶ **Visitez** *la Bretagne*
(indicatif)   *(impératif)*

je demande ⟶ *(un renseignement au fermier)*   ✗

tu demandes ⟶ **Demande** *(au fermier)*

il/elle/on demande ⟶ ✗

nous demandons ⟶ **Demandons !**

vous demandez ⟶ **Demandez !**

ils/elles demandent ⟶ ✗

b) négation.

Achète du pain !   N'achète pas de pain !   Partez !   Ne partez pas !
Prenons la voiture !   Ne prenons pas la voiture !   Entrez !   N'entrez pas !

c) conjugaison.

REGARDER	CHANGER	PRENDRE
regarde	change	prends
regardons	changeons	prenons
regardez	changez	prenez

METTRE	SORTIR	ALLER
mets	sors	va
mettons	sortons	allons
mettez	sortez	allez

VENIR	FAIRE	S'ARRÊTER
viens	fais	arrête-toi
venons	faisons	arrêtons-nous
venez	faites	arrêtez-vous

2. en et y

a) indiquent le lieu.
y = là
en = de là

il va **à** Paris - il **y** va
ils campent **en** Espagne - ils **y** campent
nous allons **au** cinéma - nous **y** allons

il vient **de** Paris - il **en** vient
nous arrivons **du** Japon - nous **en** arrivons
tu sors **de la** boulangerie ? - tu **en** sors ?

b) remplacent un nom.
y = à ça
en = de ça

elle pense **à son travail - elle y** pense
il pense aux vacances - il **y** pense
j'ai **des cigarettes** - j'**en** ai
il achète du pain, de la viande - il **en** achète

c) place de « en » et « y »

nous allons en Bretagne :
nous **y** allons - allons-**y** - n'**y** allons pas !
tu prends du pain :
tu **en** prends - prends-**en** ! - n'**en** prends pas !

1. Répondez aux questions en employant « en » ou « y ».

Est-ce qu'ils campent dans le champ ?
→ *Oui, ils y campent.*
Est-ce qu'ils prennent des pommes ?
→ *Non, ils n'en prennent pas.*
Est-ce que tu vas au cinéma ?
— *Oui ......*
Est-ce que tu achètes des glaces ?
— *Non ......*
Est-ce qu'elle habite à Londres ?
— *Oui ......*

Est-ce qu'elle connaît des Écossais ?
— *Non......*
Est-ce que tu travailles en Suisse ?
— *Oui ......*
Est-ce que tu es né dans ce pays ?
— *Non ......*
Est-ce qu'elles vont à Paris le week-end ?
— *Oui ......*
Est-ce qu'elles ont des amis parisiens ?
— *Non ......*

2. Répondez en employant « en » ou « y » et l'impératif.

Tu viens avec moi à l'aéroport ?   — D'accord, allons-y.

1. *Est-ce que nous pouvons aller au cinéma, Papa ?   — Oui ......*
2. *Tu viens avec moi acheter un journal ?   — D'accord ......*
3. *Papa, est-ce que je peux prendre du vin ?   — Non ......*
4. *Chérie, on prend des côtelettes pour ce soir ?   — Volontiers ......*
5. *Maman, est-ce que je peux aller camper avec mes copains ?   — Non ......*

3. Regardez les documents page 78 et écrivez :

une publicité sur votre ville, un extrait de guide sur votre région ou votre pays.

4. *A quels ordres (à l'impératif) correspondent ces signaux ou ces panneaux ?*

5. *Il est 5 heures du matin ! Vous partez - vous voulez laisser vos « instructions » :*

Il faut : faire des courses (acheter beurre, œufs, café, fruits)
écrire à grand-mère, à des amis...
prendre rendez-vous chez le dentiste, le coiffeur...
faire attention à...
aller chez/au...
ne pas oublier...
penser à...

Faites un mot *pour votre ami(e), mari ou femme,*
vos enfants... **Employez des impératifs.**

1. Est-ce que tu **manges**   du **poisson ?**   **oui,** j'en mange
                                et de la **viande ?**   **non,** je n'en mange pas

        Est-ce que tu **vas**   au **cinéma ?**   **oui,** j'y vais
                                et au **théâtre ?**   **non,** je n'y vais pas

2. Pierre dit à Jean de **travailler**   : « Travaille ! »
     Il veut **travailler** avec Nicole   : « Travaillons ! »
     Il dit à Paul et Anne de **travailler**   : « Travaillez ! »

3. Paul, **va à la poste !**   Non, n'y va pas !
     Chérie, **allons au cinéma !**   Non, n'y allons pas !
     Les enfants, **prenez du pain !**   Non, n'en prenez pas !

● *Le « parasite » et sa victime*

Lui :   *Est-ce que tu as, vous avez ...... des cigarettes ?*
              du feu ? de l'argent ? une voiture ......
La victime : *Oui, j'en ai ......*
                     Non, je n'en ai pas ......
Lui :   *Est-ce que tu vas au restaurant ? au cinéma ? au théâtre ? ......*
             Est-ce que tu pars à Paris, à Tahiti, aux Bahamas ?
Elle :   *Oui/non ......*
Lui :   *Je peux venir avec toi ?*
Elle :   *Oui, viens/non, ne viens pas ......*
             Allons-y ...... Non, je ne veux pas.

Imaginez la situation et le dialogue.

1. Mettre le frein à main.
2. Prendre cric, manivelle et roue de secours.
3. Dévisser les écrous de la roue.
4. Mettre le cric sous la voiture.
5. Changer la roue.
6. Revissez les écrous.
7. Descendre le cric.
8. Revisser encore.
9. Remettre roue à plat, cric et manivelle.

● *Une roue à plat.*

Il lit la notice et donne des instructions.

Imaginez le dialogue.

Lui :	*Mets le frein à main.*
	Prends le cric ......
Elle :	*Voilà/D'accord...*
	(ou) Je n'y arrive pas,
	tu peux m'aider ?

● *Qu'est-ce qu'il y a à visiter à Morlaix ?*
Faites le guide en employant :

— *Il y a ...... il faut voir ...... je vous conseille ......*

● *Vous allez au bureau de tabac*
(à la poste, à la boulangerie, à la pharmacie...).
Invitez votre voisin(e).

Vous :	*Je vais à/au ......*
	Est-ce que tu as besoin de ......
Lui/Elle :	*Oui, il me faut ......*
	Non.
Vous :	*Tu as de l'argent ?*
Lui/Elle :	*Oui/non.*
Vous :	*On y va ...... Allons-y.*
Lui/Elle :	*D'accord ...... Allons-y.*
	Non ! Attends ! Je prends ......

● *Vous conseillez votre voisin(e) pour la visite de votre pays ou de votre ville.*

Lui :	*Qu'est-ce qu'on peut visiter ?*
	Qu'est-ce que tu (vous) me conseilles (ez)
Vous :	*Va à ...... Allez à ...... Il y a ......*

3.3 Fête à Roscoff

Luc : — Ah voilà Alain ! Tu as garé la voiture ?

Alain : — Oui, à l'entrée de la ville

Luc : — C'est loin ?

Alain : — C'est à 1 kilomètre.

Anne : — Oh là là ! il faut y retourner. J'ai oublié mon sac et l'appareil de photo.

Alain : — Oh zut !

Anne : — Sois gentil !

Alain : — Bon, bon, on y va. Où est-ce qu'on se retrouve ?

Luc : — En face du café de la Marine. Dépêchez-vous !

« C'est la fête à Roscoff. La fête de la Sainte-Barbe. Aujourd'hui on rit, on chante, on danse. A 17 h grand concours de chant. A 18 h apéritif avec cidre et crêpes. A 19 h concours de danses bretonnes et de binious... »

Luc : — Qu'est-ce que c'est un biniou ?

— Un biniou c'est un instrument de musique, jeune homme.

« A 21 h fest noz* sur la place du port. »

Marie : — C'est du breton fest noz ?

Luc : — Je crois.

Marie : — Qu'est-ce que ça veut dire ?

Luc : — Je ne sais pas.

Notre concours de chant commence. Voici la première concurrente. Approchez-vous du micro, n'ayez pas peur ! Elle est jeune, elle est jolie mais elle a l'air timide ! Amis de Roscoff applaudissez bien fort ! Ah elle sourit.

Lui : — Vous êtes mademoiselle... ?

Elle : — Madame. Madame Chevallier.

Lui : — Et vous venez... ?

Elle : — De Nice.

Lui : — Et vous êtes en vacances ici ?

Elle : — Oui, avec mon mari et mes enfants. Mais c'est le dernier jour, on part demain.

Lui : — Vous avez passé de bonnes vacances ?

Elle : — Oui.

(* Fest noz : fête de nuit.)

| Lui : | — Qu'est-ce que vous avez fait ? |
| Elle : | — On est allé à la plage, on s'est baigné et on a visité la région. |

| Lui : | — C'est bien ça ! Et qu'est-ce que vous chantez ? |
| Elle : | — « J'ai pleuré sur tes pas ». |

[y]

Qu'est-ce que tu as fait ?
● ● ● ●

J'ai garé la voiture.
● ● ● ● ●

Qu'est-ce que c'est une flûte ?
● ● ● ●

C'est un instrument de musique.
● ● ● ● ● ● (●) ● ●

PROGRAMME

17 h Grand concours de chant
18 h Apéritif avec cidre et crêpes
19 h Concours de binious et de danses bretonnes
21 h FEST NOZ avec l'orchestre les Korrigans de Brest

ROSCOFF FÊTE DE LA SAINTE-BARBE
Le 6 août
sur la place du port

Le 4/8

En vacances en Bretagne,
nous pensons à vous !
Avons visité Saint-Malo
et sommes arrivés à Roscoff.
Belle région : mer et soleil !
Bons baisers et
A bientôt
hEG

VOCABULAIRE

● **la fête, le spectacle**

— **les vedettes** : chanter, danser, jouer *(la comédie)*, jouer de la musique.
Le chant *(un chanteur - une chanteuse)*
La danse *(un danseur - une danseuse)*
Le théâtre, le cinéma *(un comédien - une comédienne - un acteur - une actrice)*
La musique *(un musicien - une musicienne)*.
— **les spectateurs (le public)** :
rire *(le rire)*, sourire *(le sourire)* ;
pleurer *(les pleurs - les larmes)*
applaudir *(les applaudissements - les bravos)*
siffler *(les sifflets)*
— **le spectacle** : commencer *(le commencement - le début)* finir *(la fin)*

- **pour compter :**

Elle a gagné le concours - elle est **première**.

1 premier, (ière)
2 deuxième *(second, e)*
3 troisième
4 quatrième... dernier, (ière)

- **aujourd'hui**

Vendredi	Samedi	**Dimanche**	Lundi	Mardi
avant-hier	hier	**aujourd'hui**	demain	après-demain

- **le préfixe « re » + verbe (= une deuxième fois)**

Venir	Voir	Trouver	Prendre	Faire	Dire
Revenir	Revoir	Retrouver	Reprendre	Refaire	Redire

Mettre	Serrer	Monter	Lire	Commencer
Remettre	Resserrer	Remonter	Relire	Recommencer

GRAMMAIRE

1. Le passé composé = (présent de « avoir » ou de « être » + participe passé) (*)

a) conjugaison.

VISITER
j'ai visité
tu as visité
il/elle/on a visité (la région)
nous avons visité
vous avez visité
ils/elles ont visité

ALLER
je suis allé (ée)
tu es allé (ée)
il/elle/on est allé (ée)
nous sommes allés (ées) à la plage
vous êtes allés (ées)
ils/elles sont allés (ées)

b) formes.

er → **é**   trouver → j'ai trouv**é**   garer → j'ai gar**é**   jouer → j'ai jou**é**
      commencer → j'ai commenc**é**   aller → je suis all**é**

ir → **i**   dormir → j'ai dorm**i**   finir → j'ai fin**i**
      sortir → je suis sort**i**   partir → je suis part**i**

ATTENTION !

avoir	→	eu	venir	→	venu	lire	→	lu
voir	→	vu	pouvoir	→	pu	vouloir	→	voulu
dire	→	dit	mettre	→	mis	prendre	→	pris
être	→	été	naître	→	né	faire	→	fait

(*) **avec être les verbes** : aller/venir ; entrer/sortir ; arriver/partir ; naître/mourir...

+ les verbes pronominaux (cf. 3.4)

c) la négation.

Il visite la région
Il **ne** visite **pas** la région
Je vais à la plage
Je **ne** vais **pas** à la plage

il a visité la région
Il **n'**a **pas** visité la région
je suis allé à la plage
je **ne** suis **pas** allé à la plage

2. Les impératifs (suite)

ÊTRE	AVOIR
sois	aie
soyons	ayons
soyez	ayez

1. *Recopiez et complétez ce tableau. Faites des phrases avec les verbes au passé composé.*

[e]		[i]		[y]	
. . . . .	(être)	repris	(. . . . . .)	. . . . .	(avoir)
chanté	(. . . . . .)	. . . . .	(dire)	lu	(. . . . . .)
. . . . .	(visiter)	. . . . .	(prendre)	. . . . .	(entendre)
travaillé	(. . . . . .)	appris	(. . . . . .)	vendu	(. . . . . .)
. . . . .	(déjeuner)	dormi	(. . . . . .)	. . . . .	(attendre)
fait	(. . . . . .)	. . . . .	(mettre)	voulu	(. . . . . .)
. . . . .	(habiter)	fini	(. . . . . .)	. . . . .	(voir)
oublié	(. . . . . .)	. . . . .	(rire)	. . . . .	(pouvoir)

2. *Recopiez et complétez ce dialogue.*

Vous avez passé de bonnes vacances ?
— *Oui, on . . . . . . Bretagne.*
Vous . . . . . . camping ou à l'hôtel ?
— *On . . . . . . hôtel au bord de la mer.*
Qu'est-ce que . . . . . . fait ?
— *On . . . . . . des églises, des musées.*
On . . . . . . à la plage.

3. Recopiez la carte du fils de Mme Chevallier à sa grand-mère (Employez des passés composés).

Roscoff le 7 août

Ma chère Grand-mère,
Nous . . . . . . de bonnes vacances à Roscoff.
Nous . . . . . . à la plage.
Nous . . . . . . visité la Bretagne.
Hier soir, nous . . . . . . à la fête et maman
. . . . . . fait . . . . . . de chant. Elle a très bien
. . . . . . et les spectateurs . . . . . . beaucoup
. . . . . . Et elle . . . . . . gagné le concours.
Nous repartons demain. A bientôt.

Je t'embrasse très fort. Jean-Baptiste.

4. Vous êtes allés à la fête de Roscoff.
Vous écrivez à des amis ce que vous avez vu et ce que vous avez fait.

5. Faites une affiche (en français) pour annoncer une fête dans votre région, votre ville ou votre village.

6. *Aujourd'hui, c'est le 2 avril 1999. Qu'est-ce qu'il s'est passé le 1ᵉʳ avril?*
Écrivez: Hier...

ARRIVÉE DES MARTIENS

LES LARMES
d'une grande actrice

Une photo du YETI

DIVORCE DE G. G.

Mort de la
dernière BALEINE

Début de la course
VÉNUS - JUPITER

1. — Qu'est-ce que tu as fait?
   — (garer la voiture) **J'ai** garé la voiture
   — (retourner à la fête) Je **suis** retourné à la fête.

2. Qu'est-ce qu'elles ont fait cet été?
   Elles sont allées en Bretagne.
   Elles ont campé près d'une ferme.

● *L'animateur présente les 2 concurrents suivants et dialogue avec eux.*
Faites-les parler!

Nom :	John Smith
Nationalité :	anglaise
Adresse :	6 Castle street, Liverpool
Chanson :	« Love, love ».
Nom :	Gina Mosca
Nationalité :	italienne
Adresse :	14 via Crociferi, Rome
Chanson :	« Hier tu as souri ».

● *Vous organisez un « concours » (de chant, de danse, de poésie, de dessin).*
Présentez votre voisin(e), puis dialoguez avec lui/elle.

Voici le premier concurrent, la première concurrente.
Il est . . . . . . Il a l'air . . . . . . Elle est . . . . . . Elle a l'air . . . . . .
Vous êtes Monsieur . . . . . . Madame . . . . . . Mademoiselle . . . . . .
Vous venez d'où? Qu'est-ce que vous faites ici?
Qu'est-ce que vous faites dans la vie? . . . . . .
Qu'est-ce que vous chantez? (dansez, récitez, dessinez . . . . . .)

● *Le mot mystérieux :*
En vous aidant d'un dictionnaire demandez/donnez une explication à votre voisin sur
le modèle :

Vous : *Qu'est-ce que c'est un biniou,*
une . . . . . . ?
Est-ce que c'est un instrument de
musique, un . . . . . . ?
Qu'est-ce que ça veut dire . . . . . . ?
C'est du français, de l'anglais, du
chinois . . . . . . ?

Lui/Elle : *C'est . . . . . .*
. . . . . .
Oui/non
. . . . . .
Ça veut dire . . . . . .
Je crois/je pense/je ne sais pas
. . . . . .

● *Fixez un rendez-vous à votre voisin(e).*

Vous :	*On va au théâtre, au cinéma, au ......?*
Lui-Elle :	*D'accord/volontiers. Allons-y ......*
ou	*Non, je ne peux pas.*
Vous :	*Où est-ce qu'on se retrouve ?*
Lui-Elle :	*Chez ......, dans ......, devant, à côté*
	de ......, en face de ......, près de,
	à l'entrée de ......, à la sortie de.

● **Qu'est-ce qu'ils/elles ont fait pendant le week-end ?**
Faites-les parler.

● *Dialoguez avec votre voisin(e).*

— *Qu'est-ce que tu as fait (vous avez fait) ce week-end ?*   — *Et toi ?*
— *Où es-tu allé(e) ? Où êtes-vous allé(e) ? ......*   — *Moi......*

● *Les jeunes Suisses racontent au fermier le début de leur voyage.*

(Départ Lausanne le 26 juillet - Paris du 27 juillet au 3 août - Hôtel du Luxembourg - Visite de Notre-Dame, le Louvre, la Tour Eiffel.
Départ en Bretagne le 4 août - Nuit à Rennes - Arrivée à St-Pol le 5.)

Faites-les parler. *Nous sommes partis ......*

● *Racontez vos dernières vacances ou votre dernier voyage. Vous pouvez utiliser les* **verbes** *partir, arriver, visiter, voir, aimer, préférer, manger, dormir, ...*

3.4 Dans les pommes...

Le fermier : — Alors les jeunes, vous vous réveillez ?

Anne : — Oui, mais on a encore sommeil ! On n'a pas assez dormi.

Le fermier : — Qu'est-ce que vous avez fait hier soir ?
Vous êtes allés à la fête ?

Alain : — Oui. On a dansé, on a mangé des crêpes...

Luc : — Et on a bu !

Alain : — On a trop bu ! Moi, j'ai mal à la tête.

Le fermier : — Vous êtes fatigués ?

Alain : — Oh non, ça va. On est en vacances, vous savez.

Le fermier : — Alors je peux vous demander un service ? Je cueille mes pommes - Vous ne voulez pas m'aider ?

Tous : — Oh si - Bien sûr - Si - Volontiers.

Le fermier : — Faites attention, Marie-Claude ! Vous montez trop haut. Soyez prudente !

Anne : — Luc, tiens-lui l'échelle !

Alain : — Eh Luc, apporte-moi un panier vide !

Luc : — J'arrive.

Marie-Claude : — Ne lâche pas l'échelle !

Luc : — Au secours ! Venez vite ! Marie-Claude est tombée !

Alain : — Tu t'es cassé la jambe.

Marie-Claude : — Je ne crois pas.

Le fermier : — Vous ne pouvez pas marcher Marie-Claude ?

Marie-Claude : — Si, si !

Luc : — Tu as mal ?

Marie-Claude : — Un peu ! mais ce n'est pas grave.

Anne : — Il faut appeler un médecin.

Marie-Claude : — Non, non, je n'ai rien...

89

Luc :	— Ouf, j'ai eu peur !!		M. Legall. Excusez-moi.
*Anne :	— Qu'est-ce qui s'est passé ?	Le fermier :	— Ça ne fait rien. Des pommes, j'en ai encore !
Luc :	— J'ai lâché l'échelle et elle est tombée.	Alain :	— Ça s'appelle « tomber dans les pommes » !
Marie-Claude :	— Et j'ai écrasé vos pommes !		

[ã]
[ɔ̃]

On part en vacances dimanche.

Ils ont encore sommeil.

Attention ! Soyez prudente !

Non ! Non ! Vous montez trop haut!

FAITS DIVERS
Chute de cyclo

Hier un accident s'est produit à 6 heures du matin à la sortie de Roscoff sur la route de St-Pol.
M. Christophe Legall, 18 ans, étudiant, demeurant 15 rue des Minimes à Morlaix s'est endormi sur son vélomoteur, est tombé sur la route, et s'est cassé l'épaule droite.

BLOCS-NOTES
Dimanche 21 mars

MÉDECIN
Du samedi 20 mars à 20 h, au lundi 22 à 8 h : Dr Durand, 2 rue du Perrout, tél. : 50.16.12.
En cas d'urgence s'adresser au Centre hospitalier (médecine, chirurgie, maternité).

PHARMACIEN
Pharmacie Centrale, 217 rue Grande, tél. : 50.14.11.

AMBULANCES
Hôpital, permanence du centre hospitalier : Ambulances Avonnaises, tél. : 50.05.12.
Urgences : Ambulances Louis, 175 rue Grande, tél. : 50.08.61.
Ambulance Service, 48 rue A.-Briand, tél. : 50.61.13.

INFIRMIÈRE
Mme Fleuric, A-18, Les Peupliers, tél. : 50.18.03.

VOCABULAIRE

● le corps

le cou, le bras,

la main, les doigts,

l'épaule, le coude,...

le ventre le dos,

le foie, le cœur,

l'estomac...

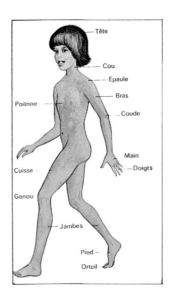

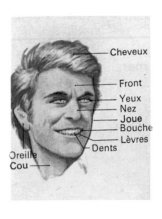

la tête

- **l'accident, la maladie,** être malade, être fatigué

avoir mal *à la tête, à la jambe, aux dents...*
se faire mal, (un mal, une douleur), se casser *la jambe, le bras,*
la cuisse..., (une cassure, une fracture), se blesser (une blessure)
c'est grave, ce n'est pas grave, ce n'est rien...
Il faut appeler un médecin, une ambulance, la police, les pompiers...

- **la sécurité**

Attention ! Danger ! Danger de mort ! Au secours !
Aidez-moi ! A l'aide ! Venez vite !
Prudence ! Soyez prudents ! Faites attention !

- **les degrés**

Il n'a **pas du tout** dormi	Il a **peu** dormi	Il a **beaucoup** dormi
Il n' a **pas beaucoup** dormi	Il n'a **pas assez** dormi	Il a **trop** dormi
Il a dormi **un peu**	Il a **assez** dormi	Il a **beaucoup trop** dormi

GRAMMAIRE

1. L'interrogation négative

Tu ne peux pas marcher ? **Non,** je ne peux pas
Si, je peux

Ça ne va pas ? **Si,** ça va
— Non, ça ne va pas

Ça va ? **Oui,** ça va
— Non, ça ne va pas

2. L'impératif et le pronom indirect

Parler *(donner, dire, demander, apprendre...)*

(à moi)	parle-moi	—	parlez-moi
(à lui - à elle)	parle-lui	parlons-lui	parlez-lui
(à nous)	parle-nous	—	parlez-nous
(à eux - à elles)	parle-leur	parlons-leur	parlez-leur

(Négation)

ne me parle pas	—	ne me parlez pas
ne lui parle pas	ne lui parlons pas	ne lui parlez pas
ne nous parle pas	—	ne nous parlez pas
ne leur parle pas	ne leur parlons pas	ne leur parlez pas

3. Conjugaison des verbes pronominaux (*) SE RÉVEILLER

Présent	Passé composé	Impératif
je me réveille	je me suis réveillé(e)	
tu te réveilles	tu t'es réveillé(e)	réveille-toi
il/elle/on se réveille	il/elle/on s'est réveillé(e)	
nous nous réveillons	nous nous sommes réveillés(ées)	réveillons-nous
vous vous réveillez	vous vous êtes réveillés(ées)	réveillez-vous
ils/elles se réveillent	ils/elles se sont réveillés(ées)	

(*) Au passé composé tous les verbes pronominaux se conjuguent avec « être ».

Négation   je me réveille   je **ne** me réveille **pas**
je me suis réveillé   je **ne** me suis **pas** réveillé

1. Remplacez les mots soulignés par des pronoms.

Exemple : *Écrivez au directeur.* =
Écrivez-lui.
Téléphonez aux journalistes. =
Téléphonez-leur.
Téléphone à tes parents : ......
Téléphone à ta sœur : ......
Téléphone à ton grand-père : ......
Apporte une bière à Marie-Claude : ......
Apporte une bière à Alain : ......
Apporte une bière à Anne et à moi : ......

2. Mettez les verbes au passé composé :

Hier soir, je ...... (sortir). Je ...... (aller) au restaurant avec des amis. Nous ...... très bien (manger). Puis on ...... (voir) un vieux film de Chaplin. Moi, j'...... beaucoup (rire). A la sortie, nous ...... (aller) dans un bar. On ...... trop (boire). Je ...... (se coucher) à 3 h du matin et ...... (se lever) à 9 heures. Aujourd'hui j'...... (avoir) sommeil toute la journée.

3. Faites des phrases en employant : *moi, lui, nous, leur,* **après.**

Donnez ..... Demandons ..... Achète ..... Tiens ..... Chantez ..... Vendons .....

4. Terminez les phrases en employant : beaucoup, trop, peu, pas assez.

Exemple : Vous fumez beaucoup ? Oui, hier j'ai trop fumé, j'ai fumé deux paquets de cigarettes.

Elle boit beaucoup ? — Oui, hier ......
Ils travaillent beaucoup ? — Non, hier ......
Elle danse beaucoup ? — Oui, hier ......

Vous dormez beaucoup ? — Non, hier ......
Vos enfants mangent beaucoup ? — Oui, hier ......

5. A quels conseils de prudence peuvent correspondre ces panneaux ?

6. Racontez la journée de M. Lemercier.
Qu'est-ce qu'il a fait ?

Réveil à 7 h. Douche. Petit déjeuner à 7 h 30. Sorti à 8 h. Au bureau de 8 h 30 à 12 h. Déjeuner avec une amie. Au bureau de 14 h à 17 h 30. Apéritif avec un copain. Retour à la maison à 19 h. Dîner à 20 h. Télévision (film italien) après dîner. Coucher à 23 h.

Racontez votre journée d'hier.

7. Vous avez été témoin de cet accident. Vous racontez.

Marie-Claude écrit à une amie pour raconter son « accident ». Faites la lettre.

1. Demandez la permission au fermier et à la fermière → Demandez-**leur** la permission.
Donne un panier à Luc → Donne-**lui** un panier.
Téléphone à Anne → Téléphone-**lui.**

2. (Anne) Qu'est-ce qu'elle a fait ?   (monter trop haut)
(prendre l'échelle)   — Parce qu'elle est montée trop haut.
— elle a pris l'échelle.   Elle s'est fait mal ? (se casser la jambe)
Pourquoi est-ce qu'elle est tombée ?   — Oui, elle s'est cassé la jambe.

● **Qu'est-ce qu'ils demandent ? Faites-les parler !**

- *Qu'est-ce qu'ils peuvent dire ?*

- *Faites-les parler :* *Hier, j'ai trop bu ; aujourd'hui, j'ai mal à la tête.*

Il/elle a l'air fatigué(e) ! Dialoguez avec votre voisin(e).

Vous :	ça va ? ça ne va pas ?	vous êtes fatigué(e) ?	vous êtes malade ?
Lui/Elle :	oui/non/si	oui/non	oui/non

Vous :	Où avez-vous mal ?	Qu'est-ce que vous avez mangé/bu ? ......
Lui/Elle :	J'ai mal au/à la	Vous n'avez pas assez dormi ......
Vous :	Vous avez trop mangé/bu	Qu'est-ce que vous avez fait hier ? ......

Anne : — On vient vous dire au revoir...

Marie-Claude : — et vous remercier.

Le fermier : — Vous rentrez chez vous ?

Alain : — Non, non, on reste encore une semaine en Bretagne, mais on va aller à Brest et à Quimper.

Le fermier : — Eh bien, bon voyage !

Anne : — Attendez ! on vous a apporté un petit cadeau. Tenez !

Le fermier : — Une boîte... Qu'est-ce que c'est ?

La fermière : — Donne-la moi. Je vais l'ouvrir... Oh ! Des chocolats suisses. Merci beaucoup. C'est trop gentil. Mais entrez, je suis en train de faire des crêpes. Vous allez les manger avec nous.

Le fermier : — Tu as du café, Yvonne ?

La fermière : — Oui, je viens d'en faire. Il est encore chaud. Tenez, asseyez-vous. Prenez des bols et des assiettes.

Luc : — Passe-moi une fourchette, Marie-Claude !

Anne : — Hmm ! Elles sont bonnes, vos crêpes, Mme Legall. Vous allez me donner la recette.

La fermière : — Bien sûr. Je vais vous l'écrire tout à l'heure.

Marie-Claude : — Arrête, Luc. Ne mange pas trop vite. Tu vas être malade ! Regardez-le ! On vient de manger et il a encore faim !

La fermière : — Laissez-le. Je vais en refaire. Allez, servez-vous. Il faut les manger. Elles vont être froides.

Anne : — On va vous écrire. Vous allez nous donner votre adresse.

La fermière : — Bien sûr, c'est route de Kertanguy à Roscoff.

Anne : — Pardon ? Je n'ai pas compris ! Vous pouvez répéter ?

La fermière : — Route de Kertanguy.

Anne :	— Kertanguy ? Comment ça s'écrit ?
La fermière :	— K-E-R-T-A-N-G-U-Y.
Anne :	— D'accord, Kertanguy.
Le fermier :	— Dites, vous n'avez pas soif ?
Luc :	— Oh si.
Le fermier :	— Tenez, voilà du cidre et du Calva. Le cidre, nous allons le boire tout de suite, et le Calva,

	c'est un cadeau.
★ Tous :	— Oh merci. Merci beaucoup !
Le fermier :	— De rien ! Allez, à votre santé ! Bonne chance et « Kenavo » !
Luc :	— Kenavo ?
Le fermier :	— C'est du breton !
Alain :	— Qu'est-ce que ça veut dire ?
Le fermier :	— Ça veut dire « au revoir ».
Tous :	— Alors Kenavo ! Kenavo !

liaisons

On reste encore une semaine en Bretagne.

Vous allez me donner votre adresse.

Nous allons vous l'écrire tout à l'heure.

FICHE CUISINE

CRÊPES BRETONNES

250 g de farine.
4 œufs.
1/2 litre de lait.
1 cuillerée à soupe de sucre.
1 cuillerée à café de sel.
50 g de beurre.
1 cuillerée à soupe de Calvados.

- Mélanger la farine avec les œufs, le sel, le sucre et le lait froid.
- Ajouter le beurre et le Calva.
- Attendre une ou deux heures.
- Dans une poêle chaude et beurrée, verser assez de pâte, mais pas trop.
- Cuire une ou deux minutes et retourner la crêpe.

1. Versez la pâte avec la louche.
2. Étalez avec le « râteau ».
3. Retournez la crêpe avec la spatule.

=== **VOCABULAIRE** ===

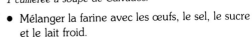

• la vaisselle (les ustensiles de cuisine)

Les cuillères, les fourchettes, les couteaux, les assiettes, les verres, les tasses, les bols...
Une casserole, un plat, une poêle...

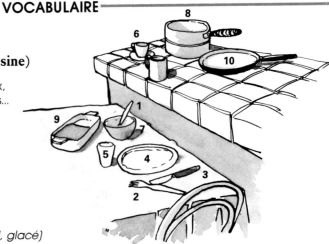

• la cuisine

Le frigidaire *(réfrigérateur)*
la cuisinière, le four
éplucher, mélanger, cuire, faire cuire,
mettre au four, servir chaud, *(tiède, froid, glacé)*

- **l'état physique : avoir...**

faim, soif, chaud, froid, sommeil...
avoir envie/besoin...
de manger, de boire, de dormir...
être... fatigué, malade, guéri...

- **les souhaits (je vous souhaite...)**

bon appétit, bonne chance, bon courage...
bon voyage, bonnes vacances, bon week-end...
(Je bois...) à votre santé ! A la vôtre !...

- **demander une explication**

Pardon ? Je n'ai pas compris !/Je ne comprends pas !

Vous pouvez répéter ?	Répétez, s'il vous plaît !
Vous pouvez épeler ?	Épelez, s'il vous plaît !

Qu'est-ce que ça veut dire ?	Ça veut dire...
Comment ça se dit *(en français)* ?	Ça se dit...
Comment ça s'appelle ?	Ça s'appelle...
Comment ça s'écrit ?	Ça s'écrit : ...

GRAMMAIRE

1. pronoms personnels (compléments directs) : le, la, l', les

remplace un nom...

masculin singulier	c'est un cadeau, je **le** prends voilà Jacques, je **le** connais	ouvre-**le** appelle-**le**	(je **l'**ouvre) (je **l'**appelle)
féminin singulier	c'est une boîte, je **la** prends voilà Anne, je **la** connais	ouvre-**la** appelle-**la**	(je **l'**ouvre) (je **l'**appelle)
'masculin ou féminin pluriel	ce sont des fruits, ce sont des crêpes, je **les** prends voilà Jacques et Luc, voilà Anne et Françoise, je **les** connais	achète-**les** appelle-**les**	(je **les** achète) (je **les** appelle)

2. présent continu, futur proche, passé récent

Présent continu

(être au présent)
je suis
tu es
il/elle/on est   + *en train de + infinitif*
nous sommes
vous êtes
ils/elles sont

Futur proche

(aller au présent)
je vais
tu vas
il/elle/on va   + *infinitif*
nous allons
vous allez
ils/elles vont

Passé récent

(venir au présent)
je viens
tu viens
il/elle/on vient   + *de + infinitif*
nous venons
vous venez
ils/elles viennent

elle va faire des crêpes
elle est en train de faire des crêpes
elle vient de faire des crêpes

3. un verbe, 4 constructions : venir

venir (+ date, heure)   : ils viennent dimanche à 3 heures
venir de (+ lieu)   : ils viennent du Japon/ils en viennent
venir + infinitif   : ils viennent dire au revoir
venir de + infinitif   : ils viennent de manger des crêpes.

1. *Transformez suivant les modèles*

a) *Est-ce qu'ils partent? → Est-ce qu'ils vont partir?*
Elle va en Bretagne. → Elle va aller en Bretagne.

b) *Ils sont partis. → Ils viennent de partir.*
Elle est allée faire des courses. → Elle vient d'aller faire des courses.

Où faites-vous vos courses?
Qu'est-ce que vous faites ce week-end?
Passez-vous vos vacances en Espagne cet été?
Ils vont au Mexique.

Nous avons acheté une nouvelle voiture.
J'ai passé une semaine en Bretagne.
Elle est sortie.
Il est allé chercher le journal.

2. *Qu'est-ce qu'ils viennent de faire? Qu'est-ce qu'ils sont en train de faire? Qu'est-ce qu'ils vont faire?*

Exemple (Alain)
Il est 8 heures :
- 7 heures réveil - 8 heures petit déjeuner - 9 heures départ au bureau.
Alain vient de se réveiller, il est en train de prendre son petit déjeuner, il va partir au bureau.

(Françoise)
- 9 heures lire le journal - 9 heures 30 écrire une lettre - 10 heures téléphoner à sa mère (Il est 9 h 30 mn).

(Didier et Brigitte)
- 11 heures 30 prendre l'apéritif - 12 heures 30 déjeuner au restaurant - 14 heures aller au cinéma (Il est 12 heures 30).

(Jeanne et Corinne)
- 21 heures dîner - 22 heures regarder la télévision - 23 heures 30 aller se coucher (Il est 22 heures).

Et vous, qu'est-ce que vous êtes en train de faire?
Qu'est-ce que vous venez de faire? Qu'est-ce que vous allez faire?
Répondez par écrit.

3. *Le jour de son accident Marie-Claude écrit à sa mère pour lui dire ce qu'elle fait, ce qu'elle a fait, ce qu'elle vient de faire et ce qu'elle va faire.*
Faites la lettre.

4. *Anne répond aux questions d'Alain.*
Notez ses réponses en remplaçant les noms par le, la, les.

Exemple : Est-ce que tu connais...? ... la recette des crêpes? (oui) Elle la connaît bien

les amis de Luc (oui)
la route de Brest (non)
la ville de Morlaix (oui)

le camping de Saint-Pol (non)
Mme Legall (oui)
les filles de Mme Artaud (non)

5. *Remplacez* LE, LA, L', LES *par un nom* :

1. *Je vais la vendre, je vais vendre la* . . . . . .
2. *Il vient de la voir* . . . . . .
3. *Elle va l'acheter* . . . . . .
4. *Il faut l'applaudir* . . . . . .
5. *On va les inviter* . . . . . .

6. *Le fils de Mme Delors a attrapé la grippe - Sa grand-mère écrit à Sophie. Faites la lettre en employant :*

il a mal à . . . . . . - *il a envie de* . . . . . . - *il n'a pas envie de* . . . . . . - *il a faim, soif* . . . . . . *je viens de* . . . . . . - *je vais* . . . . . .

7. *Écrivez la recette de l'omelette aux champignons.*

(6 œufs, des champignons, des fines herbes, du sel, du poivre, de l'huile ou du beurre)
(vous pouvez employer des verbes à l'impératif : « mélangez », à l'indicatif : « vous mélangez », ou à l'infinitif : « mélanger »)

1. Tu vas faire du café ?   Non, je viens d'en faire.
Elle va aller à la boulangerie ?   Non, elle vient d'y aller.
Vous allez téléphoner aux copains ?   Non, nous venons de leur téléphoner.
Il va acheter le journal ?   Non, il vient de l'acheter.

2. Vous avez fait le thé ?   Non, je suis en train de le faire.
Elle a écrit ses cartes postales ?   Non, elle est en train de les écrire.

• ***Il pense aux vacances. Qu'est-ce qu'il va faire ? Faites-le parler !***
Et vous, qu'est-ce que vous allez faire cet été ?

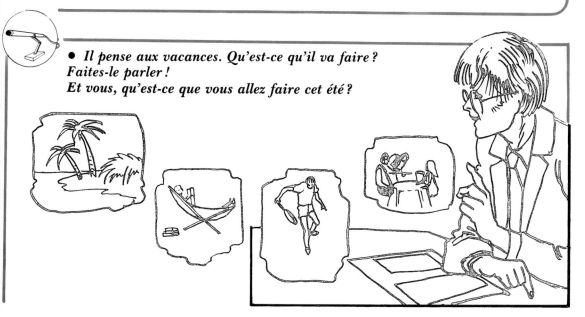

● *Qu'est-ce qu'ils viennent de faire ?*
Qu'est-ce qu'ils sont en train de faire ?
Qu'est-ce qu'ils vont faire ?

● *Dialoguez avec votre voisin(e).*

Vous :   Qu'est-ce que tu fais ?

Lui/Elle :   Je suis en train de ...... Je viens de ...... et cet après-midi/tout à l'heure/ce
soir ...... je ...... Et toi ? qu'est-ce que tu fais ?

Vous :   Moi, je ......

● *Vous demandez à votre voisin la recette d'un plat (ou d'une boisson) de son pays.*
Il vous la donne (oralement), vous essayez de noter.

Vous :   J'ai envie de faire (manger, boire) du, de la ...... Tu peux me donner la recette ?

Lui/Elle :   Tu prends ..... Tu mélanges ...... tu ......

Vous :   Attends ! Je n'ai pas bien compris ! Comment ça s'écrit ? Tu peux répéter ? Épelle s'il te plaît ! Qu'est-ce que ça veut dire ?

● *C'est l'anniversaire (la fête) d'un(e) ami(e).*
Vous apportez des cadeaux.

Il/Elle vous invite à prendre « un verre », un gâteau ....
Jouez la scène.

(L'arrivée) :   Bonjour ! ça va ? ......

Vous :   Bon anniversaire ! Je t'ai apporté .....
Merci ...... Qu'est-ce que c'est ? ....

Lui/Elle :   Tu n'as pas faim / soif ? Prends ......

(puis les « adieux ») :   Au revoir, à bientôt ......

BILAN

A. Tests

1. *Recopiez et complétez les tableaux ci-dessous :*

2ᵉ pers. sing.	mange	.....	.....	.....	va	.....	bois	.....	.....	arrête-toi
1ʳᵉ pers. plur.	.....	soyons	.....	attendons	.....	.....	...	commençons	.....	
2ᵉ pers. plur.	.....	.....	faites	.....	.....	écrivez	.....	.....	dormez	.....

je suis en train d'écouter la radio	....	....	....
....	....	....	vous allez comprendre
....	....	ils viennent de partir	....
tu es en train de l'atten-dre ?	....	....	....
....	j'ai téléphoné à ma sœur	....	....
....	....	nous venons de visiter Brest	....
elle est en train de chan-ter	....	....	....
....	....	....	nous allons dîner
....	Jacques a fait un gâteau	....	....

2. *Choisissez la bonne réponse*

Tu as garé la voiture ?
— Oui, je la gare.
— Oui, je l'ai garée.
— Oui, je vais le faire.

On va à la fête ?
— D'accord. Vas-y.
— D'accord. Allons-y.
— Oui. On y est allé.

Il y a du café ?
— Non, mais je viens d'en faire.
— Non, mais j'en ai fait.
— Non, mais je vais en faire.

Tu vas à la plage ?
— Oui, j'y vais.
— Oui, j'y suis allé.
— Oui, je viens d'y aller.

Vous avez la recette des crêpes ?
— Oui, je vais vous les écrire.
— Oui, je vais vous l'écrire.
— Oui, je vais vous en écrire.

3. *Choisissez la bonne réponse*

On peut camper ici ?
— Oui, oui, c'est défendu.
— Oui, oui, c'est permis.
— Oui, oui, c'est interdit.

On n'a pas beaucoup de pain !
— Alors, n'en achète pas.
— Alors, va en acheter !
— Alors, il ne faut pas en acheter.

Vous n'êtes pas français ?
— Oui, je suis français.
— Bien sûr, je suis français.
— Mais si, je suis français.

Vous avez encore sommeil ?
— Oui, j'ai trop dormi.
— Oui, j'ai beaucoup dormi.
— Oui, je n'ai pas assez dormi.

D'où venez-vous ?
— Nous venons manger avec vous.
— Nous venons du Café du Port.
— Nous venons vous dire au revoir.

4. Écrivez le contraire

C'est permis.
J'ai chaud.
J'ai pensé aux cigarettes.
Elle est gaie.
Ils ont trop d'argent.
J'adore le ski.
Les spectateurs ont applaudi.
Il monte les escaliers.
Vous restez ?
Ils entrent dans le magasin.

5. Trouvez les pronoms qui manquent

Vous êtes américaines ?
— Non, ... je suis australienne et elle, ... est irlandaise.
Ils habitent à l'hôtel ?
— Non, elle, ... habite chez un ami. Et ....., il habite un studio.
Alors, Jacques, vous avez passé de bonnes vacances, tes amis et toi ?
— Moi oui. Mais ......, ils ont eu un accident de voiture.
Vous êtes des touristes ?
— Elle oui, mais ..... j'habite ici.
Vous avez fait les courses ?
— Oui, nous, ... avons acheté les hors-d'œuvre et la viande.
Et ......, ils ont acheté les gâteaux et le vin.

6. Complétez en employant VENIR DE... ou ALLER...

Tu vas faire le concours ?
Il y a trois paquets de cigarettes !
Elle est neuve, sa voiture ?
Elle s'est fait mal ?
On peut camper ici ?
Vous partez quand ?
Il faut ranger le salon !
Vous leur avez dit merci ?
Il n'y a plus de café !
Il ne dort plus ?

— Oui, je ...... (chanter) « Le temps des cerises » !
— Bien sûr, je ...... (acheter) !
— Oui, il ...... (acheter).
— Oui, elle ...... (tomber).
— Je ne sais pas, mais je ...... (demander).
— Nous ne partons pas, nous ...... (arriver) !
— Bon, nous ...... (ranger).
— Non, mais nous ...... (faire).
— Bon, je ...... (faire).
— Non, il ...... (se réveiller).

7. Trouvez les questions

— Nous venons de Suisse.
— Elle est allée chez le coiffeur.
— Je pars au Mexique.
— Ils vont à Madrid.
— Elle arrive de Munich.
— Nous avons dormi dans la voiture.
— J'ai garé la voiture devant la poste.
— Elle va chez une amie.
— J'habite à Paris, place de la Contrescarpe.
— Je viens de chez Juliette.

9. Répondez en employant Y ou EN :

Vous venez de Bretagne ?   — Oui, ...
Le guide parle de Brasparts ? — Non, ...
Vos amis sont à Concarneau ?   — Oui, ...
Vous jouez du piano ?   — Non, ...
Vous achetez des disques ?   — Oui, ...
Elles habitent à Lausanne ?   — Non, ...
Tu prends du café ?   — Non, ...
Ils vont au théâtre ?   — Oui, ...
Tu as de l'argent ?   — Non, ...
Tu penses à la voiture ?   — Oui, ...

8. Choisissez la bonne réponse :

Maman, j'ai peur !
— Mais non, n'ayons pas peur.
— Mais non, n'ayez pas peur.
— Mais non, n'aie pas peur.
On les attend ?
— Non, ne les attendons pas.
— Non, ne les attends pas.
— Non, ne les attendez pas.
Vous êtes malade ? — Oui.
— Alors ne te lève pas.
— Alors ne vous levez pas.
— Alors ne nous levons pas.
Monsieur l'agent, je peux me garer ?
— Non, ne te gare pas ici.
— Non, ne nous garons pas ici.
— Non, ne vous garez pas ici.
Viens, chérie. Je n'aime pas ces gens.
— Alors ne restez pas ici.
— Alors ne restons pas ici.
— Alors ne reste pas ici.

10. Mettez le pronom qui convient :

Il est avec sa sœur. Il ...... parle.
Il est avec ses amis. Il ...... parle.
Ta voiture est trop vieille : vends ......
— Je ...... ai vendue hier !
Vous parlez à ces gens ?
— Non, nous ne ...... parlons pas.
Tu as invité les Guimard ?
— Non, je ne ...... ai pas invités.
Tu veux sa voiture ? Il faut ...... lui demander.
Je peux regarder tes livres ? — Oui, regarde ......
Je peux téléphoner à tes parents ? — Oui, téléphone ......
Tu n'as plus de vêtements !
Achète ...... un beau blouson.
Je n'ai plus de cigarettes. Tu ...... en achètes ?
On peut venir ? C'est vrai ? Vous ...... invitez ?
Les enfants veulent une glace.
— Oh oui, Papa, achète ...... une glace !
Je vous ai écrit une lettre ; vous ...... avez lue ?
J'ai une grande maison. Viens chez ......

B. Texte complémentaire

Frédéric : — Allô... ici Frédéric. Est-ce que je peux parler à Francine, s'il vous plaît ?
— Elle dort.

Frédéric : — Alors ne la réveillez pas.
— Si, si. Elle travaille à neuf heures et demie. Je vais l'appeler. Ah ! Elle vient de se réveiller. Francine ! Téléphone.

Francine : — Qui c'est ?
— Ton copain de Paris, Frédéric.

Francine : — Allô ? Frédéric ?

Frédéric : — Bonjour, Francine. Excuse-moi, je te réveille.

Francine : — Non, non. D'où est-ce que tu m'appelles ?

Frédéric : — De Roissy. Je viens d'arriver à mon travail.

Francine : — Mais quelle heure est-il ?

Frédéric : — Huit heures et demie.

Francine : — Oh là là ! J'ai encore sommeil. Je n'ai pas assez dormi.

Frédéric : — Qu'est-ce que tu as fait hier soir ?

Francine : — Je suis allée au cinéma avec des amis. Ensuite on est allé dîner et on a pris un verre dans un bar. J'ai un peu trop bu. J'ai mal à la tête aujourd'hui.

Frédéric : — Tu es rentrée à quelle heure ?

Francine : — A trois heures du matin. Et toi, qu'est-ce que tu as fait hier soir ?

Frédéric : — Je suis resté chez moi, j'ai travaillé ma guitare et... j'ai pensé à toi.

Francine : — Ah, c'est gentil.

Frédéric : — Qu'est-ce que tu fais ce week-end ?

Francine : — Je ne sais pas.

Frédéric : — Moi, je ne travaille pas vendredi. Je peux venir à Lyon ? Tu m'invites ?

Francine : — Bien sûr.

Frédéric : — Je peux être à Lyon dans l'après-midi.

Francine : — Moi, je travaille, mais je suis libre à cinq heures. Mais, dis, tu as mon adresse ?

Frédéric : — Non, je ne l'ai pas.

Francine : — Tu as quelque chose pour écrire ?

Frédéric : — Attends, je vais prendre un stylo... voilà.

Francine : — Alors, c'est 11 rue Raynouard.

Frédéric : — Tu peux répéter ? Je n'ai pas compris.

Francine : — 11 rue Raynouard.

Frédéric : — Renoir ?

Francine : — Non : Raynouard. Je vais épeler : R-A-Y-N-O-U-A-R-D. Tu as compris ?

Frédéric : — Oui, oui.

Francine : — Je viens t'attendre à la gare ?

Frédéric : — Mais non. Je connais bien Lyon. J'y ai habité deux ans.

Francine : — Bon. Alors, à vendredi ?

Frédéric : — D'accord, à vendredi. Je t'embrasse.

Francine : — A bientôt.

C. Images pour :

« Il faut voir Roscoff »

ROSCOFF est, d'octobre à mai, une petite ville de 4 000 habitants. Mais de juin à septembre, 50 000 touristes — Parisiens, étrangers (Anglais et Allemands surtout) — viennent visiter les plages de sable fin, les vieilles rues, le port. Ils viennent aussi se reposer et se « soigner » : l'eau de mer chaude est très bonne pour les rhumatismes et les fractures. Dans le vieux port, on voit des bateaux à voile et des bateaux de pêche « langoustiers ». Ils vont pêcher la langouste et le crabe près des îles anglo-normandes ou de la Cornouaille anglaise.

ROSCOFF a été un grand port de commerce et de guerre du xve au xviiie siècle. En 1404, l'amiral Jean du Penhoat est parti de Roscoff pour combattre les Anglais (bataille du Cap Saint-Mathieu). En 1548, Marie STUART est arrivée d'Angleterre pour se marier avec le « dauphin » de France, François II.

Au xviiie siècle, ROSCOFF est un « repaire de corsaires ».

AU VIEUX ROSCOFF

Trou de flibustiers, vieux nid
A corsaires ! Dans la tourmente
Dors ton bon somme de granit...
Dors : sous les noires cheminées
Écoute rêver tes enfants,
Mousses de quatre-vingt-dix ans...
Épaves des belles années...

Tristan Corbière, *Les amours jaunes* (Éd. Gallimard).

« C'est du breton, FEST NOZ » ?

Oui, c'est du breton ! Ça vient de « fest », la fête et « noz », la nuit. Le soir de la fête, on allume un grand feu. Jeunes et vieux dansent, les vieux quelquefois en costume traditionnel, les jeunes en blue jean ! Il n'y a pas beaucoup de touristes. On mange des crêpes, on boit du cidre et du « chouchen » (un alcool fait avec du cidre, du miel et du calvados) ; les musiciens jouent du biniou (une petite cornemuse) et de la bombarde (un petit instrument, mais il fait beaucoup de bruit), des chanteurs chantent en breton de très longues chansons, les « Kan ha diskan » (chant et rechant). Le premier chanteur chante la première phrase, le deuxième chanteur la répète, etc.
On danse en ligne ou en groupe la « gavotte », le « jabadao » ou « l'an-dro ».

D. Aide-mémoire

1. Les Pronoms personnels

	A	B	C	D (*)
1re pers. sing.	je (j')	me (m')	me (m') [moi]	moi
2e pers. sing.	tu	te (t')	te (t') [toi]*	toi
3e pers. sing.	il, elle, on	le, la (l') [se]*	lui	lui, elle
1re pers. plur.	nous	nous	nous	nous
2e pers. plur.	vous	vous	vous	vous
3e pers. plur.	ils, elles	les [se]	leur	eux, elles

A. Pronoms personnels sujets :
elle travaille, **nous** allons à la plage, **on** habite à Paris...

B. Pronoms personnels compléments directs :
je **le** connais, on **la** connaît, on **les** connaît
(*) avec les verbes pronominaux :
je **me** lave, tu **te** laves, il **se** lave...

C. Pronoms personnels compléments indirects (sans préposition) :
il **me** donne, il **lui** donne... des chocolats, il **leur** donne des chocolats (à Pierre et Marie)
(*) avec les impératifs : donne-**moi** des chocolats ! Approche-**toi** !

D. Pronoms personnels compléments indirects (avec préposition) :
c'est à **lui** (Pierre), c'est à **elle** (Marie)
je vais chez **eux,** je vais chez **elles.**

(*) ou pour l'insistance **moi,** je travaille ; **toi,** tu dors...

2. Les participes passés

1. Les verbes en **er** (1er groupe) font **é** au participe passé
ex. : jouer → joué

2. Les verbes en **ir** (2e groupe) font **i**
ex. : finir → fini

3. Les autres verbes (3e groupe) ont des terminaisons variées. (E. *Conjugaisons* : voir Bilan 4, page 148.)

3. Les adjectifs numéraux ordinaux

un	premier	onze	onzième
deux	deuxième (second)		....
trois	troisième		....
quatre	quatrième	dix-neuf	dix-neuvième
cinq	cinquième		....
six	sixième	cent	centième
sept	septième		....
huit	huitième	mille	millième
neuf	neuvième		....
dix	dixième	million	millionième

4. Les fêtes de l'année en 1982 :

Jour de l'An	Vendredi **1er janvier**
Mardi Gras	Mardi 23 février
Pâques	Dimanche 11 avril
Fête du Travail	Samedi **1er mai**
Armistice 1945	Samedi **8 mai**
Ascension	Jeudi 20 mai
Pentecôte	Dimanche 30 mai
Fête des Mères	Dimanche 6 juin
Fête Dieu	Dimanche 13 juin
Fête Nationale	Mercredi **14 juillet**
Assomption	Dimanche **15 août**
Toussaint	Lundi **1er novembre**
Fête de la Victoire	Jeudi **11 novembre**
Noël	Samedi **25 décembre**

4.1 Les Pellicier déménagent

à 800 Km.

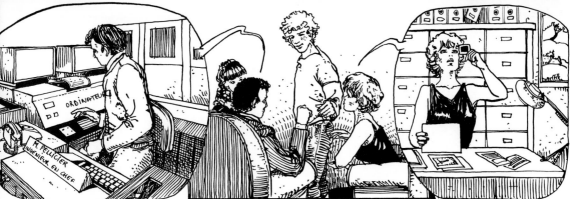

≪ M. Pellicier :	— Les enfants, j'ai une bonne nouvelle à vous annoncer : nous allons déménager !
Gérard :	— Tu appelles ça une bonne nouvelle ! Je ne suis pas d'accord ! On est bien ici. On a nos copains ; je n'ai pas envie de déménager.
Virginie :	— Moi non plus, je préfère rester là ! Et où on va, d'abord ?
≫ Mme Pellicier :	— Devinez !
Gérard :	— A Paris ou en province ?
M. Pellicier :	— En province.
Gérard :	— Oh là là !
Virginie :	— C'est au nord ou au sud ?

Mme Pellicier :	— C'est au sud.
Gérard :	— C'est à combien de km de Paris ?
Mme Pellicier :	— A 800 km environ.
Virginie :	— C'est au bord de la mer ?
Mme Pellicier :	— Oui.
Gérard :	— C'est à Marseille !
M. Pellicier :	— Non, c'est à 150 km à l'ouest de Marseille.
Virginie :	— Ce n'est pas à Montpellier ?
M. Pellicier :	— Si ! Bravo, tu as trouvé.
✱ Gérard :	— Et pourquoi est-ce qu'on va à Montpellier ?
M. Pellicier :	— Parce qu'IBM m'envoie à l'usine de la Pompignane. Je viens

	d'avoir une promotion. En septembre, je serai ingénieur en chef à Montpellier.
Gérard :	— Ah bon !
Virginie :	— Et Maman, qu'est-ce qu'elle deviendra ? Elle aura un travail ou elle sera au chômage ?
Mme Pellicier :	— Ne t'inquiète pas ! Je retrouverai un poste de documentaliste.
Gérard :	— Et mes études ? Je passe le bac cette année. L'an prochain je serai à la fac.
M. Pellicier :	— Ce n'est pas un village, Montpellier ! Il y a une université.
✱ Virginie :	— Où est-ce, la Pompignane ?
M. Pellicier :	— C'est dans la banlieue de Montpellier, à Castelnau.
Virginie :	— C'est loin du centre ?
M. Pellicier :	— Non, tout près, à sept ou huit kilomètres.
Gérard :	— Et on habitera où ? A Castelnau ?
Mme Pellicier :	— Bien sûr.
✱ Gérard :	— Alors il me faudra une moto.
Mme Pellicier :	— Pourquoi ?
Gérard :	— Eh bien, pour aller à la fac !
Virginie :	— Et moi, un vélomoteur pour aller au lycée.
Mme Pellicier :	— Ah non ! Je suis contre ! C'est dangereux les deux-roues.
Gérard :	— Mais Maman, on en aura besoin. Tu ne pourras pas nous conduire au lycée et à la fac !
Virginie :	— C'est vrai, Maman, il a raison !
Mme Pellicier :	— Bon, bon, je réfléchirai.
M. Pellicier :	— Bien sûr, et moi, je payerai.

[ʃ]
[ʒ]

En septembre je serai ingénieur en chef.

L'an prochain, je serai à la fac.

Je ne serai pas au chômage.

Je ne changerai pas de travail.

Gérard et Virginie vont déménager.

Vous voulez

- *avoir une bonne situation ?*
- *faire un travail passionnant ?*
- *habiter en province ?*
- *vivre dans une ville agréable ?*
- *être près de la mer et de la montagne ?*

... CHOISISSEZ MONTPELLIER

L'informatique a encore choisi Montpellier

Une nouvelle entreprise de montage d'ordinateurs a choisi Montpellier et s'est installée à la Pompignane, près du centre de la ville, sur un terrain de 48 hectares. Avec ses 2 390 employés (2 095 hommes, 295 femmes), cette usine sera la troisième de France. L'entreprise fabriquera un nouvel ordinateur qui servira aux grandes entreprises comme EDF, aux banques et aux centres de recherche scientifique.

Un technicien en informatique vous parle

Je suis arrivé à Montpellier en 1965 avec un brevet de technicien en informatique. J'ai trouvé un travail dans une petite usine de montage d'ordinateurs. Les années ont vite passé ; il y a eu beaucoup de changement ; l'usine a grandi ; mon travail est devenu très intéressant. L'an prochain, je serai cadre et mon salaire passera de 10 000 à 12 000 ou 13 000 F par mois. Vivre en Province ? J'aime bien. Ici la mer est à 10 km, la montagne à 90. Paris est à 1 heure d'avion et, avec le TGV, à 5 h de train. »

VOCABULAIRE

● les travailleurs

un employé	un technicien	un artisan
un ouvrier	un ingénieur	un fonctionnaire
un cadre......	un commerçant......	un agriculteur......

● les lieux de travail

Une entreprise, une usine, un magasin (un commerce), une administration (EDF, PTT, Éducation Nationale)...

● la vie professionnelle

Une promotion	: un technicien devient cadre.
Une augmentation	: son salaire passe de 10 000 à 12 000 F. Il gagnera 12 000 F.
Une situation	: un emploi, un travail, un poste.
Un chômeur	: il a perdu son emploi ; il est au chômage.

● les études

à l'école *(primaire)* — un (e) écolier *(ière)*
au collège — un (e) collégien *(ienne)*
au lycée — un (e) lycéen *(éenne)*
à l'université, à la faculté (la « *fac* ») —
un (e) étudiant (e)

un étudiant en lettres *(dans une faculté des lettres)*, en médecine *(dans une faculté de médecine)*, en droit *(dans une faculté de droit)*, en sciences *(dans une faculté des sciences)*,......

● la date

1981	1982	1983	1984	1985	1986
il y a 2 ans	l'année dernière *(l'an dernier)*	**cette année**	l'année prochaine *(l'an prochain)*	dans 2 ans	dans 3 ans

● les moyens de locomotion, les voyages

l'auto *(la voiture)*	l'avion	aller en *(voiture, taxi ......)*
la moto	le bateau	aller par ...... *(le train, bateau)*
le vélomoteur	le taxi	prendre ...... *(le bus, l'avion, un taxi...)*
le vélo *(la bicyclette)*	le bus *(l'autobus)*	voyager en ...... *(bateau, avion ......)*
le train *(le TGV)*	le car	faire ...... *(de la moto, du vélo ......)*

109

- **l'orientation, la situation (dans l'espace)**

— au nord, au sud, à l'est, à l'ouest ......
— dans le nord, dans le « Midi » ...... *(de la France)*
— dans le centre, en banlieue, à Paris, en province ......
— en ville, à la campagne ......
— au bord de la mer, tout près de la montagne ......
— à l'entrée, à la sortie *(de la ville, du village)* ......

- **pour ou contre ?**

pour

je suis pour
je suis d'accord
c'est vrai
tu as raison
j'ai envie...
moi aussi

contre

je suis contre
je ne suis pas d'accord
ce n'est pas vrai (c'est faux)
tu as tort
je n'ai pas envie de...
moi non plus

GRAMMAIRE

1. Le futur de l'indicatif (*)

AIMER	ÊTRE	AVOIR	CONDUIRE
J'aimerai	Je serai	J'aurai	Je conduirai
tu aimeras	tu seras	tu auras	tu conduiras
il/elle/on aimera	il/elle/on sera	il/elle/on aura	il/elle/on conduira
nous aimerons	nous serons	nous aurons	nous conduirons
vous aimerez	vous serez	vous aurez	vous conduirez
ils/elles aimeront	ils/elles seront	ils/elles auront	ils/elles conduiront

PRENDRE	ALLER	FAIRE
Je prendrai	J'irai	Je ferai
tu prendras	tu iras	tu feras
il/elle/on prendra	il/elle/on ira	il/elle/on fera
nous prendrons	nous irons	nous ferons
vous prendrez	vous irez	vous ferez
ils/elles prendront	ils/elles iront	ils/elles feront

(*) *Terminaisons :* rai - ras - ra - rons- rez - ront

2. Avoir ...... à ...... / Falloir ...... pour ......

avoir + nom + à + infinitif
j'ai une nouvelle à vous annoncer
il a un travail à faire
j'ai un renseignement à demander

falloir + nom + pour + infinitif
il me faut une moto pour aller à la fac
il faudra de l'argent pour acheter des fruits
il me faut une échelle pour cueillir les pommes

3. L'interrogation : Pourquoi ?

— *sur la cause*   Pourquoi vont-ils aller à Montpellier ? Parce qu'IBM y envoie M. Pellicier
— *sur le but*   Pourquoi veux-tu une moto ? Pour aller à la fac

1. Écrivez au futur les verbes entre parenthèses.

L'an prochain, les Pellicier (habiter) près de Montpellier. M. Pellicier (être) ingénieur en chef chez IBM et Mme Pellicier (avoir) un emploi de documentaliste. Leur fils (aller) à la fac et leur fille au lycée. Il leur (falloir) des deux-roues pour aller au travail. M. Pellicier (acheter) une moto et un vélomoteur.

2. Relisez le texte et complétez les phrases suivantes :

Les Pellicier habitent Paris. L'an prochain, ils . . . . . .

Mme Pellicier est documentaliste. A Montpel-lier . . . . . .

M. Pellicier est ingénieur. Là-bas, ...

Gérard passe le bac cette année. L'an prochain . . . . . .

Il n'a pas de moto. Pour aller à la fac . . . . . .

Virginie n'a pas de vélomoteur. Avec un vélomoteur . . . . . .

A Paris, ils n'ont pas besoin de deux-roues. A Montpellier, ...

3. Transformez les publicités ci-dessus en employant le futur :

a) *Choisissez IBM France, vous aurez . . . . . .*
b) *J'ai choisi IBM France, j'aurai . . . . . .*

Ils ont choisi le TGV, ils . . . . . .
Nous avons choisi le TGV, nous . . . . . .

4. Situez votre pays et votre ville.

J'habite à . . . . . .
c'est à . . . . . . km de . . . . . .

au nord, au sud de . . . . . .
tout près de . . . . . .

5. Une nouvelle entreprise s'est installée près de chez vous (dans votre ville ou votre pays). Sur le modèle des documents ci-dessus, vous présentez cette entreprise, ses employés. Vous indiquez précisément son emplacement.

au nord, au sud de . . . . . .   près de . . . . . . au bord de . . . . . . en ville, à la campagne . . . . . .

6. Choisissez la (ou les) bonne(s) réponse(s) (attention : il peut y en avoir une, deux ou trois).

J'ai envie d'acheter une grosse moto ! — Moi non plus. — C'est faux. — Pas d'accord.

Je n'irai pas avec vous à Montpellier ! — Moi aussi. — Moi non plus. — Mais non !

C'est bien, la province ! — C'est vrai. — Tu as raison. — Je ne suis pas d'accord.

Je préfère habiter dans un village ! — Tu as raison. — Moi non plus. — Moi aussi.

Que pensez-vous des deux-roues ? — Je suis pour. — Je suis contre. — C'est faux.

---

1 — Tu **es** libre aujourd'hui ?
— Non, mais je **serai** libre demain

2 Qu'est-ce que tu as fait **hier ?**
Et **aujourd'hui ?**
Et **demain ?**

— Hier, j'**ai travaillé.**
— Aujourd'hui, je **travaille** encore.
— Demain, je ne **travaillerai** pas.

● **Les bonnes résolutions**

Qu'est-ce qu'il fera l'année prochaine ?
Qu'est-ce qu'il ne fera plus ?

Faites le parler.

● **Les projets de Virginie Pellicier**

Dans deux ans passer le bac — entrer à la fac de médecine
— 1992 être médecin — 1993 aller travailler à l'étranger —
2000 revenir en France, s'installer dans une petite ville.

● **Parlez de ses projets** *Dans deux ans Virginie Pellicier* ......

● **Et vous, quels sont vos projets pour l'année prochaine ?**
pour l'an 2000 ? Que ferez-vous ?
Qu'est-ce que vous ne ferez plus ? Que deviendrez-vous ?
Où irez-vous ?

● **M. Benedetti change de vie. Décrivez !**

M. Benedetti, 38 ans :	*technicien (Renault Paris)*
Salaire :	*10 000 F/mois*
Domicile :	*Évry ville nouvelle*
Travail :	*Paris*
Moyen de transport :	*RER (Réseau Express Régional)*
	(domicile - lieu de travail)
L'année prochaine :	*Cadre (Renault-Le Mans)*
Salaire :	*12 500 F/mois*
Domicile :	*20 km du Mans (à la campagne)*
Travail :	*Le Mans*
Moyen de transport :	*voiture*
	(domicile - lieu de travail)

● « **Iles de rêves** »
Avec une carte, cherchez et situez (par rapport aux continents, aux pays, et aux villes importantes) les îles :

Galapagos, Maldives, Seychelles, Fidji, Shetland ......
C'est à ...... km de ......
au nord/au sud de ......

● **Où habites-tu ? Comment vas-tu à ......**
Dialoguez avec votre voisin(e)

Vous   *Où habites-tu ? (tu habites/vous habitez où ?)*
Lui/elle *A ...... c'est au nord/au sud de......*
            près de ......
Vous   *Tu habites en ville, à la campagne ? ......*
Lui/elle *En ville, près du centre, dans la banlieue ...*

Vous   *Tu vas à ton travail ? (à la fac)*
            en bus, en voiture ? ......
Lui/elle *Oui, je ......*
            Non, je prends le train, le car .....

● **Regardez une carte de France et situez les principales villes françaises.**

Exemple : *Strasbourg est à l'est de Paris, près de l'Allemagne, à ...... km de ...*

● **Pour ou contre ?**

Ils ne sont pas d'accord (pour déménager, pour aller en vacances).
Faites-les parler.

● **Vous avez envie d'aller au cinéma, de partir en vacances en Italie, d'apprendre le chinois...**
Votre voisin(e) n'est pas d'accord ! Elle/il préfère ......
Dialoguez !

4.2 Vivre à Montpellier

M. Pellicier : — Il y a du courrier.

Mme Pellicier : — Oui, l'office de Tourisme de Montpellier nous a répondu. C'est dans la grosse enveloppe qui est sur la table.

M. Pellicier : — Tu as regardé ?

Mme Pellicier : — Oui.

M. Pellicier : — Alors, ça te plaît, Montpellier ?

Mme Pellicier : — Beaucoup. Tu verras les photos. C'est une belle ville !

M. Pellicier : — Les enfants !

Virginie : — Qu'est-ce qu'il y a ?

M. Pellicier : — On vient de recevoir des prospectus sur Montpellier. Venez voir !

Gérard : — Ah oui ! Bonne idée !

M. Pellicier : — Les « loisirs à Montpellier », ça intéresse quelqu'un ?

Virginie : — Oui, moi ! Merci.

M. Pellicier :
* — Ah voilà quelque chose pour moi : « la route des vins ». Il n'y a pas un guide de la région ?

Gérard : — Si, si, c'est moi qui l'ai. Écoutez : « Capitale du Languedoc-Rousillon située au milieu d'une région de vignobles. Montpellier est une ville qui laisse à tous les visiteurs un souvenir extraordinaire. »

Gérard : — Il y a combien d'habitants à Montpellier ?

Mme Pellicier : — 250 000.

Gérard : — Ah bon, c'est assez grand !

Virginie : — Et il fait beau ?

Gérard :	— Oui, toute l'année. Écoute ça : « Montpellier a un climat très agréable. L'hiver est doux, l'été est chaud, il pleut un peu au printemps et en automne, mais le ciel est bleu 280 jours par an. »
Virginie :	— C'est formidable ! On ira à la plage tout le temps. On pourra bronzer et faire de la planche à voile. Elles sont loin les plages ?
✱ M. Pellicier :	— Non ! Regarde la carte ! En haut, Montpellier, avec l'autoroute qui passe au sud de la ville. Et en bas, les plages : Palavas, Carnon, la Grande Motte.
Gérard :	— Et Castelnau, où c'est ?
M. Pellicier :	— Là. Sur la route qui va de Montpellier à Nîmes.
✱ Virginie :	— Je ne vois pas la Camargue.
M. Pellicier :	— C'est là, à droite !
Virginie :	— C'est bien. On pourra faire du cheval !
Gérard :	— Et les Pyrénées ?
M. Pellicier :	— Tout en bas à gauche ! En dessous, c'est l'Espagne.
Gérard :	— Ça, je sais ! Mais c'est à combien de kilomètres ?
M. Pellicier :	— 90 ou 100.
Gérard :	— Super ! On ira faire du ski le week-end.
✱ Mme Pellicier :	— C'est ça ! Le ski, la plage, la planche à voile, le cheval. Et le lycée et la fac, vous y pensez ?

C'est une ville très agréable.

[s]
[z]

Elle laisse aux visiteurs un souvenir extraordinaire

J'ai envie de skier et de bronzer

MONTPELLIER

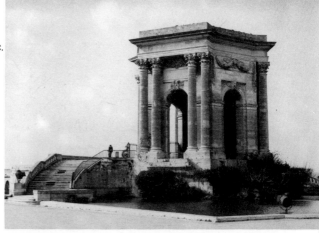

Ville d'art et de science
250 000 habitants. Capitale du Languedoc.
Gare SNCF — Aéroport de Fréjorgues.
A 10 km de la mer.
Climat méditerranéen.

Ses monuments

— l'Arc de Triomphe
— les Arceaux
— la Cathédrale

Ses jardins

— le Peyrou
— le jardin des plantes

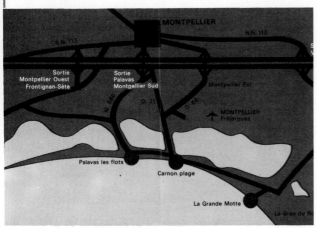

Ses maisons anciennes

(XVIIe et XVIIIe siècle)

Ses facultés

— médecine   — lettres
— droit   — agronomie
— sciences

Ses industries modernes

IBM

Ses plages

Des kilomètres de sable
fin sous un ciel bleu

- **le temps**

Le beau temps
Il fait beau, il fait chaud
Il y a du soleil
Le soleil brille
Le ciel est bleu
Le ciel est « dégagé » ......

Le mauvais temps
Il fait mauvais, il fait froid
Il y a du vent. Il fait du vent
Il pleut (pleuvoir)
Il neige (neiger)
Il y a un orage
Il y a du brouillard
Il y a des nuages, le ciel est gris ......

- **les saisons** Printemps - Été - Automne - Hiver

- **localisation** En haut, en bas, à gauche, à droite
au milieu (de ......) entre ......
en dessous (de), au-dessous (de) ......
sur la route de ...... dans la région de ......

- **donner son avis : « Ça te plaît ? »**

Oui, beaucoup	Non, pas du tout ......
C'est bien	Ce n'est pas bien
C'est extraordinaire, formidable	Ce n'est pas terrible
C'est agréable	C'est désagréable
C'est grand, beau	C'est petit, laid
joli, amusant	ennuyeux ......
(Chic ! Super ! Bonne idée !)	(Zut ! La barbe ! Ah non !)

GRAMMAIRE

1. qui — Pronom relatif sujet

— *Le pronom relatif relie deux phrases :*
Castelnau est sur la route **qui** va de Montpellier à Nîmes
phrase a) : Castelnau est sur une route
phrase b) : Cette route va de Montpellier à Nîmes.

Les photos sont dans la grosse enveloppe **qui** est sur la table
phrase a) : Les photos sont dans une grosse enveloppe
phrase b) : Cette grosse enveloppe est sur la table

La subordonnée relative sert à préciser, à définir
Qui est Mme Richaud ? C'est la dame **qui** est près de la fenêtre.
Où est Castelnau ? C'est sur la route **qui** va de Montpellier à Nîmes.

Un cric, c'est **quelque chose qui** sert à soulever une voiture.
Un journaliste, c'est **quelqu'un qui** travaille dans un journal.

2. c'est... qui (pour insister)

Il n'y a pas un guide ? — Si, si, je l'ai pris
                 Si, si, **c'est** moi **qui** l'ai pris.

3. tout - toutes - tous - toutes (adjectifs indéfinis)

tout	(Un ......, le ......, ce ......, mon ......)	+ nom masculin singulier
toute	(Une ......, la ......, cette ......, ma...)	+ nom féminin singulier
tous	(Les ......, ces ......, mes ......)	+ nom masculin pluriel
toutes	(Les ......, ces ......, mes ......)	+ nom féminin pluriel

4. Conjugaison du futur (suite)

POUVOIR	VOIR
je pourrai	je verrai
tu pourras	tu verras
il/elle/on pourra	il/elle/on verra
nous pourrons	nous verrons
vous pourrez	vous verrez
ils/elles pourront	ils/elles verront

5. Quelqu'un - quelque chose (pronoms indéfinis)

Quelqu'un *(un homme, une femme)*
≠ personne
Quelque chose *(une chose)*
≠ rien

1. Regardez les deux cartes météorologiques et faites un bulletin météo pour hier et demain.

— *Le temps hier :*
dans l'ouest, il a plu ;
dans le sud-est ......

— *Le temps demain :* il fera ......

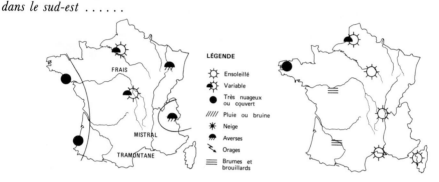

2. Décrivez le climat de votre pays ou de votre région.

3. Définissez les mots suivants, comme dans l'exemple (employez le relatif « qui » et servez-vous d'un dictionnaire) :

Un Office du Tourisme : c'est un bureau qui donne des renseignements aux touristes.
Un fonctionnaire : ...... Un deux-roues : ...... Une agence immobilière : ...... Un étudiant : ...... Un chômeur : ...... Un représentant : ......

4. Trouvez les deux phrases qui donnent les phrases suivantes, comme dans l'exemple :

J'ai un guide qui donne tous les renseignements.
a) J'ai un guide.
b) Ce guide donne tous les renseignements.
J'ai une voiture qui a quinze ans.
Il y a une autoroute qui va de Paris à Narbonne.
Je connais une dame qui travaille chez IBM.
Est-ce qu'il y a un train qui va à Castelnau ?
Nous avons des amis qui habitent à Nîmes.

5. Réécrivez, comme dans l'exemple :

Tu as le guide de Montpellier ?
C'est toi qui a le guide de Montpellier ?
J'ai cassé un verre.
L'Office du Tourisme nous a écrit.
Elle va conduire.
Ils nous ont téléphoné hier soir.
Sa mère lui a payé une moto.

6. Complétez avec tout (le), toute (la), tous (les), toutes (les)...

Ils connaissent ...... Bretagne
Tu veux ...... café ?
Elle va taper ...... lettres

J'ai fait ...... mon travail
Je ne connais pas ...... plages
J'ai vu ...... votre famille

7. Sur le modèle de la présentation de Montpellier

« *Capitale du Languedoc-Roussillon,*
Montpellier est une ville qui ..... souvenir extraordinaire.

Présentez Paris, la capitale de votre pays, une ville célèbre.

8. Situez sur cette carte les villes ou les monuments suivants en utilisant : nord, sud ...... en haut, en bas, à gauche ...... de la carte, entre ...... au milieu ...... sur la route qui va de ...... à ....

Sommières - Aigues-Mortes -
Le pont du Gard -
le château de Villevieille

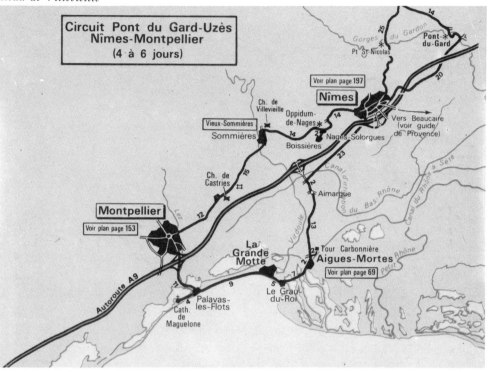

1. Il y a une enveloppe sur la table. Prends-la.
Prends l'enveloppe **qui** est sur la table.

2. Un buraliste vend des articles pour fumeurs.
Un buraliste, c'est **quelqu'un qui** vend des articles pour fumeurs.

(Avec *c'est quelqu'un qui* / et *c'est quelque chose qui*)

● ***Décrivez ce « collage » en employant :***

à gauche, à droite
en haut, en bas, au-dessus, en dessous
entre, au milieu de ......

● *« L'hiver à Venise »*
Vous parlez d'une belle ville que vous connaissez et vous conseillez à votre voisin(e)
une saison pour la visiter.

Vous :	*Vous connaissez Venise (Bagdad, Zanzibar, Tananarive...) ?*
Lui/elle :	*Oui, j'y suis allé en été (en automne...)*
ou :	*Non, où est-ce ?*
Vous :	*Ça vous a plu ?*
ou :	*C'est près de ......*

Sur la route de ......
Regarde la carte ......

Lui/elle : *C'est beau, c'est grand ......*
Il y a combien d'habitants ?
Il y fait beau ?

Vous : *Il faut y aller en hiver*
(au printemps ......)
Il fait ......

● *Où est-ce ? Est-ce que c'est grand ? Est-ce que c'est joli, beau ? Quel temps y fait-il ?*

Moscou en hiver

Paris au printemps

Saint-Tropez en été

● SUR LA CARTE ! *Prenez une carte. Vous choisissez une ville et votre voisin(e) doit deviner. Vous répondez par oui ou par non.*

C'est dans le sud ? le nord ?
C'est en haut, en bas, à gauche, à droite de la carte.
C'est sur la route de, entre, près de ...... Alors c'est ......

● *Jamais d'accord ! Vous donnez votre avis sur quelque chose. Votre voisin(e) dit le contraire.*

Vous :   *C'est extraordinaire ! Il te plaît, ce tableau ?*
Elle/lui : *Non, ça ne me plaît pas du tout. C'est laid.*
Vous :   *La marche à pied, le vélo, c'est super !*
Elle/lui : *Ah non ! C'est ennuyeux !*

4.3 A la recherche d'une villa

Monsieur et madame Pellicier sont venus à Montpellier pour chercher un logement. Ils veulent une villa assez grande (il leur faut trois chambres) et pas trop chère. Ils sont en ce moment avec Mme Talbot qui dirige l'agence Immo-34.

✶ Mme Talbot — Je vais vous montrer une villa qui vous plaira. C'est une maison moderne que je trouve très bien. Au rez-de-chaussée, il y a un grand séjour, une cuisine et une chambre, et au premier étage deux chambres et une belle salle de bains.

M. Pellicier : — Elle fait quelle surface ?

Mme Talbot : — 150 m^2 et il y a un très joli jardin avec des arbres.

M. Pellicier : — Ça c'est agréable !

Mme Talbot : — Vous verrez, c'est tout près d'un centre commercial.

Mme Pellicier : — C'est pratique. Et la villa est libre immédiatement ?

Mme Talbot : — Il y a des locataires qui partent le 1er août. On arrive...

✶ M. Pellicier : — C'est tout droit ?

Mme Talbot : — Non, vous prenez la première à gauche, c'est un peu plus loin sur la droite. Voilà, nous y sommes !

✶ Mme Talbot : — Alors, qu'est-ce que vous en pensez ?

Mme Pellicier :	— Moi, je la trouve très bien. Pas toi ?
M. Pellicier :	— Si, elle me plaît, mais... c'est ennuyeux, il n'y a pas de garage !
Mme Pellicier :	— On peut facilement garer la voiture dans le jardin.
M. Pellicier :	— Oui, c'est vrai, tu as raison, mais le jardin est petit !
Mme Talbot :	— Ah non, il est assez grand : il fait 200 m² exactement.
✱Mme Pellicier :	— Et le centre commercial est où ?
Mme Talbot :	— C'est à 500 mètres. Vous descendez à gauche, vous allez jusqu'aux feux que vous voyez là-bas. Vous tournez à droite au rond-point, et c'est en face.
✱M. Pellicier :	— Le loyer est de combien ?
Mme Talbot :	— 3 500 F par mois. C'est raisonnable !
M. Pellicier :	— Oui, ce n'est pas trop cher ! Bon, eh bien, allons la visiter.
Mme Talbot :	— Je regrette, M. Pellicier, les locataires ne sont pas là, et je n'ai pas les clés !
M. Pellicier :	— On ne peut pas la visiter ?
Mme Talbot :	— Si, vous pourrez la visiter demain. Les locataires seront là !
Mme Pellicier :	— Mais nous devons repartir demain !
Mme Talbot :	— Je suis désolée.
✱Mme Talbot :	— Attendez, voilà les locataires ! Nous avons de la chance !

Ils veulent une villa — il leur faut trois chambres

• • • • • • • • • • • •

[v] Cette villa fait 120 m²

• • • • • • • • ••

Vous voyez les feux ?

• • • • •

[f] En face vous garez facilement votre voiture.

• • • • • • • • • •

C'est vous qui choisissez ! Alors choisissez

Une entreprise qui connaît vos problèmes
Une entreprise que 10 000 familles ont choisie
Une entreprise que vous conseillez à vos amis
Choisissez Bâti Sud.

Pour aller de la gare à l'agence Immo-34 : suivez l'avenue de la gare. Aux feux, tournez à droite, continuez tout droit, traversez la Place du Marché et prenez la première à droite. Au rond-point, vous tournez à gauche dans la rue de l'église.

=== VOCABULAIRE ===

• **le logement :** un appartement *(dans un immeuble)*, un studio, une maison,.une villa
l'entrée, le couloir, la salle de séjour *(le séjour, le living = salon + salle à manger)*, les chambres, le balcon, la terrasse...
la cuisine, la salle de bains, les toilettes *(les w.-c.)*. Dans une salle de bains ; lavabo, baignoire, douche.

• **vendre, acheter, louer :**

une vente	un achat	une location
un vendeur	un acheteur	un locataire
le prix de vente	le prix d'achat	le loyer

• **dans l'ascenseur**

le premier étage, le deuxième, le troisième...,
le dernier, le rez-de-chaussée, le sous-sol
— Quel étage *(s'il vous plaît ?)*
— Le premier, s'il vous plaît.
— Moi, je vais au troisième.
— Et moi, au second.

• **pour donner son avis : Moi,ça me plaît ! Moi,ça ne me plaît pas !**

c'est grand, c'est petit, c'est cher, c'est trop cher, ce n'est pas trop cher, c'est bon marché,
c'est moderne, c'est vieux, c'est « ancien »...
c'est bien, c'est agréable, c'est pratique, c'est clair,
ce n'est pas bien, c'est sombre, ce n'est pas pratique...

• **pour demander son « chemin »**

La gare ......
L'hôtel Rex ...... ⎫
La rue de Paris ...... ⎬ s'il vous plaît ?
            ⎭

Pardon ...... Où est la gare *(la rue ......)* ?
Excusez-moi ...... vous connaissez ......
Pardon Monsieur *(Madame ......)* pour aller à la gare ?

• **pour indiquer un chemin (un itinéraire)**

c'est à gauche, à droite, tout droit
vous continuez jusqu'à ......
vous prenez la première *(la deuxième ......)* à gauche, à droite
vous tournez à gauche ...... après le/la ......
vous traversez la rue *(l'avenue, le boulevard, la place ......)*

GRAMMAIRE

1. Les pronoms relatifs (suite)

sujet : **QUI**	complément d'objet : **QUE**
Ils vont voir une villa. Cette villa leur plaira Ils vont voir une villa **qui** leur plaira	Je vais voir une entreprise. Mes amis m'ont conseillé cette entreprise Je vais voir une entreprise **que** mes amis m'ont conseillée.

2. C'est... qui, c'est... que

C'est Mme Talbot **qui** dirige l'agence
(= Mme Talbot dirige l'agence).

C'est moi **qui** paye
(= je paye)

(pour insister sur un mot)
C'est une villa **que** nous cherchons, pas un appartement ! *(= nous cherchons une villa)*
C'est lui **que** je veux voir, pas elle !
(= je veux le voir)

3. Les adverbes en «-ment »

formation = adjectif au féminin + ment
dangereuse ⟶ dangereusement
exacte ⟶ exactement
facile ⟶ facilement

difficilement, simplement,
gratuitement, immédiatement...

Les adverbes accompagnent un verbe (ou un adjectif). Ils sont en général après le verbe.

1. *Reliez les deux phrases comme dans le modèle :*

Mme Talbot va leur montrer une villa. Elle la trouve très bien.
→ *Mme Talbot va leur montrer une villa qu'elle trouve très bien.*

Les Pellicier ont une fille. Vous la connaissez.
Montpellier est une belle ville. Les touristes l'aiment beaucoup.
M. Pellicier a une voiture. Il la garera dans le jardin.
Ils ont des amis étrangers. Je les trouve très sympathiques.
Elle a une voiture de sport. Elle la conduit très vite.

2. *Mettez QUI ou QUE :*

La rue Racine, c'est la rue . . . . . . va de la gare à la Mairie. Dans cette rue, il y a une maison . . . . . . je trouve très belle. — C'est la maison . . . . . . a un jardin avec de grands arbres ? Je la connais. Des gens . . . . . . je connais habitent à côté. Ce sont les Dunod. — Les Dunod ? Ces gens . . . . . . viennent de Bordeaux ? Moi aussi je les connais. J'ai des amis . . . . . . les trouvent sympathiques, mais moi je ne les aime pas beaucoup.

3. *Choisissez l'adverbe qui convient :* immédiatement - facilement - exactement - gratuitement - difficilement - dangereusement
N'attendez pas ! Partez . . . . . .
Le dimanche, on visite le Louvre . . . . . .
Il va trop vite. Il conduit . . . . . .

Dans 2 minutes, il sera . . . . . . midi.
Il s'est cassé la jambe et il marche . . . . . .
Avec le plan on trouve . . . . . . l'agence.

4. Sur le modèle suivant, faites deux phrases avec QUI et QUE :

Mme Talbot connaît son métier. Elle dirige l'agence. Vous la verrez demain.

a) <u>*Mme Talbot, qui dirige l'agence, connaît son métier.*</u>

b) <u>*Mme Talbot, que vous verrez demain, dirige l'agence.*</u>

· *Les Pellicier vont s'installer à Montpellier. Ils viennent de Paris.*
Vous les connaissez bien.
· *Leur fils va faire des études de médecine. Vous ne le connaissez pas.*
Il passe son bac cette année.
· *Cette villa ne vous plaira pas. Je la trouve trop petite. Elle fait 100 m².*
· *M. Pellicier vient d'avoir une promotion. Il sera ingénieur en chef en septembre.*
La direction d'IBM l'envoie à Montpellier.

5. Un de vos amis cherche un logement. Vous avez vu deux annonces, vous écrivez à cet ami.

A LOUER **Villa, 130 m², 3 chambres, 2 s-d-b, gd séjour, garage, jardin 800 m², 8 km centre ville. 3 500 F.**

A LOUER **apt. F 4, tél., parking privé, 5ᵉ étage, asc., quartier calme, 2 350 F.**

Cher . . . . . .
J'ai trouvé deux annonces pour toi. La première, c'est une villa qui . . . . . .

6. Vous écrivez à un ami. Vous lui expliquez comment aller de la gare à votre lycée, votre université, votre centre d'enseignement...

7. Sur le modèle du début du texte, faites un résumé pour les leçons 1 et 2.

1. Je vais vous montrer une villa. Elle vous plaira.
Je vais vous montrer une villa **qui** vous plaira.
Je connais une petite maison. Je la trouve très bien.
Je connais une petite maison **que** je trouve très bien.

2. Monsieur Talbot dirige l'agence ? *(Madame Talbot)*
— Non, **c'est** madame Talbot **qui** dirige l'agence.
Vous cherchez un appartement ? *(une villa)*
— Non, c'**est** une villa **que** je cherche.

● **Vous êtes à la gare.**
Vous indiquez le chemin
pour aller de la gare :
— *au théâtre*
— *à l'agence des Étuves*
— *au centre commercial le Polygone*
— *à l'hôtel Métropole*

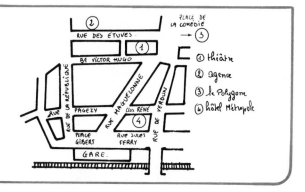

- **Vous cherchez la gare, la poste, le centre culturel, une banque, une boulangerie,... votre voisin(e) vous indique l'itinéraire.**

- **Roméo veut rejoindre Juliette. Quel itinéraire lui conseillez-vous ?**

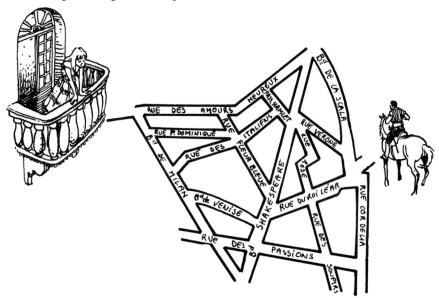

- **Vous décrivez cette villa à votre voisin(e). Il/Elle vous pose des questions.**

Vous :	*Au rez-de-chaussée, il y a ......*
	Au premier ......
Elle/lui :	*La cuisine (le séjour, ...) est grande ?*
Vous :	*Oui/Non ......*
Elle/lui :	*C'est moderne, c'est cher ......?*
	C'est pratique ......?
	On peut la visiter quand ? ......

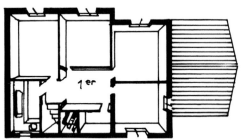

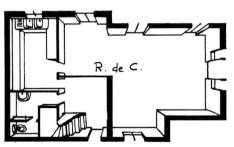

A vendre Villa
180 m² habitables
R. de Ch.: Séjour, Cuis., W.C.,
1er ét.: 3 Ch., S. de B.
630 000 F
Sur place
Sam., Dim.,de 10 h à 19 h

● *Où habites-tu? Où habitez-vous? Vous parlez avec votre voisin(e) de votre logement (ou de son logement).*

— *C'est un appartement, une chambre, une maison que tu habites?*
— *Oui/non/c'est à quel étage?*
— *C'est grand, c'est cher...? Oui/non ......*
(nombre de pièces, locataire ou propriétaire, situation des commerces)
— *Ah, ça, c'est pratique, ce n'est pas pratique, c'est agréable, c'est ennuyeux ......*
Tu as (vous avez) de la chance! Tu n'as pas de chance.

4.4 L'installation

Le camion des déménageurs est vide. Le jardin est plein de caisses et de cartons. A l'intérieur, les déménageurs installent les meubles. Les parents commencent à ranger. Les enfants sont en train de se disputer.

* Virginie : — Moi, je veux la chambre blanche. Mon placard est trop petit.

Gérard : — Ah non, je ne suis pas d'accord. Tu gardes la tienne, je garde la mienne. Elle est très bien, la chambre bleue. Elle est plus grande que la blanche. Et les placards sont pareils.

* Virginie : — Ce n'est pas vrai ! Regarde, le tien fait un mètre de plus. Moi, j'ai beaucoup de vêtements.

Gérard : — J'en ai autant que toi.

Virginie : — C'est faux, j'en ai bien plus que toi. J'ai besoin d'un grand placard. Tu vois, de ce côté je peux mettre mes jupes, mes robes et mes pantalons. Et de l'autre côté... Ah, je comprends. Il y a un lavabo dans le placard !

* Virginie : — Maman, je veux la chambre qui a un lavabo.

Gérard : — Ah non, ma vieille ! C'est ma chambre, je la garde.

128

Mme Pellicier : — Les enfants, arrêtez de vous disputer et venez nous aider. Il faut rentrer les cartons et les caisses.

* Virginie : — Bon. Moi je suis une femme, je suis moins forte que toi. Les caisses sont beaucoup trop lourdes, je vais porter les cartons.

Gérard : — Bien sûr, et c'est moi qui porterai les caisses !

* Un déménageur : — Dites Monsieur, l'armoire ne passe pas. Le couloir est trop étroit.

M. Pellicier : — Passez par l'extérieur : la fenêtre de la chambre est assez large.

L'autre : — Bon ! Allez, Maurice, on y va...

* Mme Pellicier : — Virginie, fais attention : il y a des verres dans le carton que tu portes.

Virginie : — Je sais maman, ne t'inquiète pas. Oh, zut !

Les Pellicier ont beaucoup de meubles
• • • • • • (•) •

[p] La chambre blanche est plus petite que la bleue
• • • • • • • • • • •

Le placard de la chambre bleue est plus grand
• • • • • • • • • •

[b] Il y a un lavabo dans le placard
• • • • • • (•) • •

- **le déménagement**

verbes	→ noms *(l'action de)*	charger	→ le chargement
déménager	→ le déménagement	décharger	→ le déchargement
emménager	→ l'emménagement	ranger	→ le rangement

- **le mobilier de la chambre :** une table, une chaise, un fauteuil, un lit, une table de nuit, une armoire, un bureau, une étagère . . . . . .

- **les contraires :** large/étroit, petit/grand, long/court, lourd/léger, haut/bas, plein/vide, pareil/différent . . . . . .

- **le degré, la quantité :** c'est assez lourd (*grand, plein* . . . . . .) trop, beaucoup trop, bien trop,... plus, beaucoup plus, un peu plus, moins, beaucoup moins, un peu moins, aussi

- **commencer, finir...**

commencer à . . . . . . (*se mettre à* . . . . . .)
être en train de . . . . . .

continuer à . . . . . .
arrêter de . . . . . . finir de . . . . . .

Il commence à travailler
Il se met à travailler

Il est en train de travailler
Il continue à travailler

Il arrête de travailler
Il a fini de travailler

GRAMMAIRE

1. Le comparatif

	Adjectif	Nom
Supériorité +	Gérard est plus fort que Virginie.	Virginie a plus de vêtements que Gérard.
Infériorité −	Virginie est moins forte que Gérard.	Gérard a moins de vêtements que Virginie.
Égalité =	Ma sœur est aussi grande que moi.	J'ai autant de livres que vous.

ATTENTION !
Le comparatif est souvent incomplet : Il est plus fort. Elle est moins grande. Elle a plus de vêtements. J'ai moins de travail. Ça fait un mètre de plus - Ça coûte 3 francs de moins.

2. Les pronoms possessifs :

A qui	est	ce . . . . . . ? cet . . . . . . ? cette . . . . . . ?	A moi A toi A lui/elle A nous A vous A eux/elles	C'est le mien/la mienne C'est le tien/la tienne C'est le sien/la sienne C'est le nôtre/la nôtre C'est le vôtre/la vôtre C'est le leur/la leur
	sont	ces . . . . . . ?	A moi A toi A lui/elle A nous A vous A eux/elles	Ce sont les miens/les miennes Ce sont les tiens/les tiennes Ce sont les siens/les siennes Ce sont les nôtres Ce sont les vôtres Ce sont les leurs

1. Complétez les phrases comme dans le modèle.

Gérard est aussi grand que Virginie.
L'armoire est ......
Gérard est ......
Virginie a ......
Virginie a ......
Le camion est ......
Le grand-père est ......
La fenêtre est ......
La jupe est ......
Les deux lessives coûtent ......
Les Dupont ont ......

2. Dites le contraire.

— Cette étagère est trop basse.
— C'est un paquet très léger.
— Les deux voitures sont différentes.
— J'ai acheté une grande armoire.
— Cette caisse est pleine ?

3. Complétez avec : commencer à, arrêter de, finir de, continuer à.

Le déjeuner est prêt : il faut ...... manger.
Les déménageurs ont ...... décharger à 8 h. Ils ont ...... travailler à midi.
J'ai trouvé un emploi : je ...... travailler lundi.
Les enfants, ... vous disputer !
Je connais presque tous les gens de l'immeuble. Je ...... m'habituer.
Il a ...... pleuvoir à midi. La pluie a ...... tomber toute la journée.
Quand va-t-il ...... pleuvoir ?

4. Transformez suivant le modèle :

A gauche, c'est ta chambre et à droite c'est ma chambre
→ A gauche, c'est ta chambre et à droite c'est la mienne

Nous avons des disques : j'ai mes disques, elle a ses disques.
Les habitants du Languedoc ont leurs plages. Les Bretons ont aussi leurs plages.
Moi, j'ai mes amis ; vous, vous avez vos amis.
Il y a trois chambres dans notre appartement. Dans leur appartement, il y en a quatre.
Tu as rangé ta chambre ? Moi, j'ai rangé ma chambre.
Il fait moins froid dans mon pays que dans ton pays.
Leurs enfants sont dans le jardin. Où sont nos enfants ?

5. Comparez les prix. Est-ce que c'est plus cher ou moins cher que dans votre pays ?

Prix moyens en France (en 1982) pour :
Un repas au restaurant : de 40 à 120 F.
Une nuit à l'hôtel : de 80 à 250 F.
Un petit déjeuner à l'hôtel : de 10 à 25 F.

Un café ou un thé : de 3 à 5 F.
Une bière : de 5 à 15 F.
Un paquet de cigarettes : de 3,50 F à 10 F.

6. Vérifiez ou corrigez les affirmations suivantes. Prenez un dictionnaire.

L'Espagne est plus grande que la France.
C'est faux. La France est plus grande. Elle a 36 000 km^2 de plus.

Employez : plus grand / plus petit que / moins / plus haut que . . . plus d'habitants / moins d'habitants que . . .
plus long / plus court que . . . . . .   X mètres, km de plus, de moins . . . . .

— Tokyo a plus d'habitants que Paris / Le Kilimandjaro est moins haut que le Mont-Blanc / La Seine est plus longue que la Loire / La France a moins d'habitants que la République Fédérale Allemande / Le pôle Nord est plus froid que le pôle Sud / La tour Eiffel est plus haute que l'Empire State Building (à New York).

1. A qui est cette voiture ? A tes parents ?   — Oui, oui, c'est **la leur.**
A qui sont ces cigarettes ? A toi ?   — Oui, oui, ce sont **les miennes.**

2. Gérard a moins de livres que Virginie.   Virginie a autant de vêtements que Gérard.
— C'est faux : il a **plus de** livres qu'elle.   — C'est vrai : elle a **autant de** vêtements que lui.

	livres	vêtements	disques	amis	argent
Virginie	−	=	−	=	−
Gérard	+	=	+	=	+

● **Un vendeur désagréable. Faites-les parler :**

— C'est trop court.
— Non, ce n'est pas vrai,
ce n'est pas trop court,
c'est vous qui êtes trop grand !

● **Ils se sont trompés ! Faites-les parler.**

— Eh, Monsieur ! Ce chapeau n'est pas à vous. C'est le mien.
— Ce n'est pas vrai ! C'est le mien.
— Mais non, regardez, voilà le vôtre,
il est beaucoup plus grand que le mien.
— Ah, c'est vrai. Excusez-moi !

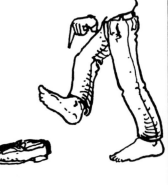

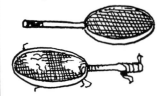

● *Comparez la première villa et la deuxième en utilisant PLUS ou MOINS.*

la première villa a plus de pièces ......

● *Avec les mêmes annonces, jouez la scène suivante : le mari et la femme ne sont pas d'accord. L'un veut la première villa, l'autre la deuxième.*

— *Je veux la villa de 6 pièces. Ma maison, ma chambre* ...... *est trop petite.*
— *Ah non, prenons la villa de 5 pièces. Elle est plus* ...... *moins* ....., *je pourrai mettre mes*
— *Ce n'est pas vrai* ...... *j'ai besoin de* ......

● **M. Dupont et M. Duval**
Comparez-les. Comparez leur maison, leur voiture, leur chien...
Qui préférez-vous ?

Employez *M. Dupont est plus, moins, aussi* ...... *que M. Duval.*
M. Dupont a un chien, une voiture ...... *plus, moins* ...... *que M. Duval.*
Le sien,/la sienne est ......
M. Duval a plus de ...... *moins de* ......

● *Avec votre voisin(e), vous décrivez et vous comparez des personnes, des animaux, des pays, des lieux, des objets... Vous dites vos préférences :*

— *Je préfère le ......, la .....*
— *Je ne suis pas d'accord ! Moi je préfère le ......, la .....*
— *Il/Elle est plus ...... moins ......*

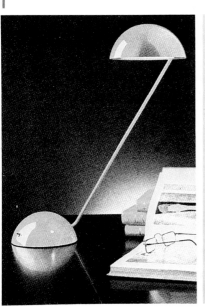

● **Une dispute. Faites-les parler !**

Le premier — *Prends l'armoire ! Elle est trop lourde.*
Je suis plus ...... (fatigué, vieux...), moins ......

Le deuxième — *Ah non. Je ne suis pas d'accord.*
Je vais ...... Et toi, tu vas ......

Un autre — *Arrêtez de vous disputer !*
Il faut aller ...... commencer à ...... continuer à ...

4.5 Le méchoui

Les Pellicier viennent de s'installer à Montpellier.
Pour la première fois, ils reçoivent des voisins et des amis de M. Pellicier qui travaillent chez IBM. Ils ont fait un méchoui dans le jardin ; un mouton est en train de cuire au-dessus d'un feu de bois.

✳ **Mme Pellicier :** — C'est bientôt prêt. Il y a des couverts sur la table. Servez-vous.

M. Pellicier : — Chérie, je te présente Jacques Morin. Il travaille au Service Développement.

Mme Pellicier : — Enchantée de faire votre connaissance, Monsieur Morin.

M. Morin : — Vous pouvez m'appeler Jacques.

Mme Pellicier : — Alors, appelez-moi Michèle.

M. Morin : — Alors, ça vous plaît le Midi ? Vous êtes bien ici !

Mme Pellicier : — Oui, on est très bien. On a eu de la chance de trouver cette villa !

M. Morin : — C'est vrai, elle est très agréable.

Mme Pellicier : — Et puis, heureusement, les voisins sont très sympathiques.

M. Morin : — Vous êtes mieux que dans la région parisienne.

Mme Pellicier : — Beaucoup mieux, c'est sûr !

✳ **M. Pellicier :** — Qu'est-ce que tu prends Jacques ? Un whisky, un porto ?

M. Morin :	— Non je ne bois pas d'alcool. Je vais prendre un jus de fruit.
Gérard :	— Papa, le mouton est presque cuit. Qu'est-ce que je fais ?
M. Pellicier :	— Attends ! Je vais aller voir ! Va me chercher un couteau, s'il te plaît.
M. Morin :	— C'est votre fils ?
Mme Pellicier :	— Oui et ma fille est là-bas. Et vous, Jacques, vous avez des enfants ?
M. Morin :	— Oui, j'en ai également deux, mais les miens sont beaucoup plus jeunes.
✱ M. Pellicier :	— Tenez, je vous ai coupé du gigot ! Ça vous va ?
Mme Pellicier :	— C'est parfait.
M. Morin :	— Hm, c'est délicieux !
Mme Pellicier :	— C'est bien meilleur qu'un gigot au four.
Un invité :	— Oh oui, c'est excellent.
✱ Une invitée :	— Vous avez déjà visité la région ?
Mme Pellicier :	— Non, malheureusement, on n'a pas encore eu le temps.
L'invitée :	— Il y a des promenades magnifiques. Le Parc National des Cévennes par exemple.
L'invité :	— Ah oui, c'est un endroit où il faut absolument aller.
Mme Pellicier :	— Où est-ce ?
L'invitée :	— C'est à environ 100 km de Montpellier. C'est près de Florac.
Mme Pellicier :	— Par où on passe pour y aller ?
L'invité :	— On va demander à Denis. Il est de Florac. Dis, Denis, par où il faut passer pour aller au Parc des Cévennes ?
Denis :	— Par Alès. C'est la route la plus rapide.
M. Morin :	— Mais c'est la moins intéressante. Moi, je vous conseille de passer par Ganges et le Mont Aigoual.
L'invité :	— Ah oui, bonne idée. Comme ça, ils pourront voir la Grotte des Demoiselles. C'est un endroit extraordinaire !
M. Morin :	— Et puis, vous revenez par les Gorges du Tarn. C'est un peu long mais la route est merveilleuse.
✱ M. Pellicier :	— Et c'est une région où on mange bien, non ?
L'invité :	— Oui, il y a de bons petits restaurants. Je vous donnerai des adresses.
Mme Pellicier :	— On y va le week-end prochain, chéri ?
M. Pellicier :	— Pourquoi pas ?

[t]

[d]

Les touristes adorent la Grotte des Demoiselles.

C'est un endroit extraordinaire !

J'ai très envie d'y aller.

Bonne idée. Quelle route faut-il prendre ?

Attendez ! On va demander à Denis.

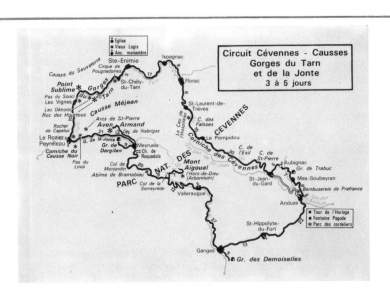

DEMOISELLES (Grotte des), à St-Bauzille-de-Putois (34).

Sur la N 986 (Montpellier à Ganges (40 km), à proximité des Plages et du Cirque de Navacelles). **Ouvert toute l'année :** du 1/10 au 31/03 de 9 h 30 à 17 h et du 1/04 au 30/09 de 8 h 30 à 19 h (arrêt pour déjeuner). En été, certains soirs : nocturne. Rens. : 3 rue Maguelonne 34000 Montpellier. Tél. : (67) 58-44-12. Carte Michelin n° 83 pli 6-7.

Cévennes-Gorges du Tarn

Entre Millau et Florac
une route splendide de 60 km qui
passe par des sites magnifiques.
A **voir absolument.**

VOCABULAIRE

- **expression du temps (adverbes)**

Ce n'est pas encore prêt, c'est bientôt prêt,
c'est presque prêt, ce sera prêt tout à l'heure,
c'est prêt, c'est déjà prêt.

- **expression de la qualité (adverbes en -ment)**

heureuse ————————→heureusement	parfaite ————————→parfaitement
malheureuse ————————→malheureusement	extraordinaire ————————→extraordinairement
merveilleuse ————————→merveilleusement	agréable ————————→agréablement

- **Une réception**

verbes ————————→noms	
recevoir ————————→une réception	les gens sont agréables, sympathiques, intéressants…
inviter ————————→une invitation	
présenter ————————→(faire) les présentations	le méchoui est délicieux,
discuter ————————→une discussion	parfait, excellent…

● **En promenade : « une sortie »**

un parc national : *le parc national des Cévennes*
des gorges : *les gorges du Tarn*
une grotte : *la grotte des Demoiselles*

une forêt, une rivière, un lac...
c'est magnifique, splendide, extraordinaire, merveilleux, très beau, très joli, très intéressant.

GRAMMAIRE

1. Le superlatif

le *(la, les)* { Plus } + adjectif
{ moins } + nom + de

	(adjectif)	(nom)
supériorité	C'est la plus belle région *(de France)*.	C'est Virginie qui a le plus de vêtements.
infériorité	C'est la route la moins rapide.	C'est Virginie qui a le moins de livres.

2. Bon, mauvais, bien, mal
(comparatifs et superlatifs de supériorité)

	comparatif	superlatif
Bon	meilleur *(que...)*	le (la, les) meilleur(e)
Mauvais	plus mauvais *(que)*	le (la, les) plus mauvais(e)
	pire *(que)*	le (la, les) pire
Bien	mieux *(que)*	le mieux
Mal	plus mal *(que)*	le plus mal
	pire *(que)*	le pire

Attention ! moins bon *(mauvais, bien, mal)* que
le moins bon *(mauvais, bien, mal)*
aussi bon *(mauvais, bien, mal)* que

On dit : « bien mieux, beaucoup mieux, bien meilleur, bien pire »
mais pas : ~~beaucoup meilleur, beaucoup pire~~

3. Où, pronom relatif (remplace un nom de lieu)

— Vous connaissez cette région ? Nous allons en vacances dans cette région
→ Vous connaissez cette région **où** nous allons en vacances ?
— Montpellier est une ville intéressante ; il faut s'y arrêter
→ Montpellier est une ville intéressante **où** il faut s'arrêter.

Attention ! Où pronom relatif ≠ **Où ?** pronom interrogatif
Où habites-tu ? C'est la ville où j'habite.

1. *Complétez en mettant BIEN ou BON et en faisant l'accord :*

En France, on mange .... ; il y a de ...... restaurants
Ce n'est pas un ...... élève. Il ne travaille pas ......
J'ai vu un ...... film hier soir. J'ai ...... aimé l'histoire
Il a une ...... situation. Il gagne ...... sa vie
Vous aimez la Bretagne ? Ah oui, c'est ......
Vous aimez la choucroute ? Oh oui, c'est ......

Ne buvez pas ce vin ; il n'est pas ......
Tu conduis trop à gauche. Ce n'est pas ......

2. *Comparez leur âge, leur taille, leur poids.*

Paul 23 ans	*1,75 m*	*72 kg*	*Paul est le plus vieux. Il n'est pas le plus grand.*
Valérie 18 ans	*1,63 m*	*49 kg*	*Il pèse le plus lourd. Il est plus petit que Jean-Pierre.*
Jean-Pierre 22 ans	*1,78 m*	*69 kg*	*Mais il est plus grand que Valérie.*

3. Complétez selon le modèle.

Restaurant « Au bon coin », menu 35 F. Restaurant « Le petit Vatel », menu 31 F.
Le restaurant « Au bon coin » est bon marché. Le restaurant « Le Petit Vatel » est meilleur marché.

Pierre 13/20. Françoise 15/20 : Pierre travaille bien. Françoise . . . . . .
Le vin blanc, c'est bon. Le champagne . . . . . .
Pour voyager, le train c'est . . . . . . L'avion . . . . . .
Fumer peu, c'est bien. S'arrêter de fumer . . . . . .
Le mouton au four, c'est bon. Le méchoui . . . . . .

4. Comparez-les. Comparez leurs résultats.

Saut en hauteur (femmes) : concurrente nº 1 mesure 1,65 m, saute 1,78 m
6 mesure 1,68 m, saute 1,75 m
3 mesure 1,72 m, saute 1,70 m
La concurrente 1 : c'est elle la moins grande, mais c'est elle qui saute le plus haut.
La concurrente 3 : c'est la plus grande, mais . . . . . .

100 mètres (femmes) concurrente nº 7 15 ans, le 100 m en 14 secondes
9 25 ans, le 100 m en 12.5 secondes
13 17 ans, le 100 m en 13 secondes
La concurrente 7 : c'est la plus jeune, mais . . . . . .
La concurrente 9 : c'est la moins jeune, mais . . . . . .

Haltérophilie (hommes) concurrent nº 5 pèse 70 kg, soulève 90 kg
8 pèse 75 kg, soulève 85 kg
15 pèse 82 kg, soulève 80 kg
Le concurrent 5 : c'est le moins lourd, mais . . . . . .
Le concurrent 15 : c'est le plus lourd, mais . . . . . .

5. Voici trois bulletins scolaires. Analysez-les.

Au 1er trimestre, Marc a bien travaillé. Au 2e trimestre, il a . . . . . .
Au 3e trimestre, ... C'est au 2e trimestre qu'il a le moins bien travaillé. C'est au 3e trimestre . . . . . . Son 2e trimestre a été le plus mauvais. Son 3e trimestre a été . . . . . .

	Moyenne sur 20	Marc Moreau	Michel Legrand	Anne-Marie Leclerc
1er trimestre		13	7	8
2e trimestre		10	6	8,5
3e trimestre		14	4	16

Au 1er trimestre, Michel a mal travaillé. Au 2e trimestre, ... Au 3e trimestre . . . . . . C'est au 1er trimestre qu'il a le moins mal travaillé. C'est au 3e trimestre . . . . . . Son 1er trimestre a été . . . . . .

Au 3e trimestre, Anne-Marie a beaucoup . . . . . . qu'aux deux autres. Son 3e trimestre a été bien . . . . . . que les deux autres.

6. *En vous inspirant des documents page 115, présentez : la région, la ville, la curiosité, le monument le plus extraordinaire de votre pays.*
Complétez cette présentation par une phrase.
Sur le modèle.

« C'est un endroit où il faut aller, qu'il faut absolument ......
C'est une région où il fait beau ...... où les gens sont sympathiques ...... où on mange bien. »

1. — C'est un beau pays !
    On y mange bien ?
 — ·Ah oui, c'est un pays **où** on mange bien.

2. C'est une belle région ?
    Oui, c'est **la plus** belle.

● *La meilleure façon de voyager.*
Le train, l'avion, l'auto-stop, la voiture, le métro, le bus, le vélo, la marche à pied...

En utilisant les adjectifs : *bon, bien, rapide, lent, cher, pas cher (ou bon marché, ou économique, ou raisonnable), intéressant, dangereux, agréable, pratique,* **dialoguez avec vos voisins(es).**

Vous :   *Comment préférez-vous voyager ?*
Elle/lui :   *Moi, je prends l'avion. C'est plus ......*
Un autre :   *Moi non. Je préfère voyager en train. C'est moins ......*
                 Le mieux pour moi, c'est ......

● *Regardez la carte des Cévennes (page 136). Choisissez deux villages au hasard.*
Commentez l'itinéraire.

● **Regardez le plan du métro et choisissez deux stations au hasard. Cherchez ensuite le meilleur itinéraire,** *(environ 1 mn 30 d'une station à l'autre).*
Ex. : *Pour aller de Corvisart à Goncourt, le plus rapide c'est de passer par la place d'Italie. Là, vous prenez la direction Église de Pantin. Vous changez à République et vous prenez la direction Mairie des Lilas.*

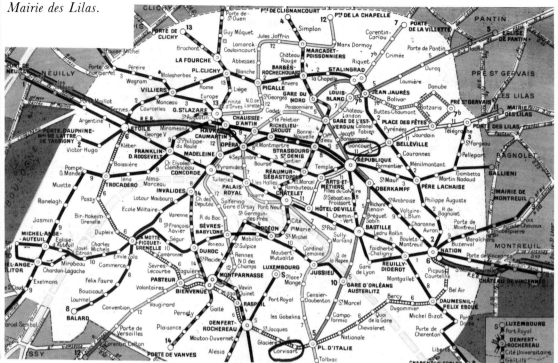

● **Choisissez votre téléviseur couleur.**
Commentez ce tableau, utilisez des comparatifs et des superlatifs.

Marques	A B C	E I N	SONAKA	S P	LUX
Fabrication	française	allemande	japonaise	suisse	française
Service après-vente	bon	bon	insuffisant	satisfaisant	médiocre
Qualité de l'image	bonne	excellente	très bonne	moyenne	moyenne
Qualité du son	excellente	bonne	excellente	moyenne	mauvaise
PRIX	3 000 F	4 500 F	3 000 F	3 500 F	2 500 F
Résultats	15/20	18/20	15/20	12/20 ·	9/20
Appréciation	C'est un bon poste et il y a un bon service après-vente.	C'est parfait mais c'est cher.	C'est bien, mais le service après-vente...	Ce n'est pas mal, mais l'image n'est pas belle.	Un poste bon marché, de mauvaise qualité.

● **Vous demandez à votre voisin(e) des renseignements sur son pays, sur la France.**
Vous : Quelle est la ville où il y a le plus . . . . . . le moins . . . . . .
Quelle est la région où il fait . . . . . . où on trouve . . . . . .
Elle/lui : La ville où . . . . . . c'est . . . . . .
Vous : Ça vaut la peine d'y aller? C'est bien, cette ville?
Elle/lui : Ah oui. C'est un endroit où il faut absolument aller
On y trouve . . . . . . il y a . . . . . . C'est magnifique, merveilleux . . . . . .

● **C'est la fin de l'année. Vous organisez une réception pour vos amis (ies), vos voisins(es). Jouez la scène (*).**

Vous présentez X à Y *Je te présente, je vous présente ......*
Vous présentez votre famille *Voilà ......, c'est ma fille, mon fils ......*
Vous servez un apéritif, un plat *Je t'ai apporté ...... ça te va ......*
Vous offrez un verre *Qu'est-ce que tu prends ? ...... vous prenez ?*
Vous prenez des nouvelles de vos amis *Alors, ça te plaît ? tu es bien ici ? ......*

Vous suggérez une promenade, une visite, une sortie, votre ami(e) est d'accord :
— *Tu veux aller à ...... avec moi ?*
— *Pourquoi pas ? Très bonne idée. Où est-ce ? ...... C'est à ......*
— *Tu verras, c'est bien. Il y a beaucoup de choses à voir ...... On ira en voiture ...... C'est extraordinaire ...... C'est une région où ......*

Votre ami(e) n'est pas d'accord :
Ah non, j'y suis déjà allé. Ça ne m'a pas plu. J'ai une meilleure idée. Allons à ...... c'est mieux. C'est moins loin ...... Il y a beaucoup plus de choses à voir ......

Vous étudiez le meilleur itinéraire.
Il faut passer par ......
Je vous conseille de ......

Vous fixez la date.
On y va le ......?
On fait ça la semaine prochaine ?

(*) **Plutôt que de jouer la scène, nous vous conseillons vivement d'organiser une vraie réception !**
Tenue « décontractée » et français obligatoire ! Bonne soirée !

BILAN

A. Tests

1. Mettez les verbes au futur

Chers amis,

Je descends à Montpellier pour mon travail et j'ai bien envie d'aller vous voir. Je *(prendre)* l'avion. J'*(arriver)* à l'aéroport de Fréjorgues vendredi soir à 17 h. Est-ce que vous *(pouvoir)* venir me chercher ? Le soir, nous *(aller)* au restaurant. C'est moi qui vous invite. Je *(passer)* le week-end avec vous. On *(avoir)* le temps de se promener. Malheureusement lundi, il *(falloir)* travailler ! Je *(repartir)* le soir par le train. J'*(aller)* à Marseille où je *(voir)* un client important.

A bientôt. Amitiés.

P.S. Est-ce que je *(pouvoir)* dormir chez vous ? Merci.

2. Complétez en employant : QUI, QUE, OÙ

1. Parlez-moi de la France. Vous connaissez le Midi ?
   — Ah oui. C'est une région . . . . . . je connais bien.
2. Quelles sont les villes les plus chaudes ?
   — Les villes . . . . . . il fait le plus chaud sont Perpignan et Nice.
3. Et quelle ville préférez-vous ?
   — La ville . . . . . . je préfère ? C'est Nice.
4. Il fait beau dans le Midi, l'hiver ?
   — Oui, c'est une région . . . . . . les hivers sont doux.
5. Et la Camargue, vous connaissez ?
   — Bien sûr. C'est un endroit . . . . . . j'aime bien aller.
6. Vous pouvez m'indiquer un bon hôtel ?
   — L'hôtel . . . . . . je vais s'appelle « Le Gardian ».
7. Qu'est-ce qu'on fait en Camargue ?
   — Les gens . . . . . . y viennent font du cheval et vont à la plage.
8. Elles sont belles, les plages ?
   — Oh oui. Il y a des plages de sable fin . . . . . . font des kilomètres.
9. Et vous, vous faites du cheval ?
   — Un peu. Mais le sport . . . . . . je préfère c'est la planche à voile.
10. Et il n'y a pas trop de touristes ?
    — Ah si ! Mais sur la plage . . . . . . je vais, il n'y a presque personne.

3. Transformez en employant C'EST... QUI..., C'EST... QUE..., comme dans le modèle

Il n'est pas technicien. Il est ingénieur. →
Ce n'est pas technicien qu'il est. C'est ingénieur.
Elle ne va pas à la fac. Son frère, y va. →
Ce n'est pas elle qui va à la fac. C'est son frère.

1. Il ne veut pas un vélomoteur. Il veut une moto.
2. Je ne fais pas la cuisine. Mon frère, la fait.
3. Ils ne vont pas à Nîmes. Ils vont à Montpellier.
4. Il n'a pas eu une promotion. Il a eu une augmentation.
5. Il ne travaille pas à l'agence. Sa femme y travaille.

4. Complétez en employant QUELQUE CHOSE, QUELQU'UN, RIEN, PERSONNE

1. Il y a du courrier ? Il n'y a . . . . . . pour moi ?
2. Je suis allé ouvrir la porte. Je n'ai vu . . . . . .
3. Tu veux encore un fruit ou un gâteau ?
   — Non, je ne veux plus . . . . . .
4. Est-ce que . . . . a téléphoné pour moi ? — Non, ...
5. J'ai parlé avec . . . . . . qui te connaît.
6. Le frigo est vide. Il ne reste plus . . . . . .
7. Je peux vous demander . . . . . . ?
8. Désolé, Monsieur. Il ne reste plus . . . . . . à louer.
9. Nous allons dîner chez eux. Il faut leur apporter . . .

5. Choisissez la bonne réponse

1. Tu peux porter cette caisse ?

Elle est assez lourde / Elle est trop lourde / Elle n'est pas trop lourde.

2. Ne prenez pas cette route !
Elle est trop dangereuse / Elle n'est pas assez dangereuse / Elle n'est pas trop dangereuse.

3. Je préfère travailler dans cette pièce.
Elle n'est pas trop froide / Elle n'est pas assez froide / Elle est trop froide.

4. Je suis très fatigué.
J'ai assez de travail / Je n'ai pas assez de travail / J'ai trop de travail.

5. Vous n'arrivez pas à faire cet exercice ?
Alors il n'est pas facile / Alors il est trop facile / Alors il est assez facile.

6. *Complétez en employant : TOUTES LES, TOUS LES, TOUTE LA, TOUT LE,*

Dans l'entreprise où je travaille, ... les cadres sont des hommes et . . . . . . secrétaires sont des femmes. . . . . . . la journée, je tape à la machine. Le soir, je rentre à la maison et j'ai . . . . . . vaisselle à faire. En ce moment, je suis très fatiguée : je vais dormir . . . . . . week-end.

7. *Posez la question qui porte sur les mots soulignés :*

1. Paris est à <u>800</u> km de Montpellier.
2. Nous nous installons à <u>Montpellier</u>.
3. Nous passerons par <u>Lyon</u>.
4. Nous descendrons <u>en voiture</u>.
5. Nous déménageons <u>le 31 juillet</u>.

8. *Voici des informations sur la famille Gautier et la famille Carnot.*

1. **M. Gautier** 39 ans	**M. Carnot** 41 ans
2. **Mme Gautier** 36 ans	**Mme Carnot** 33 ans
3. **3 enfants**	2 enfants
4. **Salaire de M. Gautier** 8 500 F	**Salaire de M. Carnot** 12 000 F
5. **Salaire de Mme Gautier** 6 000 F	**Salaire de Mme Carnot** 6 000 F
6. **Appartement des Gautier** 90 m^2	**Appartement des Carnot** 110 m^2
7. **Loyer des Gautier** 1 800 F	**Loyer des Carnot** 2 200 F

Comparez les Carnot aux Gautier :

1. M. Carnot est plus vieux que M. Gautier.   Il a 2 ans de plus.
2. Mme Carnot . . . . Mme Gautier.   Elle a 3 ans de moins.
3. Les Carnot . . . . d'enfants . . . .   Ils ont . . . .
4. M. Carnot . . . . d'argent . . . . 3 500 F . . . .
5. Mme Carnot . . . . que . . . .
6. L'appartement des Carnot . . . . que . . . .   Il fait . . . .
7. Le loyer des Carnot . . . . cher . . . .   Il fait . . . .

9. *Complétez les phrases suivantes en employant BIEN ou BEAUCOUP avec le comparatif.*

1. Les côtelettes c'est bon, mais le gigot c'est . . . . . .
2. Un vélomoteur c'est rapide, mais une moto c'est . . . . . .
3. Un appartement c'est bien, mais une villa c'est . . . . . .
4. C'est pratique une voiture, mais, en ville, un deux-roues c'est . . . . . .
5. Le vin c'est bon, mais le champagne c'est . . . . . .
6. Avoir une terrasse c'est agréable, mais avoir un jardin c'est . . . . . .
7. Un vélomoteur c'est bien, mais une moto c'est . . . . . .
8. Se casser un bras c'est ennuyeux, mais se casser une jambe c'est . . . . . .
9. C'est bien le train, mais l'avion c'est . . . . . .
10. Visiter seul un musée c'est intéressant, mais avec un guide c'est . . . . . .

10. *Complétez les phrases suivantes en employant des superlatifs :*

1. Ces deux tartes sont bonnes, mais c'est la tarte aux pommes qui est . . . . . .
2. Les chambres sont bien dans cet hôtel, mais c'est la vôtre qui est . . . . . .
3. Il y a des grottes intéressantes dans la région, mais la Grotte des Demoiselles qui est . . . . . .
4. Les amies de ma fille sont très gentilles, mais c'est Catherine qui est . . . . . .
5. Toutes ces motos sont très bonnes, mais ce sont les japonaises qui sont . . . . . .
6. Les musiciens de l'orchestre sont bons, mais c'est la flûtiste qui est . . . . . .
7. Tous les hôtels sont bien ici, mais ce sont les hôtels du bord de la plage qui sont . . . . . .
8. Toutes les caisses du déménagement sont lourdes, mais ce sont les caisses de livres qui sont . . . . . .
9. Ces deux appartements sont bien, mais c'est l'appartement du dernier étage qui est . . . . . .
10. Dans cette pâtisserie les gâteaux sont très bons, mais c'est le gâteau au chocolat qui est . . . . . .

B. Texte complémentaire

Francine : — Tu. as des vacances en février, toi ? J'ai envie de prendre une semaine pour aller faire du ski.

Frédéric : — Bonne idée. Moi aussi.

Francine : — Tu veux venir ?

Frédéric : — Pourquoi pas ? Où veux-tu aller ? Il y a une station que tu préfères ?

Francine : — Je veux un endroit où il y a de la bonne neige et beaucoup de soleil. J'ai vu des annonces dans le journal. Tiens, regarde : « Courchevel ». C'est bien Courchevel. « Studio à louer, 3/4 personnes. 2 000 F par semaine. » Ah non ! C'est trop cher. « Petit studio, 2 personnes, au centre de la station, 1 500 F la semaine. » Ça, c'est meilleur marché. Qu'est-ce que tu en penses ?

Frédéric : — Tu sais, louer un studio, ce n'est pas très pratique. Il faut faire les courses, faire la cuisine. Je n'aime pas beaucoup ça.

Francine : — Moi non plus. Mais il y a aussi les hôtels... « Méribel ». Où c'est Méribel ?

Frédéric : — En Haute-Savoie. Au sud d'Albertville.

Francine : — Alors « Méribel : Hôtel des Neiges. Février, 200 F par jour. Splendid-Hôtel, 150 F. » Ça, c'est plus raisonnable.

Frédéric : — Eh bien, moi, j'ai une meilleure idée. On va aller dans une station que je connais bien : Chamonix.

Francine : — Je veux bien, mais il va falloir trouver une location. On téléphone à l'Office du Tourisme ?

Frédéric : — Tu oublies quelque chose.

Francine : — Quoi ?

Frédéric : — je t'ai parlé de mon grand-père Félicien ?

Francine : — Ah oui, il a un hôtel à Chamonix. C'est ça ?

Frédéric : — Oh, ce n'est pas un hôtel extraordinaire. C'est petit, il y a neuf ou dix chambres, mais c'est très sympathique. Et c'est ma grand-mère qui fait la cuisine. Qu'est-ce que tu en penses ? On va chez eux ?

Francine : — Moi, je suis d'accord.

Frédéric : — Je lui téléphonerai tout à l'heure.

Francine : — C'est loin, Chamonix ?

Frédéric : — A environ 250 km d'ici.

Francine : — Et comment on y va ?

Frédéric : — C'est très simple : on prend l'autoroute jusqu'à Sallanches. L'autoroute passe par Genève.

Francine : — Et après Sallanches, il reste combien de kilomètres ?

Frédéric : — Pas beaucoup : 17 exactement.

Francine : — On ira en voiture ?

Frédéric : — Oui, c'est plus pratique que le train et là-bas on en aura besoin. On prendra la mienne. Je descendrai de Paris et je passerai te prendre chez toi. Mais, dis-moi, tu sais bien faire du ski ?

Francine : — Je suis canadienne, n'oublie pas ! Au Canada, la neige, on connaît. Mais je suis moins forte que ma sœur. Elle, elle fait beaucoup de ski. En février elle sera au Canada.

Frédéric : — Alors elle ne viendra pas avec nous ?

Francine : — Non. Elle reste là-bas tout le mois de février.

Frédéric : — Dommage. Bon. Je vais appeler mon grand-père. Heu... combien je demande de chambres ?

Francine : — Ben...

C. Images pour...

« Alors ça te plaît Montpellier? »

Vous venez d'arriver à Montpellier. En une demie journée, vous visiterez facilement le centre historique de la ville entre la place de la Comédie et le Jardin du Peyrou. Mais il restera encore bien des choses à voir : le Musée Fabre, les « Arceaux », le Jardin des Plantes, les maisons et hôtels particuliers du XVIIᵉ et du XVIIIᵉ qui font le « charme » de Montpellier. Alors, pourquoi ne pas y rester quarante-huit heures et faire un séjour qui vous permettra de sentir l'atmosphère d'une ville où il fait bon vivre !

MONTPELLIER (34000), ch.-l. de la Région Languedoc-Roussillon et du départ. de l'Hérault, sur le Lez, à 753 km au S. de Paris; 195603 hab. *(Montpelliérains).* École militaire d'administration (1948) et École d'application de l'infanterie (1967); centre universitaire d'histoire militaire (1969).
GÉOGRAPHIE. Au contact de la garrigue et de la plaine littorale, à quelques kilomètres seulement de la Méditerranée, à laquelle elle est peu liée, l'agglomération compte près de 220000 habitants; elle a connu un accroissement démographique récent considérable, sa population ayant doublé dans les vingt dernières années. Cette progression est partiellement due à l'arrivée de rapatriés d'Algérie, mais repose aussi sur une industrialisation (électronique, notamment) s'ajoutant aux traditionnelles fonctions, administrative, commerciale et universitaire. Montpellier bénéficie d'une bonne desserte autoroutière, la reliant (déjà ou à brève échéance) à la vallée du Rhône, à Toulouse et à Barcelone. À mi-chemin entre Nîmes et Béziers, elle s'affirme de plus en plus comme la métropole du Languedoc-Roussillon.
HISTOIRE. Née à la fin du Xᵉ s., la ville est dotée, en 1221, d'une école de médecine, et, en 1289, d'une université de grande renommée. Possession du roi d'Aragon puis du roi de Majorque (1204-1349), Montpellier est achetée en 1349 par Philippe VI. La ville connaît une nouvelle prospérité au XVIIIᵉ s.
BEAUX-ARTS. Bel ensemble urbain des XVIIᵉ-XVIIIᵉ s.: nombreux hôtels particuliers, promenade du Peyrou par Daviler* et le Montpelliérain Jean Antoine Giral († 1787). Faculté de médecine ayant pour noyau les bâtiments de l'anc. abbaye Saint-Benoît, fondée par Urbain V en 1564. Musée archéologique dans un hôtel du XVIIᵉ s. Riche musée des beaux-arts, portant le nom de F.-X. Fabre, un de ses donateurs (peinture européenne; école française, dont Houdon, Greuze, Delacroix, Courbet, Bazille).

« Oui, c'est une belle ville. »

L'Hôtel de Sarret, dit de la Coquille. (XVIIᵉ et XVIIIᵉ siècle).

Une vieille rue.

La Préfecture.

- *La Place de la Comédie,* l'« Œuf » pour les Montpelliérains, est la place principale et le centre d'animation du Vieux Montpellier.

- *Le Peyrou,* avec son château d'eau et la statue de Louis XIV, est un lieu de promenade dominant le sud et l'ouest de la ville.

- *Le Jardin des Plantes* qui occupe 6 ha près du Jardin du Peyrou.

- *Les Arceaux* (XVII), un aqueduc de 236 arches (800 m de long) qui amène l'eau au château d'eau du Peyrou.

- *La Cathédrale Saint-Pierre :* magnifique église du XIVᵉ siècle qui a beaucoup souffert au cours des âges. La façade, la tour et la nef sont un bel exemple d'architecture gothique méridionale.

- *L'Hôtel de Sarret,* un des cent hôtels particuliers qui font la fierté de Montpellier.

- *Le Musée Fabre :* œuvres italiennes, flamandes, hollandaises. Témoignages du Romantisme, du Réalisme et du Naturalisme français.

D. Conjugaisons

DEMANDER (*un renseignement*)

1. *Présent*	2. *Futur*	3. *Passé composé*	4. *Impératif*
Je demand**e**	Je demander**ai**	j' **ai** demandé	
Tu demand**es**	Tu demander**as**	Tu **as** demandé	Demande
Il/Elle/On demand**e**	Il/Elle/On demander**a**	Il/Elle/On **a** demandé	
Nous demand**ons**	Nous demander**ons**	Nous **avons** demandé	Demandons
Vous demand**ez**	Vous demander**ez**	Vous **avez** demandé	Demandez
Ils/Elles demand**ent**	Ils/Elles demander**ont**	Ils/Elles **ont** demandé	

ARRIVER

1. *Présent*	2. *Futur*	3. *Passé composé*	4. *Impératif*
J' arriv**e**	J' arriver**ai**	Je **suis** arrivé(e)	
Tu arriv**es**	Tu arriver**as**	Tu **es** arrivé(e)	Arrive
Il/Elle/On arriv**e**	Il/Elle/On arriver**a**	Il/Elle/On **est** arrivé(e)	
Nous arriv**ons**	Nous arriver**ons**	Nous **sommes** arrivé**s**(ées)	Arrivons
Vous arriv**ez**	Vous arriver**ez**	Vous **êtes** arrivé**s**(ées)	Arrivez
Ils/Elles arriv**ent**	Ils/Elles/ arriver**ont**	Ils/Elles **sont** arrivé**s**(ées)	
		Pierre et Françoise **sont** arrivé**s**	

SORTIR (*de la tente*)

1. *Présent*	2. *Futur*	3. *Passé composé*	4. *Impératif*
Je sor**s**	Je sortir**ai**	Je **suis** sorti**(e)**	
Tu sor**s**	Tu sortir**as**	Tu **es** sorti**(e)**	Sors
Il/Elle/On sor**t**	Il/Elle/On sortir**a**	Il/Elle/On **est** sorti**(e)**	
Nous sort**ons**	Nous sortir**ons**	Nous **sommes** sort**is(es)**	Sortons
Vous sort**ez**	Vous sortir**ez**	Vous **êtes** sort**is(es)**	Sortez
Ils/Elles sort**ent**	Ils/Elles sortir**ont**	Ils/Elles **sont** sort**is(es)**	

AVOIR (*mal*)

1. *Présent*	2. *Futur*	3. *Passé composé*	4. *Impératif*
J' **ai** mal	J' aur**ai**	J **ai** eu	
Tu **as** mal	Tu aur**as**	Tu **as** eu	Aie
Il/Elle/On **a** mal	Il/Elle/On aur**a**	Il/Elle/On **a** eu	
Nous **avons** mal	Nous aur**ons**	Nous **avons** eu	Ayons
Vous **avez** mal	Vous aur**ez**	Vous **avez** eu	Ayez
Ils/Elles **ont** mal	Ils/Elles aur**ont**	Ils/Elles **ont** eu	

ÊTRE (*malade*)

1. *Présent*	2. *Futur*	3. *Passé composé*	4. *Impératif*
Je **suis** malade	JE ser**ai**	J **ai** été	
Tu **es** malade	Tu ser**as**	Tu **as** été	Sois
Il/Elle/On **est** malade	Il/Elle/On ser**a**	Il/Elle/On **a** été	
Nous **sommes** malades	Nous ser**ons**	Nous **avons** été	Soyons
Vous **êtes** malades	Vous ser**ez**	Vous **avez** été	Soyez
Ils/Elles **sont** malades	Ils/Elles ser**ont**	Ils/Elles **ont** été	

SE LAVER

1. *Présent*		2. *Futur*		3. *Passé composé*		4. *Impératif*
Je me	lav**e**	Je me	laver**ai**	Je me **suis**	lav**é(e)**	
Tu te	lav**es**	Tu te	laver**as**	Tu t'**es**	lav**é(e)**	Lave-toi
Il/Elle/On se	lav**e**	Il/Elle/On se	laver**a**	Il/Elle/On s'**est**	lav**é(e)**	
Nous nous	lav**ons**	Nous nous	laver**ons**	Nous nous **sommes**	lav**és(es)**	Lavons-nous
Vous vous	lav**ez**	Vous vous	laver**ez**	Vous vous **êtes**	lav**és(es)**	Lavez-vous
Ils/Elles se	lav**ent**	Ils/Elles se	laver**ont**	Ils/Elles se **sont**	lav**és(es)**	

S'EN ALLER (*en vacances*)

1. *Présent*		2. *Futur*		3. *Passé composé*		4. *Impératif*
Je m'en	**vais**	Je m'en	ir**ai**	Je **suis**	all**é(e)**	
Tu t'en	**vas**	Tu t'en	ir**as**	Tu **es**	all**é(e)**	Va
Il/Elle/On s'en	**va**	Il/Elle/On s'en	ir**a**	Il/Elle/On **est**	all**é(e)**	
Nous nous en	**allons**	Nous nous en	ir**ons**	Nous **sommes**	all**és(es)**	Allons
Vous vous en	**allez**	Vous vous en	ir**ez**	Vous **êtes**	all**és(es)**	Allez
Ils/Elles s'en	**vont**	Ils/Elles s'en	ir**ont**	Ils/Elles **sont**	all**és(es)**	
				Pierre et Françoise **sont**	all**és**	

FAIRE (*du bruit*)

1. *Présent*	2. *Futur*	3. *Passé composé*		4. *Impératif*
Je fais	Je fer**ai**	J'**ai**	fait	
Tu fais	Tu fer**as**	Tu **as**	fait	Fais
Il/Elle/On fait	Il/Elle/On fer**a**	Il/Elle/On **a**	fait	
Nous fai**sons**	Nous fer**ons**	Nous **avons**	fait	Faisons
Vous fai**tes**	Vous fer**ez**	Vous **avez**	fait	Faites
Ils/Elles **font**	Ils/Elles fer**ont**	Ils/Elles **ont**	fait	

PRENDRE (*une photo*)

1. *Présent*	2. *Futur*	3. *Passé composé*		4. *Impératif*
Je prend**s**	Je prendr**ai**	J'**ai**	pris	
Tu prend**s**	Tu prendr**as**	Tu **as**	pris	Prends
Il/Elle/On prend	Il/Elle/On prendr**a**	Il/Elle/On **a**	pris	
Nous pren**ons**	Nous prendr**ons**	Nous **avons**	pris	Prenons
Vous pren**ez**	Vous prendr**ez**	Vous **avez**	pris	Prenez
Ils/Elles pren**nent**	Ils/Elles prendr**ont**	Ils/Elles **ont**	pris	

METTRE (*ses lunettes*)

1. *Présent*		2. *Futur*	3. *Passé composé*		4. *Impératif*
Je mets	mes lunettes	Je mett**rai**	J'**ai**	mis	
Tu mets	tes lunettes	Tu mett**ras**	Tu **as**	mis	Mets
Il/Elle/On met	ses lunettes	Il/Elle/On mett**ra**	Il/Elle/On **a**	mis	
Nous mett**ons**	nos lunettes	Nous mett**rons**	Nous **avons**	mis	Mettons
Vous mett**ez**	vos lunettes	Vous mett**rez**	Vous **avez**	mis	Mettez
Ils/Elles met**tent**	leurs lunettes	Ils/Elles mett**ront**	Ils/Elles **ont**	mis	

VOULOIR (*se baigner*)

1. *Présent*		2. *Futur*	3. *Passé composé*		4. *Impératif*
Je **veux**	me baigner	Je voudr**ai**	J'**ai**	voulu	
Tu **veux**	te baigner	Tu voudr**as**	Tu **as**	voulu	Veux/Veuille
Il/Elle/On **veut**	se baigner	Il/Elle/On voudr**a**	Il/Elle/On **a**	voulu	
Nous **voulons**	nous baigner	Nous voudr**ons**	Nous **avons**	voulu	Voulons/Veuillons
Vous **voulez**	vous baigner	Vous voudr**ez**	Vous **avez**	voulu	Voulez/Veuillez
Ils/Elles **veulent**	se baigner	Ils/Elles voudr**ont**	Ils/Elles **ont**	voulu	

Des verbes « difficiles » (modèles)

		PRÉSENT	FUTUR	PASSÉ COMPOSÉ	IMPÉRATIF
en IR	*COURIR*	je cours, il court nous courons, ils courent	je courrai	j'ai couru	cours courons
	DORMIR	je dors, il dort nous dormons, ils dorment	je dormirai	j'ai dormi	dors dormons
	OUVRIR	j'ouvre, il ouvre nous ouvrons, ils ouvrent	j'ouvrirai	j'ai ouvert	ouvre ouvrons
	TENIR	je tiens, il tient nous tenons, ils tiennent	je tiendrai	j'ai tenu	tiens tenons
	VENIR	je viens, il vient nous venons, ils viennent	je viendrai	je suis venu	viens venons
en OIR	*APERCEVOIR*	j'aperçois, il aperçoit nous apercevons, ils aperçoivent	j'apercevrai	j'ai aperçu	aperçois apercevons
	DEVOIR	je dois, il doit nous devons, ils doivent	je devrai	j'ai dû	dois devons
	FALLOIR (impersonnel)	il faut	il faudra	il a fallu	—
	PLEUVOIR (impersonnel)	il pleut	il pleuvra	il a plu	—
	POUVOIR	je peux, il peut nous pouvons, ils peuvent,	je pourrai	j'ai pu	—
	SAVOIR	je sais, il sait nous savons, ils savent	je saurai	j'ai su	sache sachons
	VOIR	je vois, il voit nous voyons, ils voient	je verrai	j'ai vu	vois voyons
en RE	*BOIRE*	je bois, il boit, nous buvons, ils boivent	je boirai	j'ai bu	bois buvons
	CONDUIRE	je conduis, il conduit nous conduisons, ils conduisent	je conduirai	j'ai conduit	conduis conduisons
	CONNAÎTRE	je connais, il connaît nous connaissons, ils connaissent	je connaîtrai	j'ai connu	connais connaissons
	CROIRE	je crois, il croit nous croyons, ils croient	je croirai	j'ai cru	crois croyons
	DIRE	je dis, il dit nous disons, ils disent	je dirai	j'ai dit	dis disons, dites
	ÉCRIRE	j'écris, il écrit nous écrivons, ils écrivent	j'écrirai	j'ai écrit	écris écrivons
	LIRE	je lis, il lit nous lisons, ils lisent	je lirai	j'ai lu	lis lisons
	NAÎTRE	je nais, il naît nous naissons, ils naissent	je naîtrai	je suis né	nais naissons
	RIRE	je ris, il rit nous rions, ils rient	je rirai	j'ai ri	ris rions
	VIVRE	je vis, il vit nous vivons, ils vivent	je vivrai	j'ai vécu	vis vivons

LEXIQUE

ATTENTION ! Cette liste ne présente que le vocabulaire « actif » *de la méthode, c'est-à-dire le lexique des* dialogues *repris et manipulé dans les exercices (phonétiques, exercices écrits, mécanismes, prises de parole). On n'y trouvera pas, par contre, la totalité du* vocabulaire « réceptif » *(ou « passif ») présent dans* les documents authentiques *ou les listes ouvertes de la partie* information lexicale et grammaticale. *Le vocabulaire réceptif peut toutefois être utilisé ponctuellement dans les exercices écrits et la prise de parole d'une leçon. Ne figurent pas non plus les pronoms personnels, les adjectifs possessifs, les articles... ni le* vocabulaire grammatical.*

Abréviations : n. = nom ; v. = verbe ; adj. = adjectif ; adv. = adverbe ; prép. = préposition ; loc. = locution ; m. = masculin ; f. = féminin ; pl. = pluriel ; I., II... = Unité 1, 2... ; 1, 2 = Leçon 1, 2...

A

A (de AVOIR) : Jacques a 25 ans	I. 1
À (prép.) : Il habite à Paris	I. 1
ABRICOT (n. m.) : L'abricot est un fruit	II. 5
ABSOLUMENT (adv.) : C'est absolument extraordinaire !	IV. 5
ACCIDENT (n. m.) : Il a eu un accident de voiture	III. 4
ACCORD [D'] (loc.) : Rendez-vous à 3 heures ? D'accord, à 3 heures !	I. 3
ACHAT (n. m.) : voir ACHETER	IV. 3
ACHETER (v.) : On achète du pain ?	II. 3
ACHETEUR, EUSE (n.) : voir ACHETER	II. 3
ACTEUR, TRICE (n.) : Marilyn Monroe est une grande actrice	I. 1
ADDITION (n. f.) : Garçon, l'addition s'il vous plaît !	II. 2
ADORER (v.) : Il adore le jazz	I. 4
ADRESSE (n. f.) : Adresse : 15 rue de Paris	I. 1
AÉROPORT (n. m.) : L'aéroport de Roissy-Charles-de-Gaulle	I. 3
AFFAIRES (n. pl.) : Il faut ranger tes affaires !	II. 4
ÂGE (n. m.) : Mon âge ? 36 ans !	II. 4
AGENCE [IMMOBILIÈRE] (n. f.) : J'ai trouvé mon appartement par une agence	IV. 2
AGENT [DE POLICE] (n. m.) : L'agent de police est dans la rue	I. 2
AGNEAU (n. m.) : J'aime les côtelettes d'agneau	II. 3
AGRÉABLE (adj.) : C'est une ville agréable	II. 5
AI (de AVOIR) : J'ai 30 ans	I. 1
AIDE [A L'] (loc.) : Au secours ! A l'aide !	III. 4
AIDER (v.) : Je n'arrive pas à ouvrir. Tu peux m'aider ?	III. 2
AIMER (v.) : Jacques aime beaucoup la musique	I. 4
AIR (AVOIR L') : Elle a l'air timide	III. 3
ALCOOL (n. m.) : Du vin ? Non, je ne bois pas d'alcool !	IV. 5
ALLER (v.) : Je veux aller au cinéma	I. 3
ALLUMETTE (n. f.) : J'ai des cigarettes ! Tu as des allumettes ?	II. 4
ALORS (adv.) : Un café ? — Oui ! — Oui ! Alors 2 cafés !	II. 2
ALTITUDE (n. f.) : L'Everest fait 8 900 mètres d'altitude	III. 2
AMÉRICAIN, AINE (adj. et n.) : Il est américain, il habite à New York	I. 1
AMI, E (n.) : Brigitte est l'amie d'Isabelle	II. 4
AMUSANT, ANTE (adj.) : Les films de Laurel et Hardy sont amusants	IV. 2
AN (n. m.) : J'ai 36 ans	I. 1
ANNÉE (n. f.) : L'année prochaine, je vais à Paris	IV. 1
ANNONCER (v.) : J'ai une bonne nouvelle à t'annoncer !	IV. 1
ANTIPATHIQUE (adj.) : Je n'aime pas Pierre. Il est antipathique	I. 5
AOÛT (n. m.) : Le 4 août	I. 4
APÉRITIF (n. m.) : Tu prends un apéritif ? Porto, whisky ?	II. 5
APPAREIL [DE PHOTO] (n. m.) : J'ai un appareil de photo japonais	II. 4
APPARTEMENT (n. m.) : Elle a un appartement de 200 m²	IV. 3
APPELER (v.) : Elle est malade. Il faut appeler un médecin	III. 4
APPELER [S'] (v.) : Je m'appelle Didier. Elle s'appelle Brigitte	I. 1
APPLAUDIR (v.) : Elle a bien chanté, les spectateurs applaudissent	III. 3
APPLAUDISSEMENT (n. m.) : voir APPLAUDIR	III. 3
APPORTER (v.) : On a soif ! Apportez-nous du vin !	III. 4
APPRENDRE (v.) : Elle apprend le français	II. 5
APPROCHER [S'] (v.) : N'ayez pas peur ! Approchez-vous !	III. 3
APRÈS-DEMAIN (loc. adv.) : Aujourd'hui c'est lundi, après-demain c'est mercredi	III. 3
APRÈS-MIDI (n. m. ou f.) : Rendez-vous cet après-midi à 16 heures	I. 3
ARBRE (n. m.) : Elle a des arbres dans son jardin	III. 1
ARCHITECTE (n.) : Le Corbusier est un architecte français	I. 1
ARCHITECTURE (n. f.) : voir ARCHITECTE	II. 5
ARGENT (n. f.) : Tu as de l'argent ? — Oui j'ai 100 francs !	I. 3
ARMOIRE (n. f.) : Range tes affaires dans l'armoire	IV. 4
ARRÊT (n. m.) : voir ARRÊTER [S']	III. 2
ARRÊTER [S'] (v.) : On s'arrête ici ?	III. 1
ARRIÈRE (adj. et adv.) : La roue arrière est à plat !	III. 2
ARRIVER (v.) : Jacques est en retard ! Ah il arrive !	I. 5
ARRIVER [À] (v.) : Je n'arrive pas à ouvrir ! Aide-moi !	III. 2
ARTICHAUT (n. m.) : En Bretagne, on mange de bons artichauts	III. 1
ASPIRINE (n. f.) : A la pharmacie on peut acheter de l'aspirine	II. 3
ASSEOIR [S'] (v.) : Il y a des chaises. Asseyez-vous !	III. 2
ASSEZ (adv.) : J'ai sommeil. Je n'ai pas assez dormi	III. 4
ASSIETTE (n. f.) : Mets les assiettes sur la table !	II. 5
ATTENDRE (v.) : Il est en retard. Il faut l'attendre	II. IV
ATTENTION (n. f.) : Il faut faire attention au feu	III. 1
AUJOURD'HUI (adv.) : Aujourd'hui c'est dimanche	II.2
AUSSI (adv.) : J'aime le jazz et aussi le disco	I. 4
AUTANT (adv.) : J'ai autant de vêtements que toi	IV. 4
AUTOMNE (n. f.) : L'été est fini, l'automne arrive	IV. 2
AUTORISATION (n. f.) : Il faut une autorisation pour camper ici	III. 1
AUTOROUTE (n. f.) : Il y a une autoroute de Paris à Marseille	IV. 2
AUTRE (adj.) : De ce côté la mer, de l'autre côté la montagne	IV. 4
AVANT-HIER (loc. adv.) : On est le 5. Il est arrivé avant hier le 3 !	III. 3
AVEC (prép.) : Jacques déjeune avec Viviane	I. 3
AVION (n. m.) : Le Concorde est un bel avion	IV. 1
AVOIR (v.) : Elle a 20 ans	I. 1
AVRIL : Le 1er avril	I. 4
AYONS, AYEZ (v.) de AVOIR	III. 3

B

BAC [BACCALAURÉAT] (n. m.) : Je passe mon bac cette année	IV. 1
BAIGNER [SE] (v.) : On est allé à la plage et on s'est baigné	III. 3
BANLIEUE (n. f.) : Tu habites dans le centre de Paris ? — Non, en banlieue !	IV. 1
BANQUE (n. f.) : Je vais à la banque prendre de l'argent	II. 5
BAR (n. m.) : On prend un verre au bar de l'hôtel ?	III. 4

BAS, BASSE (adj.) : Une table basse — IV. 4
BAS [EN] (loc. adv.) : Elle attend en bas — IV. 2
BEAU, BEL, BELLE (adj.) : Paris c'est beau ! — Oui c'est une belle ville ! — II. 3
BEAU [IL FAIT] loc. : Il y a du soleil, il fait beau — IV. 2
BEAUCOUP (adv.) : Vous aimez la musique ? — Oui, beaucoup — I. 3
BEL, BELLE (adj.) : voir BEAU
BESOIN [AVOIR] : J'ai beaucoup travaillé. J'ai besoin de vacances — III. 2
BEURRE (n. m.) : Le matin, je mange du pain et du beurre — II. 2
BIEN (adv.) : Tu veux du pain ? Oui je veux bien — II. 1
    C'est une bonne étudiante, elle travaille bien — IV. 3
BIEN SÛR (loc. adv.) : Il est musicien. — Il aime Mozart ? — Bien sûr ! — I. 4
BIENTÔT [A] (adv.) : Au revoir et à bientôt ! — I. 2
BIÈRE (n. f.) : J'aime la bière allemande — II. 2
BINIOU (n. m.) : C'est un musicien breton, il joue du biniou — III. 3
BLANC, BLANCHE (adj.) : Il a une chemise blanche — IV. 4
BLEU, E (adj.) : La mer est bleue — IV. 2
BLOND, ONDE (adj.) : Tu es brune ? — Non, je suis blonde ! — I. 5
BLOUSON (n. m.) : Il a un blouson de cuir — I. 4
BOIRE (v.) : Elle boit du café au lait — I. 4
BOIS (n. m.) : Une table en bois — II. 4
BOISSON (n. f.) : Le jus de fruit est une boisson — II.2
BOÎTE (n. f.) : Il a donné une grande boîte de chocolats — III. 5
BOL (n. m.) : Le matin, je prends un bol de café — III. 5
BON, BONNE (adj.) : Le restaurant est bon et pas cher — II. 2
BONJOUR (n. m.) : Bonjour Jacques ! Ça va ? — I. 2
BONNE NUIT (n. f.) : Bonne nuit et à demain ! — I. 2
BONSOIR (n. m.) : Bonsoir Pierre — I. 2
BORD [AU - DE] (loc.) : Il habite au bord de la mer — III. 2
BOUCHER, ÈRE (n.) : Le boucher a un beau rôti — II. 3
BOUCHERIE (n. f.) : Je vais à la boucherie — II. 3
BOULANGER, ÈRE (n.) : Le boulanger a du bon pain — II. 3
BOUTEILLE (n. f.) : Une bouteille de vin — II. 3
BRETON, ONNE (adj.) : Il est breton. Il habite St-Malo — III. 3
BRONZER (v.) : Je bronze au soleil — IV. 2
BRUN, BRUNE (adj.) : Il est blond ou brun ? — I. 5
BU (v.) : de BOIRE — III. 4
BURALISTE (n.) : Le buraliste vend des cigarettes — II. 3
BUREAU (n. m.) : J'ai un grand bureau — II. 1
BUS [AUTO-] : Je vais à mon travail en bus — IV. 1

————————————— C —————————————

ÇA [VA] : Ça va ? — Oui et toi ? — I. 2
CADEAU (n. m.) : Je t'ai apporté un cadeau. — Oh, merci ! — III. 5
CAFÉ (n. m.) : J'aime boire du café — I. 4
    Il travaille dans un café — III. 3
CAISSE (n. f.) : Cette caisse est lourde — IV. 4
CALVA [DOS] (n. m.) : Le calvados est un alcool — III. 5
CAMION (n. m.) : Le camion de déménagement est là — IV. 4
CAMPAGNE (n. f.) : J'aime la campagne — I. 4
CAMPER (v.) : Cet été je vais camper en Bretagne — III. 1
CAMPEUR, EUSE (n.) : de CAMPER — III. 1
CAMPING (n. m.) : Il y a un terrain de camping près d'ici ? — III. 1
CAPITALE (n. f.) : Paris est la capitale de la France — IV. 2
CARAFE (n. f.) : Une carafe d'eau, s.v.p. ! — II. 2
CARAMEL (n. m.) : Une crème caramel et un café s.v.p. ! — II. 2
CARBONE (n. m.) : Le carbone est à côté de la machine à écrire — II. 1
CARTE (n. f.) : Il y a une carte et un menu — II. 2
CARTE [ROUTIÈRE] (n. f.) : Ou est Marseille ? — Regarde sur la carte ! — IV. 2
CARTE [POSTALE] (n. f.) : J'écris une carte postale — II. 3
CARTON (n. m.) : Ce carton est plein de livres — IV. 4
CASSER (v.) : Excuse-moi, j'ai cassé un verre ! — III. 4
CÉLIBATAIRE (n.) : Vous êtes marié ? — Non, célibataire ! — I. 2
CENTRE (n. m.) : Elle habite au centre de Paris — IV. 1
CENTRE [COMMERCIAL] (n. m.) : Il y a un centre commercial à 100 mètres — IV. 3
CHAISE (n. f.) : Cette chaise est libre ? — II. 1
CHAMBRE (n. f.)) : Je vais dormir dans ma chambre — II. 5
CHAMP (n. m.) : C'est un champ d'artichauts — III. 1
CHAMPAGNE (n. m.) : Le champagne, c'est bon ! — IV. 5
CHANCE (n. f.) : Il a gagné le concours. Il a de la chance — III. 5
CHANGER (v.) : La roue est à plat ! Il faut la changer — III. 2
CHANT (n. m.) : de CHANTER — III. 3
CHANTER (v.) : Je chante « Frère Jacques » — III. 3

CHANTEUR, EUSE (n.) : Johnny HALLIDAY est un chanteur — III. 3
CHARCUTERIE (n. f.) : A la charcuterie, il y a du jambon — II. 3
CHARCUTIER, IÈRE (n.) : Voir CHARCUTERIE — II. 3
CHARGER (v.) : On part. Il faut charger la voiture — IV. 4
CHAUD, CHAUDE (adj.) : Le café est chaud — III. 5
CHAUSSURE (n. f.) : J'ai des chaussures en cuir — II. 4
CHEF (n. m.) : C'est le chef des ventes — II. 1
CHEF D'ORCHESTRE (n. m.) : Joseph Lorentz est chef d'orchestre — I. 2
CHEMISE (n. f.) : Il a une chemise blanche — II. 4
CHÈQUE (n. m.) : Tu payes ? — Oui je fais un chèque — II. 3
CHER, CHÈRE (adj.) : Cher papa, chère maman — III. 2
    300 francs un déjeuner ! C'est cher ! — II. 2
CHERCHER (v.) : Il cherche du travail — IV. 3
CHÉRI, [E] (adj. et n.) : Tu viens chérie ? — II. 3
CHEVAL (n. m.) : Il fait du cheval en Camargue — IV. 2
CHEZ (prép.) : Rendez-vous chez Paul à 3 heures ! — I. 3
CHIEN (n. m.) : Elle n'aime pas les chiens — IV. 2
CHOCOLAT (n. m.) : J'aime le chocolat suisse — II. 2
CHOISIR (v.) : Vous avez choisi ? — Oui un steak s.v.p. — IV. 1
CHÔMAGE (n. m.) : Il n'a plus de travail ; il est au chômage — IV. 1
CHÔMEUR, EUSE (n.) : voir CHÔMAGE — IV. 1
CIDRE (n. m.) : En Bretagne on boit du bon cidre — III. 3
CIEL (n. m.) : Le ciel est bleu — IV. 2
CIGARETTE (n. f.) : Tu veux une cigarette ? — Non je ne fume pas — I. 4
CINÉMA (n. m.) : Je vais au cinéma avec Marie — I. 3
CLASSEUR (n. m.) : Mes papiers sont dans un classeur — II. 1
CLÉ (n. f.) : J'ai perdu la clé de la maison ! — IV. 3
CLIENT, ENTE (n.) : Cette boucherie n'a pas de clients — II. 3
CLIMAT (n. m.) : Le climat de Montpellier est agréable — IV. 2
COFFRE (n. m.) : Les sacs sont dans le coffre de la voiture — III. 2
COIFFEUR, EUSE (n.) : Tu vas chez le coiffeur ? — I. 2
COLLÈGUE (n.) : On travaille ensemble, c'est ma collègue — II. 4
COMBIEN (adv.) : Ça coûte combien ? — 100 francs — II. 3
COMMENCEMENT (n. m.) : voir COMMENCER
COMMENCER (v.) : Les musiciens sont prêts. Le concert commence — I. 4
COMMENT (adv.) : Comment ça va ? — Bien ! — I. 2
COMPRENDRE (v.) : Allô ! Je ne comprends pas ! Épelez s.v.p. ! — II. 5
CONCERT (n. m.) : Un concert de jazz — I. 4
CONCIERGE (n.) : Le concierge est dans l'escalier — I. 2
CONCOURS (n. m.) : Elle a gagné le concours de chant — III. 3
CONCURRENT, ENTE (n.) : Voici la première concurrente — III. 3
CONDUIRE (v.) : Vous savez conduire ? — IV. 1
CONFITURE (n. f.) : J'aime le pain et la confiture — II. 2
CONNAISSANCE (n. f.) : Enchanté de faire votre connaissance ! — IV. 5
CONNAÎTRE (v.) : Vous connaissez Jacques Martineau ? — III. 3
CONSEIL (n. m.) : voir CONSEILLER — III. 2
CONSEILLER (v.) : Je vous conseille ce restaurant — IV. 3
CONSEILLER [DE] (v.) : Je vous conseille de partir — III. 2
CONSERVE (n. f.) : A l'épicerie on vend des conserves — II. 3
CONTENT, ENTE (adj.) : Il est en retard. Elle n'est pas contente — I. 5
CONTINUER (v.) : Il veut continuer son travail — IV. 3
CONTINUER [À] (v.) : Il continue à fumer — IV. 4
CONTRE (prép.) : On déménage ? Ah non, je suis contre ! — IV. 1
COPAIN (n. m.) : C'est mon copain, c'est mon ami — II. 4
COPINE (n. f.) : voir COPAIN — II. 4
CÔTÉ (n. m.) : C'est de ce côté ! Non c'est de l'autre côté ! — IV. 4
CÔTÉ [A - DE] (loc.) : Le bureau est à côté de la fenêtre — II. 1
CÔTELETTE (n. f.) : 3 côtelettes de mouton, s.v.p. — II. 3
COUCHER [SE] (v.) : Je me suis couché à minuit — III. 4
COULOIR (n. m.) : Ce couloir est étroit — II. 1
COUPER (v.) : Je coupe la viande ? — D'accord ! — IV. 5
COURRIER (n. m.) : Il y a du courrier — Oui une lettre — IV. 2
COURSES [FAIRE LES-] (n. f. pl.) : Il fait les courses au supermarché — III. 2
COURT, E (adj.) : Ce pantalon est trop court — IV. 4
COUSIN, INE (n.) : C'est mon cousin, le fils de mon oncle Paul — II. 5
COUTEAU (n. m.) : Prends un couteau pour couper ta viande ! — III. 5
COÛTER (v.) : Ça coûte combien ? — 100 francs ! — II. 3
COUVERT (n. m.) : Les couverts sont sur la table — IV. 5
CRÈME (n. f.) : J'aime la crème caramel — II. 2
CRÈMERIE (n. f.) : Je vais à la crèmerie acheter du lait — II. 3
CRÉMIER, IÈRE (n.) : de CRÈMERIE — II. 3
CRÊPE (n. f.) : Les crêpes bretonnes sont bonnes ! — III. 3
CRIC (n. m.) : Prends le cric dans le coffre ! — III. 2
CROIRE (v.) : C'est Jacques ? — Oui, je crois ! — III. 3
CROISSANT (n. m.) : Un café et un croissant s.v.p. — II. 2
CUEILLIR (v.) : Je cueille des pommes — III. 4

154

Q

R

S

──────────── Y ────────────

──────────── W ────────────

──────────── Z ────────────

Système de transcription phonétique utilisé : l'Alphabet Phonétique International.

[i]	midi		[w]	oui, moi
[e]	chanté		[p]	petit
(*) [ɛ]	chantais, tête		[b]	bord
[a]	ta		[t]	tu
(*) [ɑ]	pâte		[d]	dans
[ɔ]	porte		[k]	quand
(*) [o]	métro		[g]	gare
[u]	goutte		[f]	faire
[y]	tu		[v]	va
[ɸ]	eux		[s]	assez
[œ]	bonheur		[z]	rose
[ə]	cheveux		[ʃ]	chat
[ɛ̃]	faim		[ʒ]	jardin
[œ̃]	un		[m]	homme
[ã]	temps		[n]	nous
[ɔ̃]	monter		[ɲ]	montagne
[j]	fille		[l]	la
[ɥ]	bruit		[R]	rêve

(*) *Attention ! Cette distinction phonétique n'est pas marquée en Français dans toutes les régions.*

Limites de département
Limites de région
● Préfecture de département
● Préfecture de région

NORD PAS DE CALAIS
PAS-DE-CALAIS 62 ● Arras ● Lille
59 NORD
80 SOMME ● Amiens
● Charleville-Mézières
SEINE -MARITIME 76 ● Rouen
HAUTE- PICARDIE
OISE 60 ● Beauvais
● Laon **AISNE 02**
ARDENNES 08
50 MANCHE ● St-Lô
● Caen **14 CALVADOS**
NORMANDIE
● Metz
MOSELLE 57
BASSE
EURE 27 ● Evreux
51 MARNE
Châlons-sur-Marne ● **MEUSE 55** ● Bar-le-Duc
54 MEURTHE- ET- MOSELLE ● Nancy
BAS- RHIN 67 ● Strasbourg
29 FINISTERE ● St-Brieuc
COTES-DU-NORD 22
● Quimper
BRETAGNE
61 ORNE ● Alençon
EURE 28 ● Chartres
ET LOIR
● Troyes **AUBE 10**
CHAMPAGNE
ARDENNE
● Chaumont
HAUTE-MARNE 52
88 VOSGES ● Epinal
LORRAINE
ALSACE
● Colmar **68 HAUT- RHIN**
56 MORBIHAN ● Vannes
53 MAYENNE ● Laval
ILLE-ET-VILAINE 35 ● Rennes
SARTHE 72 ● Le Mans
PAYS DE LA LOIRE
YONNE 89 ● Auxerre
HAUTE- SAÔNE 70 ● Vesoul
● Belfort **90**
FRANCHE- COMTÉ
● Besançon
25 DOUBS
44 LOIRE- ATLANTIQUE ● Nantes
49 MAINE-ET-LOIRE ● Angers
● Orléans **LOIRET 45**
41 LOIR-ET-CHER ● Blois
INDRE- ET-LOIRE 37 ● Tours
CENTRE
COTE-D'OR 21 ● Dijon
85 VENDEE ● La Roche-sur-Yon
DEUX- SEVRES ● Poitiers **VIENNE 86**
36 INDRE ● Châteauroux
18 CHER ● Bourges
58 NIÈVRE ● Nevers
BOURGOGNE
39 JURA ● Lons-le-Saunier
17 CHARENTE- MARITIME ● La Rochelle
● Niort **79**
CHARENTE 16 ● Angoulême
23 CREUSE ● Guéret
LIMOUSIN
● Limoges **HAUTE-VIENNE 87**
● Moulins **03 ALLIER**
71 SAONE-ET-LOIRE ● Mâcon ● Bourg
01 AIN
HAUTE-SAVOIE 74 ● Annecy
PUY-DE- DOME 63 ● Clermont-Ferrand
LOIRE 42 **RHÔNE 69** ● Lyon
● St-Etienne
RHÔNE-ALPES
● Chambéry **73 SAVOIE**
DORDOGNE 24 ● Périgueux
19 CORRÈZE ● Tulle
AUVERGNE
CANTAL 15 ● Aurillac
HAUTE- LOIRE 43 ● Le Puy
● Grenoble
38 ISÈRE
GIRONDE 33 ● Bordeaux
46 LOT ● Cahors
12 AVEYRON ● Rodez
48 LOZÈRE ● Mende
07 ARDÈCHE ● Privas
26 DROME ● Valence
HAUTES-ALPES 05 ● Gap
ALPES-DE- HAUTE- PROVENCE 04 ● Digne
AQUITAINE
LOT-ET- GARONNE 47 ● Agen
TARN- ET- GARONNE 82 ● Montauban
30 GARD ● Nîmes
VAUCLUSE 84 ● Avignon
PROVENCE
ALPES- MARITIMES 06 ● Nice
40 LANDES ● Mont-de-Marsan
GERS 32 ● Auch
31 HAUTE- GARONNE ● Toulouse
TARN 81 ● Albi
MIDI- PYRÉNÉES
34 HERAULT ● Montpellier
LANGUEDOC
Bches-DU- RHÔNE 13 ● Marseille
CÔTE-D'AZUR
VAR 83 ● Toulon
● Bastia **2 B HAUTE-CORSE**
CORSE
64 PYRÉNÉES- ATLANTIQUES ● Pau ● Tarbes
65 HAUTES- PYRÉNÉES
● Foix **ARIÈGE 09**
● Carcassonne **11 AUDE**
ROUSSILLON
PYRÉNÉES- ORIENTALES 66 ● Perpignan
● Ajaccio **2 A CORSE-DU-SUD**

0   200 km

ÎLE-DE-FRANCE
Pontoise **95** ● **VAL D'OISE**
Nanterre **92** **93** ● Bobigny **SEINE St-DENIS**
YVELINES 78 ● Versailles **HAUTS DE SEINE** ● Paris ● Créteil **94 VAL DE MARNE**
77 SEINE ET MARNE
Evry ● ● Melun
91 ESSONNE

0   50 km

ÎLE-DE-FRANCE

MIGHTY MYTH

A Modern Interpretation of Greek Myths for the Classroom

Myths--Insights--Questions--Activities--Role Play

By Greta Barclay Lipson, Ed.D.
Sidney M. Bolkosky, Ph.D.
The University of Michigan--Dearborn

Illustrations by Helen Sturges Nadler

Copyright © Good Apple, Inc., 1982
ISBN No. 0-86653-064-9
Printing # 9876543

GOOD APPLE, INC.
Box 299
CARTHAGE, IL 62321-0299

All Rights Reserved - Printed in United States of America by Copy Cats, Ltd., East Peoria, Illinois.

DEDICATION

For my lustrous friend
Douglass Campbell
Taller than most men--
Within easy reach of the stars.

To Lorrie Bolkosky, whose Spanish
name is Luna, the mythical goddess
of learning, writing and mystery.

On the one hand, a myth always refers to events alleged to have taken place long ago. But what gives myth an operational value is that the specific pattern described is timeless; it explains the present and the past as well as the future.

Claude Levi-Strauss

Structural Anthropology
© 1966 Doubleday

TABLE OF CONTENTS

MIGHTY MYTH

I. BEGINNINGS	**I. BEGINNINGS**
II. WHAT'S IN MY FUTURE? THE FATES	**II. WHAT'S IN MY FUTURE? THE FATES**
III. IDENTITY CRISIS-- ATHENA	**III. IDENTITY CRISIS--ATHENA**

FOREWORD

Acknowledging Greek culture as the direct antecedent of our own, the authors profess that art, architecture, philosophy, great conquests, political institutions like democracy and cultural glory were attained at the cost of human happiness and the well-being of women and children. As in modern America, great achievements and ideals often existed alongside gross injustices and anxieties; democratic practices and expressions of equality coexisted with perceptions of women as social and political nonentities forced into abject roles. Since even scholars who retell the Greek myths proceed from different points of view and construct radically different interpretations, a systematic exploration of the myths can lead into lively discussions of contemporary American values, problems of everyday life, and virtually every major theme in the lives of modern children and adults. Such an approach would have the secondary benefit of teaching children about classical mythology in ways that give it new meaning. The ethos of Greek culture was embodied in their myths, and much that is reflected in them affects our own view of society and humankind.

FORMAT

HOW TO USE THE BOOK:

This book of Greek myths has been organized to engage and inform students in grades 5-12. It is an instructional teacher aid which condenses the most salient aspects of the stories; is intended to be read aloud; suggests insights for the teacher; and proposes reflective questions for discussion and gives some possible answers. Each story is followed by activities and a related role-play situation which extends or adds other dimensions to the story as the teacher may wish.

The format is as follows:
a. Narrative (the myth)
b. Insights for the teacher
c. Reflective questions and answers
d. Follow-up activities
e. Role play

A Note About Role Play

A class review following role play is critical to the experience and gives it meaning and purpose. Students should be given time to "debrief," which helps them divest themselves of their roles and take off their imaginary masks. Then, as a group, they should analyze and discuss what took place in their perception. The teacher may also want the pupils to write out their impressions of the event as a way of summing up.

WHY A MODERN INTERPRETATION FOR THE CLASSROOM?
Modern and Ancient Issues

Among the issues addressed in this interpretation of the myths are:

1. The nature of heroism
2. The nature of success
3. The attitude toward women
4. Competition versus cooperation
5. Love and commitment
6. Models of behavior
7. Brain versus brawn
8. Peer group pressure
9. Loneliness
10. Experience versus inexperience
11. The perils of change and progress

The authors see the myths addressing the interests and concerns of modern children. The social attitudes and feelings of Greek children were shaped by the myths, and it is possible for these very same stories to talk to modern children. This relevance has been obscured when we view the myths only as adventure fantasies. It is possible to trace the continuity of mores from the Greeks to the present time through storytelling and discussion. For the most part, only professional classical scholars talk about the persistence of Greek attitudes in our culture. Most people do not consider these stories applicable to us and our world because the tales are so removed in time. But a reading of the themes listed above clearly establishes modern relevance.

For example, children are concerned about losing in competitive sports. "It's not whether you win or lose, but how you play the game" is an empty cliche and children know it. Everything they hear and see belies such protestations of good sportsmanship. Greek children admired Achilles not because he fought fairly or showed compassion or mercy, but because he won.

2

Peer group pressure might force a child to make extravagant claims to impress his friends or move him to take risks which are genuinely frightening. A modern child might then easily understand Phaethon who was driven by the ridicule of his friends to travel to the sun at great personal peril in order to prove something to his schoolmates.

Just as TV tends to promote macho models of behavior for boys, Greek myths promoted similar models like that of the muscular Heracles. For girls, our media tend to foster derogating models of domestic females who are portrayed as mindless. This is paralleled by the instruction of Greek children who are taught to see women as having the characteristics of Pandora and Echo--women who were irresponsible, thoughtless troublemakers.

Greek myths, then, can be a rich medium through which children can discuss areas of interest and relevance in the classroom. The original meaning of the word relevance is "re-raising" or bringing back to the surface. It is with this view that the teacher in the classroom can approach these timeless stories and tie them to the present day.

Since an understanding of the values of our culture can be achieved through discussion of modern stories as well as myths, then, one may ask, why not use more contemporary forms of narrative?

The Greeks had the same option and chose to use mythology as well as history and contemporary events. Myth has more power to engage the imagination than history. Myth is "once removed from reality" but nevertheless deals with very real questions. The distance created by a fantasy element is crucial because, like fairy tales, it allows a more flexible approach. But, unlike fairy tales, myths demand attention precisely because they are concerned with reality.

Greek mythology provides another benefit. For centuries, Westerners have assumed a knowledge of classical mythology to be an integral part of a well-educated person's background. There are reasons for this: Greek culture is the parent of ours, and classical philosophers--even skeptical Plato--used mythological references to demonstrate important and serious matters. These stories, then, will offer a beginning to a sound Western education. They contain the seeds of basic questions that Western civilization has been posing for more than 2500 years. Education, we believe, ought to include an examination of our own origins so that it can proceed reasonably forward.

INTRODUCTION

Greek myths were stories created by an ancient people to explain and justify the origins of values, the physical world, the vagaries of fate, the capriciousness of nature, the wanton and wonderful ways of humans, *and* to provide role models for good and evil. The Greeks' word *paradeigma* meant education by example, and their myths offered *paradigms* or models to imitate. The myths were peopled by beautiful gods and goddesses in human form who bore a melancholy resemblance to man at his best and worst.

We have tried to capture the fascination of these stories without compressing the colorful landscape to a mere black and white snapshot. At the same time, while we have included a graphic family tree, we were deliberate in our efforts to eliminate as much allusion as possible to complicated genealogy. Those convoluted branches often strangle and discourage understanding and appreciation of the myths by students.

Myths were the main form of education for the Greeks and, because of this, represent more than the charming stories of an ancient culture. The stories were the basis for great classical works because they carry a significance for humankind and the society in which we live as descendants of Greek culture. Here are stories of attitudes between generations, between men and women, and between men and gods. The myths reveal the nature of relationship between parents and children, penetrate to the origins of human love and fear of nature, explore the conflict between children and authority, and explain why evil exists alongside or together with good.

Myths, after all, have traditionally been much more important than mere entertainment. As speculative thought, they have served to explain natural and social phenomena; to convey a sense of morality and justice; and have offered some order to the chaos and mystery of life. "Myth" means "plot" or "order," and mythologic has meant communication in words about the order and origin of things.

All of this surely ought to be at the heart of education, whether of Greek boys or American children. What Greek myths reveal can be startling for making profound connections between people who are separated by the passage of more than 2000 years.

ABOUT THE GREEK GODS AND GODDESSES

Greek gods and goddesses had a checkered history. Their origins often were Asian, not Greek, which means they were timeless, reaching far beyond Western, Greek civilized history to primitive nature worship. The names of the deities reveal their Oriental roots. Most probably, the myths traveled with various ethnic tribes from Asia Minor, Crete and the Greek Islands to Mainland Greece (Hellas). Greek myths were therefore older than Greek culture but were formalized, written down, and ritually recited beginning in the seventh century B.C. by Greek poets such as Hesiod. They duplicate far Eastern, Mideastern, and other mythologies. This suggests that the stories and characters personify eternal ideas and raise profound questions about nature, life and death. Yet they were significantly altered in the transition to Greek culture, as they clearly express Greek values as opposed to Asian ones.

Goddesses of Crete and Asia Minor, for example, were *fundamentally* different from their Greek counterparts, many of whom bore the same names. The former were protectresses and nurturing figures; the Greek goddesses often mean-spirited, persecuting shrews who inspired fear, hatred and anxiety in Greek men. Greek mythology, then, conveys both universal questions and issues as well as specifically Greek ones. For both reasons, myths continue to address contemporary Westerners.

Greek gods and goddesses were most often portrayed in human forms. The deities, we are told, did not have blood running through their veins as you and I, but also a substance called *ichor* which made them invulnerable to the injuries suffered by mortals. They were, however, immortal and could change to any form they chose. They consumed heavenly foods called nectar and ambrosia as well as the animal sacrifices offered by humans. They lived on Mt. Olympus and they acted all too human! Their time was spent toying with the lives of human beings, using them for their own vengeance and pleasure; causing suffering or happiness at will. In short, they behaved like the people who had created them. They embodied fears and hopes, explained what seemed mysterious and altogether reflected the aspirations and nature of Greek culture.

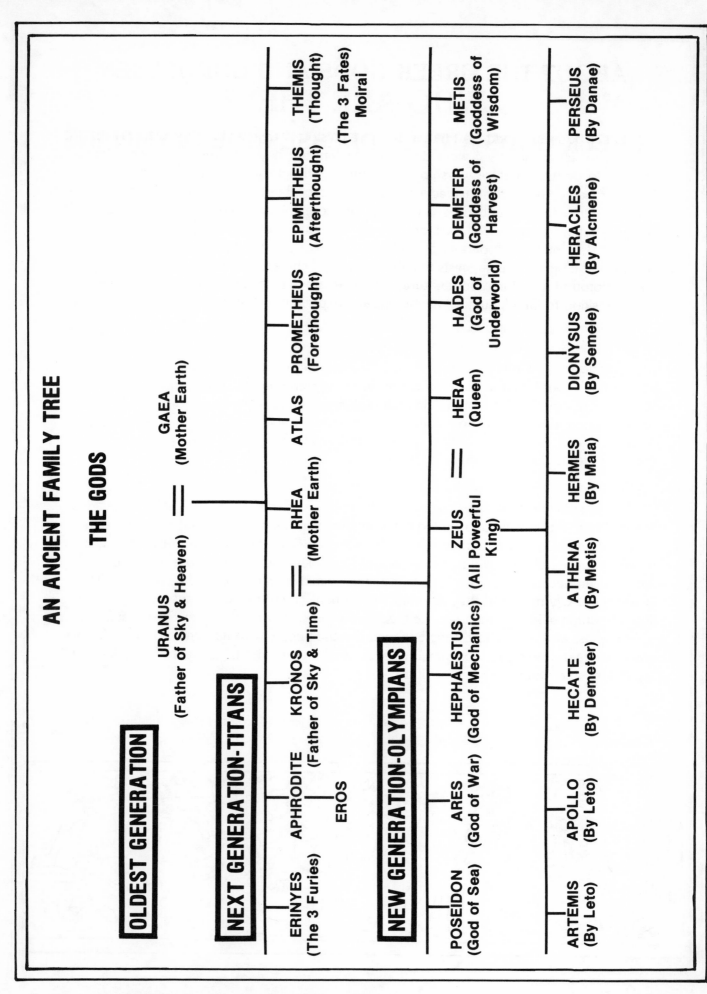

AN ANCIENT FAMILY TREE

THE GODS

OLDEST GENERATION

URANUS
(Father of Sky & Heaven)
=
GAEA
(Mother Earth)

NEXT GENERATION-TITANS

KRONOS
(Father of Sky & Time)
=
RHEA
(Mother Earth)

APHRODITE

EROS

ERINYES
(The 3 Furies)

ATLAS

PROMETHEUS
(Forethought)

EPIMETHEUS
(Afterthought)

THEMIS
(Thought)

(The 3 Fates)
Moirai

NEW GENERATION-OLYMPIANS

ZEUS
(All Powerful King)
=
HERA
(Queen)

HEPHAESTUS
(God of Mechanics)

ARES
(God of War)

HADES
(God of Underworld)

DEMETER
(Goddess of Harvest)

METIS
(Goddess of Wisdom)

POSEIDON
(God of Sea)

ARTEMIS
(By Leto)

APOLLO
(By Leto)

HECATE
(By Demeter)

ATHENA
(By Metis)

HERMES
(By Maia)

DIONYSUS
(By Semele)

HERACLES
(By Alcmene)

PERSEUS
(By Danae)

WHO ARE THEY?
GREEK GODS AND GODDESSES-THE OLYMPIANS

Roman Name

1. Zeus--Ruler of all gods and men — Jupiter or Jove
2. Hera--Wife of Zeus, Queen of the gods — Juno
3. Poseidon--God of the seas — Neptune
4. Hades--Ruler of the land of the dead — Pluto
5. Demeter--Goddess of grain, Earth and harvest — Ceres
6. Aphrodite--Goddess of love and beauty, wife of Hephaestus — Venus

THE NEXT GENERATION

7. Athena--Goddess of wisdom — Minerva
8. Apollo--God of the sun (light), reason, prophecy, music and archery — Apollo
9. Artemis--Goddess of the moon, archery, the hunt, twin sister of Apollo — Diana
10. Hephaestus--Lame god of fire and smiths — Vulcan
11. Ares--God of war — Mars
12. Hermes--Messenger of the gods; god of speed and commerce — Mercury
13. Dionysus--God of wine — Bacchus
14. Persephone--Goddess of Springtime, daughter of Demeter, wife of Hades and Queen of the underworld — Proserpine
15. Eros--God of love, son of Aphrodite — Cupid
16. Pan--God of shepherds and goatherds — Pan

In reading the Greek myths it helps to remember, throughout the perils and adventures, that the Titans and the gods were immortal. The demigods and heroes, like all other humans, were mortal.

I. BEGINNINGS

URANUS

KRONOS

GAEA

APHRODITE

RHEA

PROMETHEUS

HADES

ZEUS

POSEIDON

HERA

FURIES

PERSEPHONE DEMETER

I. BEGINNINGS

CAST OF CHARACTERS

OLDEST GENERATION

URANUS (you RAY nus):	Father Sky, ruler of the world
GAEA (JEE uh):	Mother Earth, mother of all things and oppressed by her husband

NEXT GENERATION: TITANS (GIANTS)--FIRST CHILDREN OF MOTHER EARTH

KRONOS (KRO nus):	god of time, youngest son of Uranus, clever and bold
RHEA (REE uh):	wife of Kronos, Earth goddess
APHRODITE (af ro DY tee):	beautiful goddess of love, charged to make people fall in love
THE FURIES-ERINYES-(AIR in eez):	three ugly goddesses of vengeance, charged with guaranteeing the punishment of criminals
THE FATES-MOIRAI-(MOY rye)--three sisters: CLOTHO (CLO thoh) LACHESIS (luh KEE sis) ATROPOS (AT ro pos):	daughters of Themis, goddess of necessity

NEW GENERATION: OLYMPIAN GODS AND GODDESSES

ZEUS (ZOOS):	new god of heaven and Earth, keeper of lightning and thunder, his weapons
HERA (HAIR uh):	queen of heaven, jealous and vengeful, wife of Zeus
POSEIDON (po SY dun):	brother of Zeus, new god of the sea. His sceptre is the trident.
HADES (HAY deez):	brother of Zeus, new god of the underworld, the dark kingdom of death and punishment
DEMETER (DEM uh ter):	sister of Zeus, new goddess of Earth and harvest

OLDEST GENERATION: PARENTS OF THE GODS

Uranus (Father Sky) and Gaea (Mother Earth)

At first there was only chaos. There was no order, no life, no nature--only a great misting and formless upheaval. The solid mass known as Earth did not exist. There was no sky with its celestial companions, sun, moon and stars; there was no water in lakes and oceans and not even air to breathe. But yet, from this state of confused primordial matter there arose, from an infusion of supreme power, the sky and the earth who were the parents of the gods. Father Sky was Uranus, and Mother Earth was Gaea, and the two became the parents of the Titans, the first race of mythological giants known as "the Noble Ones." Uranus, Father Sky, liked peace and heavenly quiet. He thought that in order to keep this peaceful Golden Age of his, nothing should change or move. Some say he cherished the Golden Age so much he refused to let his children alter it. Others say he was jealous and afraid of his children. And so, as each of them was born, he kept them cruelly imprisoned deep within their mother, Gaea, who was the Earth.

Mother Earth grieved for her captive children and with her youngest and cleverest son, Kronos, plotted to overthrow Uranus. This was accomplished violently one dark night when Kronos fiercely injured his father with a sickle given him by his mother, Gaea. The father, Uranus, now wounded gravely, no longer had his former powers. Saddened and defeated, he knew he would be parted from his wife forever and that the first Age of Heaven was over. And so it was that his story explained the separation of the earth from the sky in Greek mythology. When the injured Uranus was to depart, the blood which flowed from his wounds churned in the sea. The blood, the waves and the roiling water produced a thickened foam. And from this foam there rose a goddess, iridescent with sea water. The glorious Aphrodite, goddess of love, was born, and the heavens sighed with admiration. But there was more, for when the blood of the deposed Uranus mixed with the earth, the vicious Furies were born. These three goddesses, the Furies (known as the Erinyes), were the last children of Uranus and Gaea. They were given a relentless thirst for blood and justice, for they were the punishers, the avengers of victims of violent crimes, especially within families. Their job suited them well since they themselves were born from such a crime. They were terrifying to see with their sharp talons and wings of brass. The whips they carried were a reminder of the torture they inflicted upon the guilty.

NEXT GENERATION--TITANS

Kronos (Father) and Rhea (Mother)

Kronos, intoxicated with his new power, replaced his father and rose to a mighty height as King of the Titans. He quickly saw that peace and quiet was much to be desired and, like his father before him, he demanded that the new Golden Age be unchanging. But now, inevitably, it was Krono's turn to suffer violent trouble. He had been warned by his departing father, Uranus, that when it was his time to have a son, the story would repeat itself. It would be his own precious offspring, too, who would overthrow him ruthlessly. Kronos knew from his own experience that children create noise and unrest in a family as they grow. More importantly, he feared that with their increasing strength and power, his sons would begin to challenge the authority of their father. Wanting to keep life in his control, Kronos unwittingly made the prediction come true. With god-like treachery and no remorse, he swallowed each of his helpless children as they were born to his wife Rhea. Each babe in swaddling clothes disappeared with one convulsive gulp. Frantic and deeply saddened by this unloving treatment of her five children and the selfish indifference to her own wishes, Rhea courageously substituted a rock wrapped in infant's clothes for her last born son, Zeus. Her cunning was rewarded, for Kronos was deceived as he swallowed the rock believing it to be the baby. Rhea was then free to carry out her secret plan. She hid her last, most cherished infant in a cave on the island of Crete. Rhea attended to his care and nurture. He grew to manhood and was distinguished by his beauty and his smoldering desire for revenge.

NEW GENERATION--OLYMPIAN GODS AND GODDESSES

Zeus (Father) and Hera (Mother)

Zeus was not willing to hide for the rest of his life which meant for all eternity, for he knew his fate was intended to be luminous and greater--greater even than his father's. Zeus realized, however, that he would need extraordinary help to overthrow the mighty Father Kronos. With his vengeful mother, Rhea, he schemed cleverly to release his swallowed brothers and sisters so they might help him in his ambitious plan. Rhea concocted a dish which contained a tasteless emetic. She served this to her unsuspecting husband and stood by gleefully as she watched him vomit in great spasms--first the stone and then all their children, one by one. The plan was clearly a success,for they were all freed at last, and in the way of the gods, emerged fully grown from their father. With no time to lose, the clever Zeus immediately formed an alliance with his brothers and sisters. From their citadel on Mt. Olympus they waged a bitter war against their Father Kronos and his fellow Titans. Except for the wisest Titan, Prometheus, Zeus utterly defeated the race of giants.

And so began the rule of the Greek gods we know best, under the reign of Zeus, the all powerful. Zeus, the first one to know the sweetness of freedom, could not ignore his brothers and sisters because of their important participation in the monumental defeat of the Titans. As the first among equals, he struck a compromise of power with them. He gave the underworld and the dark domain of death to his sombre brother Hades, the deep mystery of the powerful seas to his brother Poseidon, and the life-giving fields, harvests and bounty of nature to his sister Demeter. All that was left over, in the sky and on the earth, he took for himself and his queen, Hera. It was in this way that the third Golden Age, some say the Silver Age, began under the rule of Zeus and his fellow gods and goddesses, collectively known as the Pantheon. Contented with new power and grace, they all agreed most amiably, to keep peace in the world and make no further changes. But we shall read more about the peace and quiet they created!

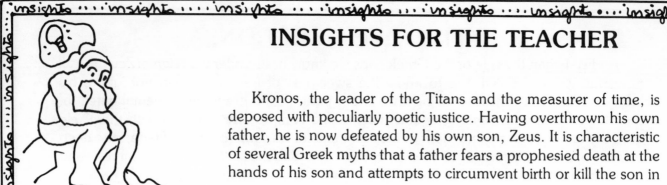

INSIGHTS FOR THE TEACHER

Kronos, the leader of the Titans and the measurer of time, is deposed with peculiarly poetic justice. Having overthrown his own father, he is now defeated by his own son, Zeus. It is characteristic of several Greek myths that a father fears a prophesied death at the hands of his son and attempts to circumvent birth or kill the son in infancy. Zeus, too, will later be warned of such a fate. Kronos' victory over his father Uranus is affected with the cunning aid of his mother. Zeus' victory, too, is accomplished through his mother, but his is not a heroic (or titanic), single-handed triumph. Zeus wins by means of a legal coalition made with his brothers and sisters and some renegade Titans. Zeus thus comes to represent law and order, political alliance and compromise.

After the creation, the roles of the feminine deities come to reveal the harsh basic Greek attitudes toward women. Aphrodite, beautiful goddess of love, is born from the violent overthrow of her father, Uranus; so there are three feminine Furies (or hell hags). Gaea, Mother Earth, displays her cunning in the plot to defeat her husband; Rhea, wife of Kronos, does the same as she conspires against her husband. These are themes that will develop more fully in the subsequent myths.

While "origin" myths from other cultures emphasize fertility or knowledge of good and evil, the Greek origin stories seem to stress violence and generational conflict. Fathers are pitted against sons from the start (as are wives against husbands). Creation, then, is a bittersweet achievement. That quality will accompany the idea of progress throughout western history and mythology.

One point should be stressed from the outset: myths often require a suspension of "rational" thought. Metamorphosis, or change, takes place miraculously and there is, of course, a constant element of fantasy. Most myths serve multiple functions: among those are the attempted fanciful explanations of natural events and of the origins of certain attitudes, values, conventions and traditions. In focusing on this latter group of origins it is necessary to omit scientific questions like: where did the Olympians come from if they were contained in Kronos? How could the god have swallowed his children and then have them emerge full grown and alive? What is important in these stories are the complex questions concerning the hostility between parents and children, husbands and wives and the infinite number of human problems which continue to beset us throughout life. Like the ancient Greeks, we, too, search for answers to timeless questions in order to give our existence some meaning, sense and harmony.

REFLECTIVE QUESTIONS

1. Some parts of the Greek myths are like fantasy. What do you think is the definition of fantasy?

    Possible Answer--A definition of a fantasy in literature is that which is not real in the world *as we know it today*. A fantasy may also be defined as a daydream or the free play of creative imagination as expressed in writing, speaking and listening.

2. What stories have you read, heard, or seen that may be described as fantasy? What happened in these stories which could not happen in the real world today?

    Possible Answer--Stories which fall under the heading of fantasy may be folktales, fairy tales, tall tales, science fiction, the supernatural, etc.

3. Uranus and Kronos (both fathers) had fears about their children who might disturb the order of things. What attitudes and worries do modern parents have about their children?

    Possible Answer--Parents want their children to develop their minds, to be respectful, to be happy, to act properly, to learn, and to be solid citizens. They also want them to be careful of their physical safety. Mothers and fathers aspire for a peaceful world for their children to grow in.

4. Kronos was like his father Uranus. How was Zeus like his father Kronos? In what ways do you think you are mentally and physically like your parents? How may you be more like your parents as you grow older?

Possible Answer--Both Kronos and Zeus rebelled and they overthrew their fathers. As adults they became tough, authoritarian figures just like their fathers. Children may see themselves resembling their parents physically, in temperament, in skills and in opinions and beliefs. As children grow, they confront the same problems as their parents. They may then be forced by circumstances and maturity to assume attitudes that are similar to those of their parents.

5. What is meant by the older generation and the younger generation? What differences in attitude between the two generations might lead younger people to disagree with older people?

Possible Answer--Older people have learned from a lot of experience and want children to listen to their acquired wisdom in order to avoid problems. Many believe that children must learn from their own experience and not from the mistakes and advice of others. Older people have power and authority and may be unwilling to "listen" to what younger people have to say or, as with Kronos and Uranus, will not allow them freedom to gain experience and express themselves. Younger people may not understand the reason for many rules and regulations. Both young and old may not be able to put themselves into the shoes of another and try to understand generational points of view.

FOLLOW-UP ACTIVITIES

1. Each generation draws from previous generations to produce new forms of civilization. Plan a time capsule which is to be buried for the information of a future civilization. What artifacts will be included which will give clues about our civilization to a future generation? Brainstorm a list with the class. Give a reason for each item to be included. What message or information will it give to a citizen of the future?

2. Describe a world of the future which will be developed by humans on this planet, in space, underground, or any place of unknown origin.

3. Make up your own story about the beginning of the world. Include a myth about at least one of the following: the creation of man and woman, the reason for a ritual or holiday, the origin of a particular part of nature.

4. Look up the word "utopia." Organize into small groups and decide what your utopian society would be like. Each group will make an oral presentation. You may include details about government, education, the economy, social life, recreation, religion, fashion, entertainment, attitudes, etc.

5. Find myths from other cultures (American Indian, Hawaiian, Eskimo, Japanese, Norse, etc.), each of which gives accounts of the beginning of the world. Many can be found. Describe one of these stories to your class. What are some similarities with the Greek story of creation? What are some differences?

AT HOME WITH
MR. & MRS. ADAM EVELY

ROLE PLAY

Statement: The creation story deals with family history, family related stress, and generational conflict.

The Scene: A modern family evening at home which dramatizes possible domestic discord.

Characters:

Father:	Wants to enjoy the evening in peace and quiet.
Mother:	May be on the father's side. May be on the children's side. May be an arbiter or peacemaker in the middle.
Younger Child:	Acting up and making noise.
Older Child:	Trying to do homework, arguing with sibling.
More children or relatives, if desired:	Someone wants to watch a TV program.

Objective: To demonstrate the possible conflicts that may occur between generations because of different needs, energy levels, and attitudes. How does each character perceive an ideal environment that makes for a satisfying and happy evening at home?

Discuss the Skit:

1. With whom did you agree? With whom did you disagree?

2. Were there issues about which you couldn't make up your mind? Did you recognize familiar conflicts?

3. Why did you sympathize with certain characters?

4. If you were to put yourself in the role of a grown-up, would your attitude be different? Why?

5. What are the reasons for conflict between sisters and brothers?

Write your feelings about the class role-play experience and discussion.

II. WHAT'S IN MY FUTURE?
THE FATES

CLOTHO

ATROPOS

LACHESIS

II. WHAT'S IN MY FUTURE? THE FATES

CAST OF CHARACTERS

**THE FATES, ALSO CALLED
THE MOIRAI (MOY rye):**   The daughters of Zeus and Themis

CLOTHO (CLO thoh):   The Spinner. She spins the thread of life with light and dark lines which stand for degrees of happiness and sadness.

LACHESIS (luh KEE sis):   The Apportioner. She twists the threads which make a life strong and weak.

ATROPOS (AT ro pos):   The Inflexible. She cuts the thread which measures the length of a life.

Fate means the power which is thought to determine the pattern, the happiness, the sadness and all the events in a person's life. Some people think that fate is determined for us from the moment we are born. The Greeks firmly believed that everything that would happen to each person was decided in advance by the Fates who were three sisters by the names of Clotho, Lachesis, and Atropos. Each sister had an important role in planning the lives of humans and gods. They knew the past and everything in the future. Once the plan was set by the sisters, even the gods in all their power and fury, could not change the inevitable course of events.

Every life, it was thought, had a different pattern like a rich tapestry or a complicated textured weaving. Clotho, the first sister, spun the thread of a human life with light and dark lines which stood for degrees of joy and despair. Lachesis, the second sister, ever so carefully twisted the thread which made a life strong or weak. The last sister, and the most dreaded, Atropos, made the final decision as she worked ruthlessly with a pair of scissors. It was she who cut the strands of life. A long thread meant an enduring and extended life into old age. A short thread meant a brief stay, ended perhaps in youth with a death that came all too soon, to be sure. It was the unswerving duty of all three sisters to see that the future, as they decreed, would be carried out with no mistakes and no interference. This idea of fate meant that nothing could be done by an individual that would influence the grand plan designed for each person. Sometimes, it would seem that the strangest most outrageous events helped the predictions come true, but those, too, were part of the mystical authority of the sisters at work. The gods, who were luckier than mortals, would often be told what the future held for them, but in many ways it was more hideous to know, for there was no way for them to cheat their destiny.

Zeus, the great god, respected and even feared the Fates. He knew their power, yet they knew his, too. They avoided his battle with the giant Titans, and he generally did not oppose them. Wisely, they all kept their distance, free to work mischief in their own domains.

The children of Zeus, however, were not as smart. Apollo especially opposed the Fates, calling them old crones and deities of Mother Earth whom he hated. Apollo and the younger gods defiantly believed that they could control their own destinies. They tried to do this by planning for the future (foresight), avoiding unnecessary danger and exercising self-control. When these failed, they would use brute force or threats in order to bend fate to their purposes. But, always they lost--for they could not win in this contest of power as the sisters diligently spun and twisted and cut--arranging the lives of humans with divine confidence.

Many people went to consult with professional oracles in hopes that they could unlock the secrets of the future. In dark and sacred places where vapors rose from scarps, the oracles used their mysterious gifts to prophesy the events that would come to pass. Both great and common folk would listen to the oracles in frightened fascination. They did not always understand the predictions which were often told in riddles--most difficult to fathom. But the gods for their part used the forecast of the oracles to plan mischievous pranks to play on men. It was indeed an entertaining pastime to tease and worry mortals who longed to know their fate.

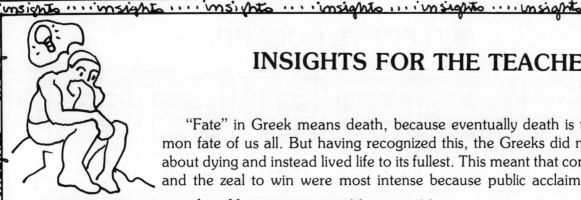

INSIGHTS FOR THE TEACHER

"Fate" in Greek means death, because eventually death is the common fate of us all. But having recognized this, the Greeks did not worry about dying and instead lived life to its fullest. This meant that competition and the zeal to win were most intense because public acclaim was the surest way to conquer fate. Victory guaranteed fame, and fame insured a name that would never be forgotten but would live forever. In the Greek system the losers were quickly forgotten, but the winners lived on as heroes in the memories of people and stayed there larger than life.

In modern times, fate has come to mean much more to us than death. For us, it means the outcome of events throughout our lives.

The Greeks personified the Fates, or the Moirai, as sisters who are deities. These three goddesses are often depicted as a young maiden, a mature woman, and a very old woman. The mature figure, Lachesis, might be considered the most influential since it is she who determines the strength or weakness of life. The activity of all three, so critical to deciding the destiny of people, revolved interestingly around the household tasks of spinning and weaving. That may imply that a person's fate was shaped most by family, home and feminine influence--particularly the mother figure.

This brings us, then, to the ageless question as to which has the strongest effect upon our lives--nature or nurture. Are we born with qualities that strongly shape our destiny, or are we nurtured by social surroundings which determine the course of our lives? Can nature be overcome by the influence of environment? Can background be overwhelmed by the strength and weakness given us by nature? Or--are both factors influential in the course of our fate?

REFLECTIVE QUESTIONS

1. What does this mean: "You are the master of your own fate"?

   Possible Answer--To be master of your own fate is to be able to determine or influence everything that happens to you in your life. This implies the ability to control other people's lives as well and neglects the effect that the fate of others would have on your life.

2. In what ways do you think your life would be different if you had different parents, brothers, sisters, and friends?

   Possible Answer--Where a person lives determines the nature of the role models. One might live in a different setting, either urban or rural. Interests are tied to environment, friends, and family. So, too, are skills or talents which are esteemed. Older brothers and sisters may teach and influence. One may be the oldest or the youngest child in a family, which in itself would affect personality traits.

3. If you had different parents, in what ways do you think you would be the same? Why?

   Possible Answer--Some people believe they are who they are because of nature since chemical and physiological components are often thought to be strong factors in shaping our personalities. (Consider this question in conjunction with question and answer 2.)

4. How could circumstances have been different in your life if you had become involved in a particular situation (either trivial or important)? If you had not become involved? Explain.

Possible Answer--Solicit responses from students. Some things can seem unimportant at the time they occur but may telescope into something with large and unforeseen developments. Suggest asking "What if...." questions. For example: What if I hadn't made the baseball team last summer? What could have happened to me? To the team? What if I broke my leg on my bike? How might it affect my year at school? Make it positive, grand and stretch your imagination.

5. Name some small things that could have the power to change the course of events in your life.

Possible Answer--Solicit answers from students. You tore your jeans on your way to school; you won a pair of roller skates in a raffle; you got a set of drums for your birthday; you walked home one day with the class genius. All of these might alter the course of events.

FOLLOW-UP ACTIVITIES

1. Write a prophecy of your own life from this moment on. Describe your future based upon your present friends, interests, strengths and weaknesses. What will come to pass? Can you make more than one prediction about what your future life and career may be?

2. Write and develop a chain of events that started from one seemingly minor occurrence. For example: a new student comes into your class. What will happen and how many things could change in a long sequence of events because of this new arrival? Brainstorm together as a class; produce a change chart or a time line.

3. Pretend you have won a large sum of money in a lottery. Some people who have won fortunes claim that this stroke of fate will not change their lives. As a big winner you are being interviewed in front of the class. Will your life change or not? How?

4. Discuss the meaning you infer from the following statement: "When I started to work harder, my luck changed." Do you believe in luck? What is it?

5. Choose a famous modern personality. This person may be a politician, sports figure, writer, musician, etc. Without knowing the true story, have the class speculate or make up a story about the *moment* of fate which contributed to the success of that person's career. Call it "The Big Break!"

KISMET HIGH SCHOOL

27

ROLE PLAY

Statement: The Fates raise the question of how much control people have over their own lives.

The Scene: The school conference room after losing a debating competition. Star debater has laryngitis.

Characters:

The Teacher Sponsor:
Wants to discuss the performance of the two debating teams-- winners and losers--in order to examine his team's weaknesses.

Star Debater of the Losing Team:
Has laryngitis (expressing the element of luck), depressed and feeling guilty.

Reporter from the School Paper:
Trying to get the story.

Two or more Team Members:
Blaming each other for goofing off, their star for getting laryngitis, and the luck of the winners.

Star Debater from the Winning Team:
She describes her hard work, practice, research and cooperative team effort that won the debate.

Objective: To demonstrate that fate or luck can be influenced by our own actions.

Discuss the Skit:
1. Do you feel that "some people have all the luck!"? Explain.
2. What characters had your sympathy? Why? With whom did you disagree? Why?
3. What do you think is the relationship between luck and hard work?
4. Considering the cooperative effort of the winning team, would laryngitis have killed their chances?

Write your feelings about the class role-play experience and discussion.

III. IDENTITY CRISIS--ATHENA

CAST OF CHARACTERS

ZEUS (ZOOS): King of the gods and father of Athena

METIS (ME tis): Titaness, goddess of wisdom and good advice; Athena's mother

ATHENA (uh THEE nuh): Daughter of Zeus and Metis; goddess of technology, prudence, domestic skills, war, justice, and protectress of heroes

ARACHNE (uh RACK nee): Very young, simple country girl, gifted weaver and pupil of Athena

HEPHAESTUS (huh FES tus): Lame god of machinery and fire, smiths and forges; a skillful craftsman. Son of Hera

ORESTES (o RES teez): Defendant at first jury trial; murdered his mother to avenge his father's murder

CLYTEMNESTRA (kly tum NESS truh): Wife of Agamemnon, leader of the Greek forces against Troy. Mother of Orestes, Prince of Argos

Not long after the overthrow of his father Kronos, Zeus fell in love with a Titaness named Metis. Her name means "wisdom, intelligence and skill." She was a radiantly bright creature, but she spurned Zeus and fled from him every time he proclaimed his love and approached her. He would chase her tirelessly and she would try to trick him by flying into the sky as a bird, diving into the sea as a fish or assuming the body of an animal that was swift and elusive. But Zeus was not to be put off by the rejection of the lovely Metis, and as quickly as she transformed herself, he, too, would change into whatever form she took. At last the game of pursuit became too much for Metis and she willingly gave in to the persistent and longing Zeus who loved her. Soon after, Metis was happy to learn that she was to have a child, but she did not know that the news frightened Zeus. For he had learned from prophecy that if Metis gave birth, the child would be more powerful than the father! So, without warning, and without pause, he swallowed his beloved Metis and the child she carried, just as his father Kronos had earlier swallowed his own children, out of fear for his power.

But the matter was not settled, for there quickly grew in Zeus' head a pain which he could not endure. He held his brow, he cried out, he drank magic potions, but no way could he find blessed relief. For Zeus suffered from the most monumental, unremitting, tortuous headache in the universe! Something inside his skull was stabbing, prodding, and throbbing until his wailing brought his devoted son Hephaestus, the metal smith, who knew immediately the cause of his father's distress. He kindly placed Zeus' head on an anvil and with one great, measured blow of his silver ax, he opened the skull of his father. Wondrously, out of Zeus' head sprang a beautiful young woman, already grown and in full military regalia with armor, shield, helmet and spear. This luminous creature was Zeus' daughter and her name was Athena. In this way Zeus had given birth to this lovely girl from his head, and he escaped the terrible prophecy which warned him of danger if Metis had given birth to his child as mortal women do.

Even though boy children were always favored, it was Athena who became the favorite child of Zeus. Like some fathers do, he treated his daughter as a son, and so she became interested in warfare, athletics and all the pursuits considered to be masculine. She invented the taming of horses and use of chariots for men. She became the keeper of her father's thunderbolts and protectress of great heroes whom she admired and advised. In this role, she helped Perseus, Heracles, Achilles, and Odysseus tirelessly in a great round of incredible adventures.

Perhaps the hero she helped the most was Orestes, son of Agamemnon, King of Argos. Orestes had taken the law into his own hands and killed his mother Clytemnestra. The Furies hounded him for that; with their hair of snakes and horrible countenance they were driving him mad--screaming, lashing and pursuing him relentlessly over all of Greece as they demanded punishment for his crime. Orestes came to Athens and begged for a trial. He had committed a crime, that was true, but he believed he was right, for he had avenged his father's murder in doing so.

Athena was the judge at this first historic trial by jury, and Apollo, god of the sun, acted as the defense lawyer. But the results were disappointing when the jury of noble Athenians cast their votes. Half thought Orestes was guilty and half thought he was innocent. Apollo, however, pleaded for his client most cleverly, for he did not deny that Orestes had killed his mother. Instead he expressed the view that mothers were not all that important.

"Is it not true that our honored judge, the goddess Athena, herself had no mother? The circumstances of her birth, from the head of her father, is proof enough!"

Athena merely gave a grave nod of her head in agreement, and thus it was declared that Orestes' crime was really not so serious. Athena broke the tie by deciding for the innocence of the defendant and so Orestes was saved. Apollo and Athena believed they had proven legally that mothers were unnecessary. Athena then openly declared that she was always on the side of men in any argument with women. Right or wrong, her loyalty was to the men. For this, she was honored as a clear thinker and a fair-minded judge!

Because Athena was born from the brain of Zeus, she had superintelligence, which many of the gods could not match. And using that intelligence, she taught man many crafts. She taught women domestic skills like cooking, spinning and weaving. Clearly, she was a combination of masculine and feminine talents, blending what she inherited from Zeus with the inherited wisdom of her mother, Metis. Yet there was a strange quality in Athena's nature, for it was unmistakable that she wished she were a god instead of a goddess. She competed vigorously with other male gods like Ares, the god of war, whom she often defeated in battle because she was more clever and skillful. She hated Aphrodite, goddess of love and femininity, and saw her as an arch enemy because Aphrodite did not use her mind in her daily existence. Instead, Aphrodite preferred to use her beauty and wile to get whatever she wanted. Athena felt only contempt for those who neglected the power of their intelligence. This is why scholars and men of wisdom prayed to her for support and inspiration.

Although Athena aided many heroes, she loved them all like a sister, or protectress. When Hephaestus, the god of mechanics, wanted to marry Athena, she refused, repelled by him and the thought of marriage altogether. The role of wife or mother was not for her!

Athena was a ferociously jealous goddess as seen by her treatment of a beautiful young woman from Lydia who had a reputation as a gifted weaver. Her name was Arachne and her work was praised as the equal of Athena's--but there was great danger in assuming that a mortal girl could possibly compete with the goddess who had invented the spindle. The girl unfortunately believed the praise she heard.

"She uses colors," people said, "that appear to be spun from jewels and one is too much in awe to touch her tapestries for fear they will move and come to life."

But the girl went too far. She boasted recklessly to all who would listen that she was better at weaving than Athena. It was inevitable that Athena make a visit to the irreverent girl.

"Since you dare to compare your artistry to mine, you vain and senseless child, I challenge you to a contest which everyone is invited to judge."

The girl Arachne knew at once that she would fail, but in her gentleness she offered to the regal Athena a gift of a cloak which had come from her very own loom. Athena accepted graciously, but was not to be put off, for seven days later the contest began. Arachne sat in a meadow and all her creative energy directed her fingers as she wove an extraordinary tapestry depicting birth and love, the care of mothers for their babies, the pride of fathers for their sons and the memories of joy and sadness which animate every human life. People exclaimed and sighed with the array of color, the refraction of light, and the exquisite display of feeling and emotion Arachne captured in this work.

Then it was Athena's turn to wield her craft; and with all eyes turned upward, they watched as she used clouds for yarn, the azure blue of the sky for the backdrop, the ethereal lights of the sun and stars, the luminosity of the moon, and the intensity of tidal pools for texture. All of this took from the domination of her superiority as a goddess. She created a tapestry of blinding majesty which told the story of the world from its beginnings-- about the creation of man, the treachery and caprice of gods and humans, and the munificence and wonder of the universe. She captured illusory hopes, dreams and fierce reality, the marvel of the celestial spheres, all earthy creatures and the infinite wonders of existence. The tapestry was ended with a chilling prediction for the future of humankind. All who observed were stunned into silence.

Arachne watched in awe; and, as she watched, she knew she had lost. In great despair the poor maid walked far into a secluded glen, took herself to a tree and hanged herself to end her grief. Athena came across the lifeless form of the pathetic girl with its popping eyes and blackened face. Out of mercy she gave the wretched creature restored life. She shrunk the body, enlarged the eyes, gave it multiple legs, and lastly turned the rope around the neck into a gossamer web. Now Arachne, no longer human, could weave endlessly as a black, frail spider, without competition or interruption--forever. Today, the scientific name Arachnid has been given to all spiders in memory of that horrible event and the sad fate of the sweet maiden who wove too well.

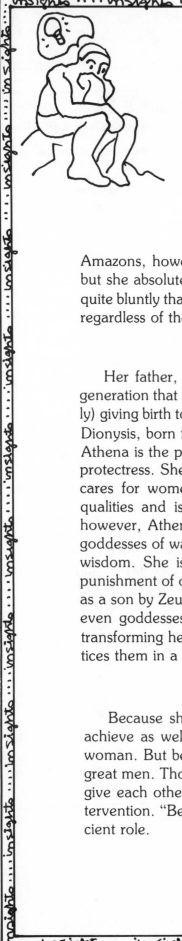

INSIGHTS FOR THE TEACHER

Athena's name is not Greek, but probably Minoan or Cretan or even Oriental. This means she was certainly a mother goddess before being transported to Greece and transformed into a masculine figure. She strongly disliked women and what they represented, at the same time resenting her own femininity. Thus she is the model aggressive, athletic, competitive, Amazon-like image. What differentiates her from Amazons, however, is her affection for men--always nonerotic. Hephaestus chases her, but she absolutely rejects him and the idea of love and marriage. What is more, she says quite bluntly that when the issue is men versus women, she will choose always for the man, regardless of the virtue of his cause or the sins he has committed.

Her father, Zeus, displays the same distress and worry over the threat of the next generation that his own father did. But he defeats the prophecy, single-handedly (mindedly) giving birth to Athena from his head. This implies that Athena is a brain child (as against Dionysis, born from Zeus's thigh, and accordingly a sensual deity). Because of her birth, Athena is the product and servant of male wisdom. She is its bearer, its devotee, and its protectress. She is a far cry from the mother protectress of Asia Minor, who, if anything, cares for women, family, home and children above all else. (Demeter reflects these qualities and is probably another form of the mother goddess.) Still the protectress, however, Athena has been converted to a masculine defender, opposing the gods and goddesses of war and love with her own warlike attitude coupled to skill, intelligence and wisdom. She is perhaps a counterpart to Prometheus, and while Prometheus suffers punishment of one kind, Athena must live with being feminine as her punishment. Raised as a son by Zeus, she longs for masculinity, for male activities and competition. But, alas, even goddesses were stuck with their gender. So Athena does the next best thing to transforming herself into a male deity and refuses to practice feminine tasks, or else practices them in a competitive fashion (as with Arachne).

Because she has been given masculine attributes in Greek mythology, Athena can achieve as well as men and even surpass them. Athena represents the strong, striving woman. But because she is a woman, she is forced to become the influence *behind* the great men. Though she is directly responsible for the victories of heroes and athletes, they give each other credit for their status but do not readily acknowledge her support or intervention. "Behind each great man is a woman" is the modern reflection of Athena's ancient role.

REFLECTIVE QUESTIONS

1. At the trial of Orestes, Athena makes it clear that she thinks mothers are unimportant. Why would Athena and the Greeks dislike mothers?

    Possible Answer--The answer to why Athena dislikes mothers (or women) may be that she herself has all the abilities to achieve in a strictly male dominated society. She admires force, competitive heroism, coldness in human relationships, and noncaring. These traditionally masculine values were the important ones in Greek society. The opposite to each of these values--love, cooperation, closeness in human relationships, and caring--are the hallmarks of a society in which mothers lead the way. As the model for masculine dominated Greek and western culture, Athena must reject motherhood and all it symbolizes.

2. Why do you think Athena wanted to be a god instead of a goddess?

    Possible Answer--This question is directly related to number 1. Only men (or gods) were allowed places of honor in Greek society. With all her talents, Athena could *not* achieve recognition to the degree she deserved because, like it or not, she was a woman. And she does not like it. Athena suffers from "self-hatred," an attitude experienced by many minority group people who want to be someone else because society pronounces and insists upon their inferiority.

3. What qualities does Athena have that are admirable or that women today would admire?

Possible Answer--She is intelligent, independent, and a strong individual. Athena rejects physical violence and believes that females and males alike should use good sense and wisdom.

4. What qualities does Athena have that modern women may not like?

Possible Answer--She does not acknowledge the value of women as worthy persons equal to men. She sees the role of women as being domestic and inferior. In the heroic world, both domestic tasks and those who perform them--no matter how necessary--are devalued. Therefore, Athena does not accept her womanhood comfortably. She is admittedly unfair to women in matters of justice, stereotypes them as superfluous and evil.

5. Athena opposes and tries to destroy all the characters with whom she seems to have so much in common. Hephaestus is the god of mechanics, Athena is the goddess of technology; Aphrodite is a beautiful goddess like Athena; Ares is the god of war and Athena is the goddess of war; Arachne, the student, is a magnificent weaver like Athena. Why would people with common interests and skills oppose each other?

Possible Answer--In a highly competitive society, where being "Number One" is important, the possibility of someone else being Number One is threatening. In a competitive atmosphere (like classical Greece or Modern America), many people feel diminished by the success of others. There seems to be no willingness to share the credit or the praise.

FOLLOW-UP ACTIVITIES

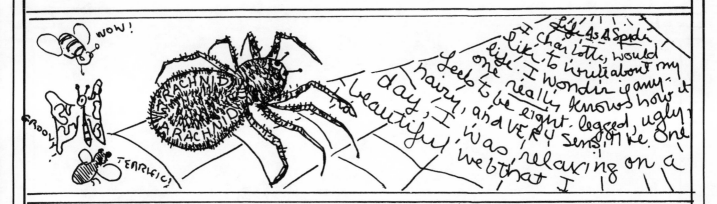

1. Imagine that you are the object of Athena's treachery and have been turned into an insect. Write an account from a spider's eye view of your strange new condition and your relationship to the world. Use your scientific name, "Arachnid."

2. Many people are at a loss to name important women in the modern world. Research for the names and backgrounds of ten outstanding *modern* women in all fields of endeavor. You may choose only one person in any one classification, i.e., the media, sports, science, politics, religion, art, literature, music, etc. Each class member may add the names and brief profiles of these famous women to a bulletin board. How many can be discovered? How many are new names to you?

3. Athena was not happy as a woman and obviously would have preferred being a man. Perhaps it was because there were greater benefits in ancient Greece as a man and little pride for women. Pretend a space creature came down to our planet Earth and noticed different sexes, colors, etc. On the creature's planet, all living things look *exactly* alike. Explain to this alien the *positive* aspects of your gender, race or creed--since the alien does not know what there is about you which is a source of pride. Describe your good qualities, your potential, your future and what you can contribute as a citizen. "THE POSITIVE ME" I am a female...male...a Black, a Latino, a Japanese, etc.

4. When Athena and Arachne competed in a weaving contest, all the citizens flocked to the event. As a person in the communications business, produce an advertisement with pictures and slogans that would attract paying customers to this unusual spectacle.

5. Athena helped the heroes Perseus, Heracles, and Odysseus, among others. Many of their adventures were frightening and gory. Look up the story of at least one of these heroes. Write a movie review of the myth you chose which you considered the best thriller of all, just as if you had seen it in your local theatre.

ATHENA ANGELS

ROLE PLAY

Statement: The story of Athena raises the question of self-hatred. Athena represents an attitude which stereotypes groups. She categorizes women as domestic and nonthinking, and therefore despises them, although she is a woman herself. Athena suffers from self-hatred and has a narrow view of women.

The Scene: In the schoolyard near the baseball diamond. A group of students are having a discussion.

Characters:

Miriam: She is a very competent athlete and wants to join the all-boy baseball team. She has a strong sense of equality and is proud to be a girl.

Lori: Miriam's friend who does not believe any girl is good enough to compete with boys. In addition, she views Miriam's ambition as unconventional!

Gabriel: He is opposed to girls on the team no matter how good they may be.

Steve: He believes that all girls should be allowed to participate in any school activity and need not always be cheerleaders. He doesn't believe that all boys have to be good at sports either and may want to participate in other, more reflective extracurricular activities like glee club, orchestra, debate society or journalism club.

Other Children: All taking sides, including the class.

Objective: To demonstrate that denying your identity can diminish you. Being positive about sex identity and your unique interests is more a source of pride and fulfillment than denying it. You don't have to do what everybody else does to validate yourself as a person.

Discuss the Skit:

1. What characters did you agree with? Why?
2. What characters did you disagree with? Why?
3. Why does Lori express the opinions you heard from her?
4. Which of the characters do you think expresses the most popular opinion?
5. Why was Miriam's cause a difficult one to defend?

Write your feelings about the class role-play experience and discussion.

IV. THE POWER OF LOVE--
DEMETER AND PERSEPHONE

IV. THE POWER OF LOVE--
DEMETER AND PERSEPHONE

CAST OF CHARACTERS

DEMETER (DEM uh ter):	Fertility goddess of the harvest, Earth, grain and life.
PERSEPHONE (per SEF uh nee):	Young lovely daughter of Demeter and Zeus; goddess of spring, flowers and young life.
HADES (HAY deez):	Mighty king of Hades, the underworld, ruler of death; brother to Zeus and Demeter.
HERMES (HER meez):	Transported the dead to the river Styx.
CHARON (CARE un):	The ferryman who took the dead to the gates of Tartarus in the underworld for a fee.
CERBERUS (SIR ber us):	The three-headed dog who guarded the gates of Tartarus.

Hades, the lord of the underworld, wanted a wife and fell desperately in love with the beautiful Persephone, daughter of Demeter and Zeus. She was like spring itself, all radiant and bright as she sang and danced among the flowers and trees. Her mother loved her very much and was proud of such a splendid and devoted daughter. Both were at home in the joyous domain of nature. Because Demeter, the mother of all growing things, was so happy, she caused the earth to bloom everywhere and all living creatures rejoiced in her gifts.

It was hard to believe that below this bright world was the frightening land of the dead where Hades thrived on the wails of the shadow people and adored the tears of the mourners crying for their loved ones. Above and below ground Hades commanded respect, for people were terribly afraid even to mention his name for fear it would attract his attention. He was never known to complain, for he always had room for more souls and never lamented the crowded conditions in his kingdom. He was sublimely patient and always "got his man." Hades ruled this populace of helpless and tortured ones with a cold and unyielding heart, though he did have his favorites. Among these was Cerberus, the three-headed dog who guarded the gates of Tartarus. Each head was a grotesque variation of the other, snarling and turning on a body of iron, with teeth like spikes and a razor tail that sliced the flesh of interlopers. Another henchman was Hermes, forever running errands, guiding the dead to the brink of the river Styx where he turned them over to Charon, the ferryman. In preparing the dead, the living relatives would put a coin under the tongue of the dead person to pay for the fare across the water. If Charon didn't find it there, he would refuse to take them across. Those who died penniless would wander about endlessly in search of a pauper's entrance hoping to find some final peace. For the heroes and great ones, there was a special place in Hades called Elysian Fields. This was a place apart from the moaning and misery of the shadows of ordinary mortals. Here the heroes constantly remembered the triumphs of their past lives. This was, perhaps, their own special kind of torture!

Such, then, was the kingdom in which the melancholy Hades ruled in his gloomy palace thinking about and yearning for Persephone. Who could imagine such a marriage joining the sombre, joyless god with this lovely young girl? Wisely avoiding Persephone's mother, Hades decided to go directly to Zeus to ask permission to wed her. Zeus, for his own reasons, agreed to this marriage and gave his blessings to this unlikely union. But for Hades, there was another problem to be solved. He knew in his fierce heart that Demeter would never permit her daughter to leave and forsake her home among the flowers to live in the land of the dead--nor would Persephone ever go willingly! With grim determination, he made his plan and stalked the unsuspecting girl. One afternoon she moved among the blooms with her paint pot dabbing colors on petals and leaves when she encountered a flower in the distance which stopped her in her path with its dramatic splendor! Never before in all her experience had she seen such a wild creation thrust out of the earth so bold and compelling. Indeed the other flowers paled in its shadow! She felt irresistibly drawn to its glory. It was a mass of black and crimson shoots with filaments of flaming hair. Its bold face was circled by great succulent spikes along a stalk of deepest emerald green. It lured her. It beckoned. She yielded to its command and touched its satin flesh. All at once in a rage of flying stones and Earth, the ground opened into a fearsome yawning bottomless abyss of terror as Hades, the god of death, tore to the surface in his chariot of onyx and shining ebony. He swept Persephone into his arms as his black steeds made that swift and sure retreat down the dark pit to carry their master and the maiden to the dreaded land of the dead.

Back in his kingdom, Hades pledged his love to the terrified girl if she would only be his bride--but she refused. He promised to make her the all-powerful queen of the underworld--but she refused. He offered her jewels, gowns, slaves and all that was in his power to bestow--but still she refused. She would not eat but wept all the time for she knew now that her father Zeus had approved the marriage and all was lost. She was torn from her mother's side and separated from everything she loved.

Meanwhile, Demeter was frantically searching for her beloved daughter. She roamed over all the vast world, and in her grief neglected to keep the earth in bloom. As goddess of Earth and all the life it gave, she held great and mysterious powers. Grain, trees, flowers, plants withered and died; streams and rivers dried up; animals began to starve and men mourned for their lost bounty praying to Demeter, mighty goddess, to replenish the starving earth, all to no avail. Even birth ceased. But as a mother, she could not bring herself to stop searching for her missing child while all other things seemed trivial and unimportant.

At last the dispirited Demeter went to Zeus. Driven to the end of her endurance, she asked the all-powerful god if he had seen their daughter Persephone. Because he saw the hideous misery of the world deprived of Demeter's life-giving hand, and because even *he* was powerless in the mysteries of birth, he told her of the marriage of Hades and the girl. Demeter raged while Zeus urged her to accept the situation.

"Consider that she is a queen now, matched to a husband who gives her luxury and privilege and all that a woman could possibly want in life. She is elevated by the power of her husband."

Trembling with anger Demeter responded, "My love means more than all the riches and majesty which can be bestowed. Her home in the fields and forests with me is where she belongs--always happy and carefree, secure in a mother's love."

Zeus tried to strike a bargain with the distraught goddess, but instead she warned him darkly, "I want her back and you may tell your brother, that sullen King of the Underworld, to release her--for until then, the earth will know only blight and famine. I will show you the power of my love and it will defeat that of force."

And so it was that nothing grew and the land was barren. Humans and animals alike suffered. The gods, too, were displeased because there were no bounteous offerings of food from humans. People forgot to worship their gods in the face of this terrible fate.

43

Zeus brooded--more willing now, in desperation, to return the girl to her mother Demeter. But there was another problem to be solved. There was an ancient law which decreed that once having eaten food in the underworld, one could never again be totally free. Word had reached Zeus that Persephone had refused to eat for days, but hunger had finally made her yield to temptation. She had sealed her doom by eating six pomegranate seeds in secret. But there were no secrets from the gods and this problem had to be resolved. Zeus summoned Demeter and Hades and together they struck a compromise. First, the gods apologized to Demeter--Zeus for his deception and Hades for his violent abduction of Persephone. It was then agreed that for each pomegranate seed eaten, the young woman would spend six months with her husband in the underworld and the next six months of the year with her mother. It would seem, too, that Persephone, despite her protests, was beginning to grow accustomed to the role of a queen and was perhaps coming of age. Everyone was satisfied.

It is because of this bargain that for six months each year Demeter withholds her warmth and nurture from the earth and its living creatures while she mourns for her daughter. In the following six months Persephone joins her mother in jubilant reunion bringing spring and summer with its new growth and regeneration. In this way the Greeks explained the change of seasons.

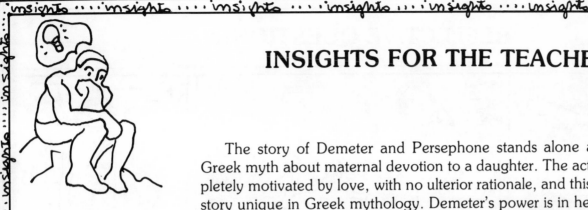

INSIGHTS FOR THE TEACHER

The story of Demeter and Persephone stands alone as the only Greek myth about maternal devotion to a daughter. The action is completely motivated by love, with no ulterior rationale, and this makes the story unique in Greek mythology. Demeter's power is in her life-giving abilities which she shares, as a mother to all on Earth. It is noteworthy that Zeus, the father, willingly hands over his daughter, but Demeter's bond to Persephone is much stronger than any other. This introduces the issues of mother/daughter relationships, the mother as the nurturing parent, and the parent/child closeness. Persephone is a product of her mother's care. And Demeter, perhaps seeing herself in the growing young woman, clings to her protectively with deepest sympathy. The situation reflects an ancient society in which mothers fear for their daughters, knowing they will be treated as they, the mothers, were: as property, as gifts, as tradeable commodities, and as the childbearers relegated to isolation in the homes and lives of men.

Historically, Demeter personified the Eastern (Asia Minor) Mother Goddess or Great Mother--mysterious, fecund, protectress of all life, and overseer of birth. Clearly Zeus has some fear of her, as does Hades. The two males cannot make demands upon her; instead they plot secretly because this is one of the few times that a woman's power is equal to theirs. Here, then, is a fundamentally human family dilemma: Zeus, the father, legally rules, yet it is Demeter who has some tacitly recognized authority which must be acknowledged. Violence belongs to Zeus; and should it come to some showdown with anyone else, he would openly wield or threaten thunderbolts. Not with Demeter. Just as in many households, the mother stands with a final veto and has the capacity to make life uncomfortable--so it is here. She, after all, holds life in her hands, and without the mother, the world (family) would crumble. Here is a bitter pill for any patriarchal culture such as the Greek (or our own). Demeter and Persephone are not weak, unthinking, or ineffectual chattel as most women and girls of Greek mythology. The compromise represents, perhaps, the uneasy truce between Greek husbands and wives at home.

Ultimately Persephone must leave Demeter, yet the ties between mother and daughter are never completely broken and Persephone becomes a regal figure, with powers in the underworld equivalent to those of her mother on Earth. There are even hints that, recognizing this, Persephone willingly accepts the bargain, lured by the rare prospect of the role of authority for herself--though always second to the man.

REFLECTIVE QUESTIONS

1. Apart from the peculiar and sinister nature of Hades as the king of the underworld, why would Demeter (the mother) not want to part with Persephone (the daughter)? Why would *any* parent not want to let a child leave the family home? Why would a child not want to leave home?

   Possible Answer--Demeter did not want to part with Persephone because she loved her as a mother loves a child. Like Demeter, a parent may not want a child to leave home for the same reason. It is never easy to give up one's children. A parent may not want to see a child who is not mature or responsible leave home. In such cases, a parent's concern for a child may be the motivating factor. A child may not want to leave home because home is a familiar, safe, comfortable and secure place to be.

2. Persephone missed her mother, the flowers, trees, and the grandeur of nature. But there are hints that she was beginning to enjoy herself as Queen of the underworld and that her attitude might change. Can you imagine why her attitude changed? When do you think young people are prepared to leave home?

   Possible Answer--Young people are prepared to leave home when they finish school, or when they are able to earn a living, or when they can assume the responsibilities of adulthood.

3. Demeter told Zeus that the power of love would defeat the power of force. What is power? What is meant by the "power of love"? Is power good or bad?

   Possible Answer--Power may be defined as the ability to control oneself and others--the ability and freedom to act--to be able to do something. Power may be good or bad depending upon what one chooses to do with it. The power of love is caring and is a positive expression. It nourishes people emotionally and gives them a sense of personal worth. As with Demeter, the power of love can accomplish great tasks!

4. Demeter and Persephone represent the strong bonds of family love. What other relationships in families are lasting and important? What relationships outside your immediate family are important to you? Why?

   Possible Answer--Grandparents, aunts, uncles, cousins, and friends, because they live outside one's home, can extend love and understanding in different ways than parents. Friends or young relatives closer in age share similar experiences and common bonds. Authority figures (clergymen, teachers, doctors) can "listen" and give counsel and support to aid growth and maturation.

5. The Greeks considered women less important than men, as demonstrated by Zeus's attitude toward Persephone, his own daughter. In Greek (Athenian) democracy women were denied citizenship; men regulated their every move and did not permit them to vote. In American democracy, have women always had the right to vote? If not, why not?

   Possible Answer--For forty years women's suffrage groups fought long and hard to gain the vote for women. Women received that right in 1920 with the passage of the Nineteenth Amendment to the Constitution which reads: "The right of citizens of the United States to vote shall not be denied or abridged by the United States or by any state on account of sex." Thus women's suffrage finally became a fact 132 years after the ratification of the Constitution! There were, of course, numerous arguments against this law, many that sound remarkably Greek: opponents of the amendment said women were naturally inferior and unimportant; they were flighty and stupid (like Pandora), could not possibly understand issues of importance because of defects in their minds and bodies; they were irrational (like Aphrodite) and suited only for domestic tasks (just as Athena had believed).

FOLLOW-UP ACTIVITIES

1. Research the scientific reasons for the change of the seasons. As a class activity, list all these scientific reasons on the chalkboard. Determine if the seasons come at the same time all over the world. If not, why not? How do the seasons affect the moods and spirits of people?

2. The meaning of Demeter, the goddess of agriculture, is "Barley Mother." The Romans called her Ceres, which related to grain and is the derivation of the word cereal. Use the dictionary to look up interesting words and write down their derivations. Select some curious words and make up your own derivations or root words just as they would appear in the dictionary. What is the meaning of etymology? You may want to consult *Words from the Myths* by Isaac Asimov. (See "From Myths to English" in this book on page 141.)

3. Conjure up a mental picture of the god Hades, the sombre ruler of the underworld, in his magnificent black chariot drawn by six horses as he emerges through a yawning hole in the earth. Write a newspaper headline and a vivid human interest story that captures that dramatic moment when Persephone was kidnapped.

4. Poseidon, the god of the sea, was anxious to win Demeter's love. She was determined to discourage him and so asked him to give her a gift of a magnificent animal which would thrill the imagination. Poseidon responded to her by creating the horse (and later the sea horse) but only after a few failures which resulted in the donkey, mule, and zebra. Choose a real animal which has creative possibilities and design a mythical history of its existence, temperament and habits. You may also create a fictitious creature by combining two animals and naming it accordingly. A cat and a dog = a cog; a snake and an eagle = a sneagle.

5. Describe yourself, or a person your age, on an adventure after leaving home in modern times. Make diary entries explaining your trials and difficulties in a world away from the security of your home. What kind of work could you do? Where would you sleep? What would you eat? End your wandering (odyssey) with an account of your return home.

ROLE PLAY

Statement: The story of Demeter and Persephone deals with the separation of children from mother and home. It raises the questions: Should children leave? When should they leave? Why?

The Scene: Persephone Garden in Demeter Park, outside of town. The characters are assembled to talk earnestly to Penny, daughter of Mrs. Spring, about her future plans. They are sitting around and addressing their remarks to the young woman and to one another for serious consideration.

Characters:

Penny:	Undecided about her future. Loves her home.
Mrs. Spring:	Wants Penny to stay at home.
Penny's Boy-friend, Harold:	Wants Penny to marry him and start a new household.
Favorite Teacher:	Wants Penny to finish school with a plan to go to college or a training school to learn more and increase her opportunities for her future.

Objective: To demonstrate the positive and negative feelings about leaving home and to investigate the reasons for going.

Discuss the Skit:

1. What do you think Penny should do?
2. Do you think each person cared about Penny and had her best interests in mind?
3. What alternatives do young people have when they finish high school?
4. What affects these alternatives?
5. What is the advantage of making a plan and discussing it with family and friends?

Write your feelings about the class role-play experience and discussion.

V. IS CHANGE ALWAYS GOOD?
PROMETHEUS

V. IS CHANGE ALWAYS GOOD? PROMETHEUS

CAST OF CHARACTERS

Prometheus (pro ME thee us): Creator of man, giver of the gift of fire to man, belonged to the race of Titans, (giant cousins of the gods), a friend of humankind, a rebel. His name means forethought.

Epimetheus (ep uh ME thee us): Brother to Prometheus, responsible for creating animals. His name means afterthought.

Force and Violence: Two henchmen belonging to Zeus.

Heracles (HAIR uh kleez): The strongest man in the world, legendary hero, favorite son of Zeus and Alcmene.

Prometheus was one of the powerful Titans, a race of giants who lived before man. After Kronos dethroned Uranus, the universe was under their dominion, and the very earth trembled at their command. Prometheus was Zeus' strongest and most willful lieutenant and had helped Zeus in his battle to defeat the giants. "Prometheus" means foresight or foreknowledge; and since he could see into the future, Prometheus knew that Zeus would win that war. Prometheus was responsible for the victory--for without him, it would never have happened. Zeus had such faith in Prometheus that he entrusted him with the job of creating man. Prometheus did this by mixing clay and water in his huge hands and shaping the new creature in the stately image of the gods. Prometheus meant to make man the noblest creature of them all. Man did not walk on all fours, looking down at the ground like the lowly animals, but was instead set apart, since he was made to walk upright with dignity. With a superior mind and shining spirit, he could look toward the horizon, lift his eyes heavenward to the sun and stars and fulfill a unique destiny.

After Prometheus created man, the job of refining and finishing the task was given to his slow brother Epimetheus. Unfortunately, Epimetheus could not always be depended upon to use his head. With little consideration, he had already bestowed all the very important gifts upon the animals. He had given them swiftness and strength for protection, claws, sharp teeth and wings for survival, cunning and instinct for hunting and defense. Alas, there seemed nothing left over to give man to make his life better and safer. Zeus, then, was obliged to watch over this weak being called man. He cared for him as a father cares for a dependent child, providing him with the fruits and nourishment of nature in a garden of innocence.

But for Prometheus this was not enough! Man was *his* creation; and Prometheus, proud of his skill, was determined to make him not equal but vastly superior to animals. For this reason, he asked Zeus to give man the comforts and benefits of fire. The great god refused the request fearing that man would grow too proud and strong--strong enough to rival the gods. Prometheus, angry and resolute, then knew what he must do. With the help of Athena, the goddess of wisdom, he travelled swiftly to the sun, lit his torch with blazing flames from that molten ball of light and carried the precious gift of fire down to humans. By this one supreme act, he had changed the quality of their lives forever.

Now Prometheus had made man superior to the animals since man would no longer be at the mercy of the climate, freezing and dying in the cruel, cold of winter. What is more, with fire, people could cook their food, make tools for farming, domesticate the beasts, fashion weapons to hunt and defend themselves against animals. They could introduce craftsmanship, build houses, fashion ships, have trade, travel and commerce. Finally and inevitably, they could wage wars against each other.

Zeus was forever a vengeful god. He was witness to these changes and quickly decreed a punishment for Prometheus for having stolen divine fire. Zeus did not care if men ate meat raw and lived like beasts in the world. He preferred that man remain innocent and childlike and now he was in a fury, for the gift of fire, once given, could not be taken back. He predicted that man would surely poison the universe and then destroy himself as well.

Zeus sent two of his servants named Force and Violence to seize Prometheus. They travelled with their helpless prisoner to the very height of the Caucasus Mountains, where no one could see them at their foul task. With chains that could not be broken, Prometheus was shackled to a great boulder by his arms and legs. His back was arched in pain against the harsh points of the rock, and they made sure that he could never move or release his body from this racking punishment. There was no one alive who could free him from his sentence of torture. He was to be punished for his "man-loving ways" and though he was a god himself, he had defied the power of the greater god, Zeus, the keeper of order in the universe. His Titan behavior, for a god, was truly improper.

Force and Violence promised Prometheus no relief, no rest, no sleep--but only misery and the sound of his own moaning. Forevermore, he would remain a prisoner of the rock as the bed of his agony. And Zeus was not finished with his mighty revenge. To increase the suffering of Prometheus, Zeus sent a vulture to tear at the blackened liver of the hapless hero. And strangely, every day his liver grew back to provide the next meal for the hungry bird who took his meal wet with blood.

Prometheus withstood his torture, however unjust, because he believed that he was right to have taken pity upon the helplessness of men. He had no regrets--knowing that if given a second chance, he would bravely do the very same thing again! He knew, too, that he had won the everlasting worship and affection of man and was to be seen as the heroic and suffering savior of mankind. After many centuries, there came another heroic sufferer named Heracles. It was this son of Zeus who climbed to the peak of the mountain and, with his super strength, greater than all mortals, broke the chains that bound Prometheus to the rock. He waited for the vulture as well; and when the giant bird swooped down for his daily repast, Heracles struck a blow that finally killed the vile condor.

INSIGHTS FOR THE TEACHER

Perhaps the unqualified western hero has been Prometheus. He is variously known as the creator of mankind, the civilizer who taught man architecture, writing, the arts and sciences, etc. He is the great gift-giver because of fire, the spark of life that symbolizes intelligence and enlightenment. He was always a rebel--first against Kronos, joining the children who overthrew the older god. Following the successful rebellion, Prometheus single-handedly conducted his own rebellion against the new father figure, Zeus. Prometheus means "forethought" or "foresight"; Prometheus appears to have been able to foresee the future. Thus, knowing the outcome of the war between the Titans and Olympians, he pragmatically and wisely joined Zeus. But Zeus's later neglect of man made them enemies and led Prometheus to steal fire. Angry over the theft, Zeus swears revenge.

Prometheus' motivation for stealing fire is questionable. He may be trying to gain something for man, yet it seems he is trying to prove himself more clever than Zeus. It is hubris--overbearing pride--that moves him. So, too, with the stealing of fire, another successful trick on Zeus to aggravate and defy him.

Prometheus has, however, raised mankind up to heavenly heights, threatening the gods with the bestowal of his precious gifts that culminate with fire. Fire seems the key here: it symbolizes superiority and control, transformation and regeneration, life itself, indeed, immortality. Philosophers and scholars of all sorts have pointed out ritual parallels between fire and life and energy; it captures the essence of ingenuity and creativity, spirituality, and, most importantly, of human thought or enlightenment. The spark of curiosity and adventure planted by Prometheus brings man to the brink of deification. This is hubris of the most excessive and serious type, handed down to man from Prometheus--another gift, the fatal one.

Prometheus acts knowing his terrible fate--he has foresight even in this--a reason the West has seen him as its greatest cultural hero, suffering for all mankind. Yet, for all his heroism, *Prometheus is responsible for ending the Golden Age*. If man did not have fire, he was, nevertheless, content and happy in nature. If there were no tools, there were also no weapons. If there was no knowledge, there was adversity or strife, no discontent, and no thought of climbing to godlike greatness. In short, man was naturally free from hubris and more than satisfied in Paradise. Why does Zeus want to withhold the magic knowledge of fire?

Is fire (thought, curiosity) altogether good? Should man have been kept in a more brutish but happy state, eating raw meat but not worrying about it and not getting burned? Perhaps Zeus had the good of man at heart when he withheld fire, and restless, mischievous Prometheus is a sort of serpent responsible for driving man from an idyllic existence. The spirit of defiance seems to go hand in hand with the yearning for new knowledge. That spirit is embodied in Prometheus; brazenly defying authority, accepting punishment only to elevate man. Yet, again, there lurks a secret desire to aggravate his superiors or the members of the ruling generation.

Prometheus' story is inseparable from Pandora's. Man's knowledge of fire is linked to his knowledge of evil, his plagues, his worries, old age, troubles, and sins. In short, to the Greeks, good came alongside women and evil. It should be clearly noted that Prometheus *stole* fire from the chief authority, from the being who had brought law and order to the universe. As a hero, then, his methods are somewhat suspect--as are his motives. Having sided with Olympians against Kronos, Prometheus then ridicules them and joins an obscure creature (man) whom he uses as an excuse to trick Zeus. So much for loyalty and fidelity. Finally, Prometheus has been compared to the Judaeo--Christian God: he creates man from clay, gives him dominion with fire, language and agriculture, and then is directly responsible for Pandora's birth which, in the Western view, represents the act of visiting evil upon mankind.

REFLECTIVE QUESTIONS

1. Why is fire so important and what would life be like without it?

   Possible Answer--Fire not only brings warmth, it is the start of technology, farming, industry, transportation and war. It might be useful to discuss connections between making tools, heating homes, fueling cars, trains, airplanes and fire.

2. Why would a hero like Prometheus endanger himself just to make life better for man?

   Possible Answer--Prometheus is traditionally viewed as sacrificing himself altruistically for the sake of man. However, this act may have been self-serving. He may also be seen as striving to prove his superior intelligence and to challenge authority. Such a victory over Zeus would make Prometheus the greatest of the gods and earn him the everlasting respect and awe of man. Such pride is called hubris.

3. What is your definition of a hero?

   Possible Answer--In Prometheus' case heroism meant that he was a winner, a champion of freedom, and an opponent of tyranny. Each person's definition of a hero reflects personal values. These may be brains, strength, athletic ability, wealth, good looks, intellect, etc. If we have sports heroes, TV heroes and movie heroes, what does this tell us about our values in America?

4. Are there good and bad things about technology?

   Possible Answer--The answer here, of course, is yes. If one sees "progress" as technological advancement alone, technology is a wonderful thing. But, if one considers that changes in technology may also mean destruction by mechanized warfare, the dehumanization of human relationships, the transformation of persons into numbers, the pollution of the environment by technology, then technology is a "mixed blessing."

5. Prometheus thought that to deny man the gift of fire was to deprive him and keep him at the level of animals. Zeus, however, believed that man, without fire, lived in a state of protected innocence--blissful, happy, and serene. Who was right?

   Possible Answer--The answer here, too, is that each in his own way was right. The question allows for examination and consideration of different points of view.

FOLLOW-UP ACTIVITIES

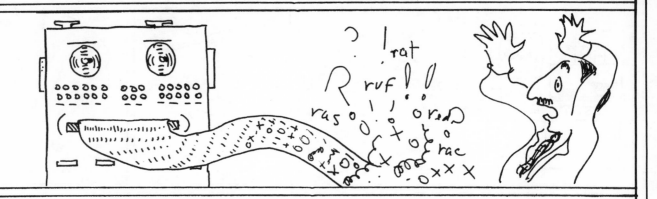

1. Like Prometheus, computers sometimes create new problems while solving old ones. Imagine that a company computer keeps demanding payment for a bill you have already paid. Write to the company and express your anger and the confusion caused by the computer.

2. Research and name forms of energy and how they are made usable for the modern world (fossil fuel, nuclear energy, mechanical energy, electrical energy, chemical energy, solar energy).

3. Zeus argued that with the gift of fire, man would discover his capacity for power and therefore would finally be responsible for his own destruction. With a partner, or with the entire class, make a list of good and bad technological inventions which can bring destruction or improvement to society. Which inventions fall into both categories? For example, the airplane can be a mode of transportation or a carrier of bombs.

4. There is a difference of opinion about the good or evil Prometheus may have caused. Find the names of great women and men in books, magazines or newspapers who have caused controversy and about whom there is a strong difference of opinion. Write down what you think the conflict is all about. Explain your famous personality to the class describing the attitudes for and against this person and what they did. The editorial section of the daily newspaper is a good place to start. You may select personalities from science, politics, law, sports, music, the arts, etc.

5. Zeus said that man lived in a state of innocence without fire, but Prometheus argued that man lived like an animal without fire. Many descriptive words depend upon a point of view. Write two sets of sentences which express two opposing points of view about the same person or thing. For example:

   a. Emily has a clever sense of humor.
      Emily is a ridiculous clown.
   b. Jack is concerned about other people.
      Jack is a nosey busybody.
   c. Cynthia really appreciates fine food.
      Cynthia will eat anything just because it's weird.
   d. Brian has a creative style of dressing.
      Brian must find his clothes at a garage sale!

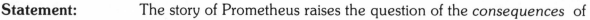

ROLE PLAY

Statement:　　The story of Prometheus raises the question of the *consequences* of the introduction of fire to man and the subsequent development of technology.

The Scene:　　A town meeting in the Prometheus City Community Center to vote on a proposal to build a factory.

Characters:

Businesswoman:　Presents a proposal to build a factory that will produce synthetic food. She must convince the citizens that the factory will be good for the community, will produce jobs, and bring prosperity.

Inventor:　Argues that the invention of synthetic food is important because it will provide nourishment cheaply for needy people everywhere.

Forest Ranger:　Has concerns about the dumping of industrial wastes, the pollution of the air, the destruction of trees, and the inevitable ruin of the land in the technological process.

Worker:　Needs a job desperately to support a family. He cannot afford to consider things like ecology and pollution when he needs money for basic necessities.

Farmer:　Has concerns that he will be out of a job and is afraid there will be no need for his crops.

Objective:　　To point out that technology can be a mixed blessing--both good and bad.

Discuss the Skit:

1. Is it possible to agree with two opposing points of view? Explain this position. Give an example.
2. What is a dilemma? Describe the dilemma in this role-play experience.
3. If the factory were built in Prometheus City, what good and bad consequences could result?
4. As a citizen of Prometheus City, how would you vote? Why?

Write your feelings about the class role-play experience and discussion.

VI. PANDORA

VI. A WOMAN'S ROLE--ANCIENT AND MODERN--PANDORA

CAST OF CHARACTERS

PANDORA (pan DOR uh): The first mortal woman created by the gods. Her name means "all gifted."

EPIMETHEUS (ep uh ME thee us): Brother of Prometheus, husband to Pandora.

HEPHAESTUS (huh FES tus): God of fire, smiths and forges.

HERMES (HER meez): A young god known for his winged scandals and pot-like hat as the messenger of the gods. God of commerce and patron of liars, gamblers and all who practiced deceit. Conducted the dead to Hades. He made Pandora deceitful.

After punishing Prometheus, the all powerful Zeus had still not satisfied his desire for revenge. It was now time to inflict punishment also upon man for having received fire. Most properly, Zeus went to Hephaestus, the god of fire, with a cunning scheme to remind the little creatures of his authority.

Until this time there were no women on Earth, so Zeus, in his anger, instructed Hephaestus to create the first mortal female who would be deliberately designed to bring misery and unhappiness to the world. Hephaestus created a maiden named Pandora from clay. Her name means "all-gifted," for all gods and goddesses gave her the best and the worst qualities that each had the power to bestow. Athena breathed life into her and gave her useful skills--knowledge of the loom, cooking, and other domestic talents; Aphrodite bestowed charm and exceptional beauty; and finally, perhaps most important, Hermes, the patron of liars, thieves, and other shady characters, made her deceitful. With such a creature to deal with, Zeus thought, man would certainly be occupied forever, unable even to *think* about rivaling the gods.

The result was that Pandora was the most beautiful, the most talented, and the most accomplished young woman one could ever imagine! But the rest of the evil plan was to give Pandora a great curiosity which she could not in any way control.

Zeus then offered this *first* magnificent woman as an irresistible bride to Epimetheus, the brother of Prometheus. Craftily, the god made it seem as though this expansive gift was a sign that all bitterness toward Prometheus and his family was magically forgotten. As expected, Epimetheus eagerly received the girl--enchanted by her radiance. When the gods sent Pandora down to Earth, they gave her a wedding present. So awesome was the gift that when they presented it, the bride was heard to gasp in wonderment! The box was fashioned with inlaid woods of warm and burnished hues. It was set with white and amber diamonds shimmering with facets of piercing light. Lustrous green emeralds were captured in plaits of golden leaf, replete with regal purple amethyst. Blood rubies and blue sapphires swirled on scrolled enamelled edges. Matching jet and creamy white pearls were paved in fanciful clusters like seeds. It was a dazzling sight to see.

But Pandora was bewildered, for she was warned by Hermes that she must never open the box under any circumstances. How strange, she thought, to receive a wedding gift that was not to be opened, and how unhappy it made Pandora that she could not enjoy what was hidden inside the box. What good was a gift that could not be enjoyed?

Daily she polished the splendid box and the vision of it filled her every waking moment. She set it on a table and watched the streaming sunlight play on its lustrous surface. She tried desperately to ignore the box, but its beauty lured her. She felt her curiosity grow with every day that passed until she could no longer sleep for thinking about the fascinating treasure that must be hidden inside. Besides, she thought, who would ever know if she took the smallest peek inside? Whom would it hurt? What difference could it make to anyone?

And so she made her plan. She was determined to wait until no one was in the house and she was absolutely alone. Then, one day, in the privacy of her room, she picked up the box and felt a rush of pleasure run through her. Her excitement deepened and her heart beat madly. Her cheeks burned with anticipation and her hands trembled as slowly, deliberately, she lifted the lid.

Time stood still, enveloping Pandora in silent expectation. All at once, with a great rush of screaming, frightful sounds, there was a whirring of stinking, winged creatures flying free out of the box. They smeared her skin with their viscous slime. They flapped at her eyes and ears, entangling her hair. They swooped, screeching through the room--their foulness clouding the air in a choking vapor. The filthy horde swarmed briefly in the rafters above-- winking as if in a final salute. They took their leave, in haste, snarling angrily at one another as they escaped on that eternal flight to the unsuspecting world outside. That moment was a disaster. For Pandora had released upon man all the evils of disease, misery, and corruption that would visit humankind with misfortune forever and ever.

In mortal fright, when all these hideous creatures escaped, Pandora held fast to the fateful box and struggled desperately to shut the lid on the last, single creature contained inside. Alone at the very bottom, it clawed and scratched wildly, but the lid was safely secured. Pandora did not realize it, but that one thing she had trapped in the box was called HOPE. This meant that whatever terrible events might befall man, he would always have hope that life could be happy and better. For it is hope that helps us face the future and each new day with optimism and good cheer.

When Pandora collected herself, she was desperately afraid of her husband's anger. Quickly a plan formed in her mind. She would divert him in all the ways she could conspire to avoid punishment. Although Epimetheus would, of course, discover her foolishness, somehow she must make him forget--at least while he was at home with her. Calling upon the gifts and skills given her by the goddesses Athena and Aphrodite, she prepared elaborate delicacies for her husband's table. Then, with great care and guile, she bathed herself in oil and essence attending with intense vanity to the makeup on her features. At her next task, she quickly spun a gossamer fabric of vibrant colors and fashioned it into an enchanting tunic which clung to the lines of her perfect form. Satisfied with all these deliberate preparations to make her husband love her, she met him at the door with a vessel of the sweetest and most aromatic wine.

Epimetheus was unprepared for the affection of this welcome when he arrived home. His anger was softened by the loveliness of his tender bride. And so, in her deceit, Pandora was spared the full force of her husband's wrath. But then, forever after, she and all other women were fated to serve, to beguile and to cater to the needs of men. Responsible for all evils released from Pandora's box and for the origin of death and disease, woman was forced to atone by caring for man throughout his entire life and into the decay of his old age.

INSIGHTS FOR THE TEACHER

Because of his anger at Prometheus, Zeus promises to create an evil in which all would rejoice, "a beautiful evil." Hesiod wrote: "Thus was born the damnable, destructive race of women, who live as a great source of woe among mortal men." This portrayal is in sharp contrast to Pandora's Eastern counterparts. In the myths of Asia Minor and Crete, for example, she is the Great Mother, goddess of all gifts to mankind, a protectress and one who guarantees life. Her primary function is fertility and she is an unequivocal symbol of life and wisdom. There are historical and sociological reasons for the transformation in Greece, but the point here is that in Greece she was considered the root of all evil for man. Her name bears a double meaning, for she will confer many terrible "gifts" on man.

But woman suffers, too. In fact her suffering is worse than man's. She is twice a victim because not only is she, too, heir to all the evils of the world, but she is made to bear the burden of guilt, and her punishment is bondage. There is a profound injustice here in that she was intended to pay for the sins of man and Prometheus. Yet, *she did not even exist when those acts were committed.* Pandora was created deliberately as a punishment and then was herself punished. It must be emphasized that modern women are regarded, unfortunately, in the same demeaning fashion and have inherited Pandora's status as victim. This is an important part of the Greek legacy to modern times, the magnitude of which is rarely understood.

Why does Pandora open the box? She is made to be curious, deceitful, meddling, as her female descendants were designed to be. She is furthermore, as Hesiod again points out, a drone, who gives nothing in return for her keep. But she is *not* all bad, but will serve a purpose in the scheme of things. Having turned loose sickness, strife, warfare, and most importantly, old age, she and her kind will look after old men when they are helpless and sick. This story reveals fundamental assumptions about the nature of human existence: men grow old and sick, and this condition is worsened by the abandonment of men by their children--ungrateful and uncommitted; worsened, too, by being at odds with each other. There is never a thought of a community of individuals who care for one another as comrades. Instead, all men are alone, forsaken by Zeus, distrustful of each other. Mortality is not the issue here because man was previously intended to die, but he died free from disease. Now, old age looms before him. Pandora, responsible for this condition, also alleviates it. Women will forever be a mixed blessing created to look after their husbands. Perhaps man's curse is to be forced to cleave to woman, yet better this than loneliness.

Like Eve, Pandora, then is guilty for the loss of paradise. Or is she? The curse of Zeus is a consequence of Prometheus' act, and he endures the punishment. Yet Pandora has taken the blame. This myth clearly provides a portrait of how the Greeks perceived women: meddling, scatterbrained, deceitful, charming, domesticated, and the cause of man's misery. This pernicious view of women will be reconfirmed in stories with Athena, Orestes, and others. Greek society, like all others, demanded that individuals conform to established cultural patterns of masculine and feminine behavior in order to be accepted as a member of the community. For this reason, when drastic social changes occur, as in our modern society, it is often difficult for some people to feel comfortable with modified, new views of traditional roles without being threatened and uneasy.

REFLECTIVE QUESTIONS

1. How could this story have been changed if woman was created first and Pandora was a man?

    Possible Answer--Presumably men would be regarded in the same way that women are regarded in modern times, with all the negative traits attributed to females. That it is so difficult to conceive of men like this shows the depth of our own cultural prejudices.

2. What are some of the personality traits that men and women have in common?

    Possible Answer--This can be answered by listing so-called feminine traits and masculine traits and establishing that both men and women have characteristics which can cross over the boundaries of sex.

3. What is a stereotype and what is the stereotype of women this story presents? How are sex stereotypes bad for men and women alike?

    Possible Answer--A stereotype is a fixed mold or pattern and all the individuals of a particular group supposedly share the characteristics of the pattern. It is naive, trite, and a surface level perception of individuals. Stereotyping ("stereo" means solid in Greek) solidly and rigidly classifies people. Women are considered made in Pandora's image. It is important to emphasize here that stereotyping is based on prejudice and dangerous for both men and women. Men and women alike should have freedom of choice to be what they want to be--not what others rigidly expect them to be. Women are entitled to feel fulfilled as single people, as mothers, as homemakers, or as career people. Men, too, should not have to conform to ideals of macho men, athletes, and hard-driving competitors unless that is their personal choice. We must be what we perceive ourselves to be for a happy and healthy existence--true to ourselves, with an open view of being the best we want to be.

4. Pandora was blamed for the consequences of Prometheus' crime. Zeus created her for the purpose of making men less powerful than gods, and women have had to bear the punishment for his act.   Who do you think is responsible for the evils Pandora let loose on the world?

Possible Answer--Pandora is, of course, the obvious culprit. But she never intended harm. Her guile comes from Aphrodite and is defensive, used to ward off harm from Epimetheus. Prometheus, who presumably knew the outcome of his theft of fire, nevertheless went ahead--deliberately setting out to spite Zeus. And Zeus, of course, designs the diabolical scheme. He *uses* Pandora, manipulates and punishes her. Zeus escapes all blame. In almost all other cases, the Greeks liked to pursue consequences back as far as they could to uncover the origin. With Pandora, they stopped far short of the beginning.

5. Pandora's punishment, shared by all women who followed her, is supposed to be her task of menial domestic work and care for children and old men. This means she bears the critical marital responsibilities of caring for the home and family. What seems to be the ancient and modern attitude toward this vital role of homemaker? How can these responsibilities be shared by others in the modern family?

Possible Answer--This aspect of the Pandora story reveals much about Greek and Western values. Here is the vicious, logical circle: because Pandora is evil, she is given what the Greeks considered "degrading" work, that is, domestic work. Domestic work, in turn, is considered humble because it is done by Pandora, who everyone knows is guilty and therefore only qualified for menial labor. In other words, Pandora is bad because she does the work of slaves, which is humiliating. We know the work is humiliating because Pandora is the one who does it--and whatever she does must be terrible. Greek culture was one that did not consider home, family and children to be important. By denigrating women, their responsibilities were also denigrated. Greek history (and modern Western history) testifies to this: laws were calculated to destroy family ties* and there is a clear bias against women, children, and whatever is associated with them.

*Beginning around the 7th century B.C. the following laws were passed in Athens, Sparta, and other city-states (nations): laws assigning residence by district (deme) and thus destroying family physical nearness and cohesion; laws eliminating family names and replacing them with district names; laws identifying people not with families but with territory (you and your country); laws regulating frequency and places men and women could fraternize; and laws removing the education of children from the home and placing it in the public sphere. There were numerous other laws which, over a period of about two hundred years, eroded family and kinship allegiances.

FOLLOW-UP ACTIVITIES

1. Stereotypes (fixed images) "happen" for many reasons. One need only watch TV for a steady diet of Americans as stereotypes. Keep a log for one week in which you include the day, time and title of the program. Indicate whether it is a situation comedy, a police show, a soap opera, a movie or a children's show. Look carefully at the *roles* that are given to women, men, children, single people, husbands, wives, old people, racial minorities, professional people, workers, and any others that come to your attention. How many times are women characterized as being involved with the laundry, the softness of toilet tissue, diverting hubby with good food, or entertaining as an enchanting hostess? Don't forget to watch the commercials, especially. How many times are women or minorities featured as significant or professional people? How often are working men macho figures? How are children dealt with? How often are old people seen as wise, helpful and contributing members of the community? How are children and old people teamed up?

2. Working in groups, read as many different folktales from other cultures as you can find which deal with the creation of humans. How was the first woman created in all these tales? What are some similarities and differences? One person in each group may make a presentation of the likenesses and differences of the origins of women. For example: in Hawaiian mythology, woman was created out of man's shadow.*

*See Martha Beckwith, *Hawaiian Mythology*, (Honolulu: University Hawaii, 1970)

3. Many women must work outside the home to support their families. Considering the entry of women into all kinds of jobs, write out at least five sentences that recognize the new status of women and break the stereotype of the usual jobs women had in the past. For example:

   a. The pilot landed the hydroplane neatly as she waved to her family through the window.

   b. I recognize the clatter of my boss's heels as she walks through the plant checking work stations.

   c. We waited as the surgeon took off her sterile mask and flashed us a smile of success.

   d. The cab driver knew her way around New York like the palm of her hand.

   Since sexual stereotypes harm both sexes, now break the stereotype for men with five sentences which recognize the ability of men to assume different nontraditional roles.

   a. He was the most loved nursery school teacher at school.

   b. Dad cradled the baby in his arms and sang her a lullaby.

   c. Steve, the male nurse, took care of me with tender, loving care.

   d. The male coauthor of this book, *Mighty Myth*, did the final typing because he is a faster and more accurate typist than our secretary!

   e. My uncle Bill had tears in his eyes as he watched the soap opera on TV.

4. Construct and decorate a fantasy box. Imagine that this box holds something that could change the lives of people. Write about and explain what this force or object is and what it can do for the country or the world. Make the contents of your box positive!

5. Here are some language arts activities to expand the Pandora story:

   a. Conduct a television interview with Pandora after the box is opened.

   b. Write a diary which tells how you feel (from day to day) about a gift given to you in January with the instructions "DO NOT OPEN UNTIL CHRISTMAS."

   c. Write an objective newspaper account about Pandora which includes the five W's: *Who, What, Where, When, Why* (and sometimes *How*).

   d. Write a script of a conversation between Pandora and a famous modern person of your choice.

ROLE PLAY

Statement: One of the questions throughout the story of Pandora deals with guilt. Who is responsible for the outcome of a series of acts? Pandora was created at Zeus's command to punish Prometheus and man for the theft of fire. She was not created to act as a free, thinking individual. Prometheus was guilty, Zeus was guilty, and the gods who created her were guilty, but it is she who has been regarded as guilty down through the ages.

The Scene: A meeting in the school building. The discussion is heated as the disappointed students try to determine who is to blame for the cancellation of a long-awaited field trip.

Characters: (The class may decide on the choice of characters. Here are some possibilities.)

Principal, Ms. Culp:	The actual announcement came from her in support of the teacher's decision.
Teacher, Mr. Harris:	Mr. Harris set down guidelines for proper attitudes and behavior weeks before the trip. He claims everyone knew the rules which would make the trip a rewarding experience for deserving students who acted responsibly.
Parent:	Can't believe his child was responsible for behavior that would make it necessary to cancel the trip for everyone. Claims to have a well-behaved child.
Student who is usually good:	Does not understand why entire class should be penalized.
Student who usually lacks self-control:	Claims to have made a small slip in behavior.

Objective: To demonstrate that there are multiple factors which contribute to any event. In attempting to determine responsibility, different people may have different perceptions of the same situation.

Discuss the Skit:

1. What good does it do to find out who is responsible?
2. How do you feel about a classroom situation in which everyone is punished for the actions of one person?
3. Considering all the facts, whom do you think is the culprit in this situation?
4. What would you do in a similar situation as the principal or the teacher?

Write your feelings about the class role-play experience and discussion.

VII. WHY CAN'T YOU LOVE ME? ECHO AND NARCISSUS

CAST OF CHARACTERS

HERA (HAIR uh):	Queen of the gods, Zeus's jealous wife, daughter of Kronos and Rhea, the Titans
ECHO (ECK oh):	A wood nymph; a lovely maiden
NARCISSUS (nar SISS us):	A handsome and vain young man
ARTEMIS (ART uh mis):	Goddess of the moon, hunt, wild animals--patroness of young lovers, sister to Apollo

Echo was a lovely nymph who lived in the woods of ancient Greece. She lived with many others just like herself in the streams and among the trees and flowers.

She was much loved for her warmth and liveliness by all her friends, but there was just one problem. She talked too much. Her conversation was pleasant and entertaining, to be sure, because she was genuinely interested in her companions. She asked endless questions and rarely waited to hear the answers. Poor girl, she could not control herself. More than anything in the world, she enjoyed gossiping. Warming to the news of the day, she would talk and talk and talk. It all came tumbling out while she hardly stopped for a breath. Her listeners would wilt with fatigue as she bombarded them with words. Their eyes grew glassy and inattentive. Inevitably their tempers grew ragged. Would she ever remain quiet? They longed for her silence.

It happened one day that her friend Zeus, the king of all the gods, asked her to help him. He knew about her reputation for idle chatter and wanted to turn it to his own use. It seemed that he was trying to avoid his wife, Hera, who was following him around suspiciously and was much too interested in his constant mischief. On that day Zeus wanted Echo to talk to his wife for a long time so that it would divert her. He hoped that after a weary time with Echo, it would grow too late for Hera to find him, as he pursued his latest pleasures. Of course Echo agreed. Imagine someone asking her to gossip as a special favor! It was the easiest thing in the world for her to do. She played her part well and detained Hera for hours.

When the goddess discovered that Echo had played this trick on her, she was in a mounting rage and decided out of anger to work her spiteful powers on the girl.

"Since you love to talk so much, you foolish girl, and you deliberately wasted my time so that I could not find my husband, I will make sure that you will never talk again. This should teach you a lesson not soon forgotten. From now on, the only words you will ever be able to say will be the last words you hear that have been spoken by others. For the rest of your life, you will only be able to repeat what someone else has said."

Echo was filled with anguish and shame. There was nothing she could do or say to soften this hard punishment. That same day she left her friends and wandered far into the deepest reaches of the woods where she would be alone, since it was no longer possible for her to speak or laugh with anyone again.

One day a young man named Narcissus had been hunting in the woods alone, enjoying the keen sport of the chase. He was tired after a long outing and paused to recover himself. As he rested he was observed by Echo, who recognized him immediately. She had heard about this handsome youth from the other nymphs who had fallen desperately in love with his good looks the moment they set eyes on him. Unfortunately, Echo was no different from the rest; and as she studied his fine features, his hair as fair as wheat and his straight, slender form, she, too, fell hopelessly in love with him.

Everyone spoke of the beauty of Narcissus, but the trouble was that Narcissus heard all this extravagant praise everywhere he went. And, what was worse, he too believed that he was the most prized and wonderful of young men to look upon. This was bad for Narcissus because he became very vain and proud. After a time he was convinced that no one in the world was splendid enough to match him or be his beloved. He walked with his head up high and his nose slightly atilt which discouraged those who would approach him.

In the days that followed, whenever Narcissus appeared, Echo could not speak but followed him around faithfully in the woods. She was full of love and yearned to tell him of her feeling. This, of course, was impossible. One day, Narcissus heard rustling in the trees behind him. He turned and called out,

"Come out, whoever you are. I have heard your footsteps for a long time. Please don't be so shy."

The answer was returned by Echo, "So shy."

He called out engagingly, "I'm sure we can be friends."

"Be friends," she said softly.

"Everyone tells me that they love me," he boasted.

"Love me," said Echo, as her pulse raced with expectation. And with this last statement she stepped bravely out of the brush to meet him, her heart infused with love. She had been lonely for so long and she was certain this beautiful youth had come to rescue her. She extended her arms with anticipation, smiling sweetly all the while. But once he saw her looking at him with such deep and sincere affection, he was no longer interested. Quickly he reminded himself that no one could possibly be good enough for him, and he was not moved by Echo's loving expression. He stared at her with cold empty eyes, turned his back and left without a word of good-bye.

Echo, foresaken, was bereft as a beggar by the cruel rejection of Narcissus, and she walked the forest dispirited and sadder with each day that passed. She pined for him and began to grow thinner with grief until finally she became so frail there was nothing left of the sweet maid but her haunting far-off voice which can still be heard by all of us. If we listen when the waves of sound bounce back to us from hills and cliffs and empty rooms and lonely halls, it is Echo we hear.

Long after Echo's sad departure, Narcissus continued to come to the woods to hunt, always happy and unconcerned about anyone else but himself. He did not know that Echo in her despair had called to the goddess Artemis, whom she knew favored her with affection. She prayed to the goddess and wished that the beautiful young man would fall deeply in love with someone and be hurt in the same way he had so often made others suffer. The goddess Artemis was the patroness of young lovers. She felt a great tenderness toward Echo and decided it was indeed time to punish Narcissus soundly for his conceit.

The plan began to work as one day Narcissus returned to the woods and stopped to rest by a clear pool. When he bent down to drink he saw a most exquisite face mirrored in the water. He was seized with longing and instantly he fell in love. The expressive eyes he saw moved his soul, the lush golden hair begged to be touched, the gentle lips were like a budding flower--such delicate features he had never encountered nor beheld before. Narcissus, the proud and conceited youth, had fallen madly, passionately in love with the reflection of his own face! He tried to kiss the face in the pool, gently, gently, but the water shimmered at the contact of his lips and the face disappeared. He tried to touch the face when again it reappeared, but it quickly departed. He cried plaintively. He pleaded patiently for the wondrous creature to speak to him, to love him, to stay with him--to favor him with the same affection that filled his breast to bursting. It was to no avail. Finally he made a vow to stay by the pool until his new love responded to his blandishments and appeared to him as a person. But the face in the pool never answered. He kept a lonely vigil by the pool day after day. He did not eat. He did not sleep. He became wan and sickly. His hair grew long and his legs weakened as his entire body was bent toward the reflection. With passing time he became forever rooted to the side of the pool. As days and weeks followed one upon the other, his human form began to change, and all that could be found in his place was the fragile narcissus flower looking down into the crystal blue water with its delicate yellow center framed by white petals. The narcissus flower may still be seen in the spring, a fragile sentinel, standing alert on its long slender green stalk watching its own image in the water.

INSIGHTS FOR THE TEACHER

This story may be regarded as a nature myth which describes the origin of the beautiful narcissus flower and explains the phenomenon of an echo. But if we read more carefully, we recognize that the story is more than that; it has sweeping psychological overtones. Narcissus, of course, is the archetypal (original) narcissist: he bears excessive self-love, to the exclusion of all others. Narcissism has also come to include a total preoccupation with one's own appearance and indifference to the plight or welfare of others. The name means "numbing" or "narcotic"; Narcissus is indeed numb to everyone and everything but himself. All this is demonstrated in the encounter with Echo. Perhaps no group of characteristics better describes the Greeks--and modern Westerners--as that of Narcissus. His mother was told that he would live long if he did not know himself. What he knew, instead, was the superficialities of external appearance. And that was what his unre-quited lovers admired about him, for who could love such a self-centered egoist for his per-sonality? Unfortunately for him (and for Echo, among others) there was no more to Nar-cissus than his external facade. He was distant, uninvolved, and vain, like so many other Greek gods and heroes.

Self-love is important for a person's health, but Narcissus, in typical Greek fashion, took this too far, to excess. Students should consider the possible consequences of neglecting others because of absolute love for self: it is detrimental to community, personal relationships, and ultimately to the individual.

Echo, too, is archetypal. She resembles Pandora in her irresponsibility and chattering, a stereotype of how the Greeks viewed women again. It is his cruel rejection of Echo that brings Narcissus' downfall as he is punished by Echo's patron goddess, Artemis. Yet *Echo* is the sufferer, not Narcissus. Her plight is basically undeserved, her penalty an overreac-tion. The other issue in Echo's tale is her incessant talking (apart from stereotyping it as a purely womanly trait). Silence is an important quality that Echo seems to lack. These two mythological characters ironically complement each other: the one, Narcissus is silent and self-indulgent, and the other Echo, is talkative to excess and selflessly devoted to another.

REFLECTIVE QUESTIONS

1. Narcissism is a term used in modern psychology. It describes someone who loves himself to excess. What could be the result of a relationship with such a person?

    Possible Answer--Like Echo, one who tried to form a close relationship with a narcissist probably would be disappointed because his affection would not be returned. In many cases, narcissistic people are overwhelmingly obsessed with their own prestige, honor, status, glory, material trappings, victory or success. They have few close relationships and those they do cultivate (as in every case of Greek mythology) end in disaster. Narcissistic self-love excludes loving others and makes lasting relationships difficult if not impossible. Narcissists' main attachments are to themselves.

2. What is the opposite of narcissism? Why is it important to care about yourself?

    Possible Answer--The opposite of narcissism is empathy. "Em" means "he" in archaic Greek and "pathy" means feeling. Thus, empathy means to "enter into his feelings" (or the feelings of another). Empathy is the power to *understand* someone or something outside ourselves. Empathetic people *understand* the feelings, fears, and hopes of others. Unlike narcissists, they can put themselves into the minds of others or they extend themselves to others. It is important, as healthy individuals, to have esteem for ourselves in order to care about others. Without self-respect, respect for other human beings is difficult. There is a middle ground between excessive self-love and self-hatred. The examples of Narcissus and Athena represent the two extremes.

3. What are the dangers of interfering in the private business of other people or taking sides, as Echo did when she interfered with Hera and Zeus? Why might such involvement create trouble if you were only trying to help?

Possible Answer--It seems that, as in the case of Echo, the affairs of family members are often best left alone by outsiders. Family ties often allow great flexibility even in arguing, and what may be accepted from a family member may not be accepted from an outsider.

4. What is a beauty contest? What is there about these contests that many people find offensive?

Possible Answer--Feminists and others have attacked traditional beauty contests because they present women as physical objects to be admired for only superficial or external qualities. These contests now include a demonstration of "talent" or "intelligence" (usually a 30-second response to a universal question). But the focus remains the same--the value of *external* beauty of the contestants.

5. Assume that a person is admired for good looks only--with no consideration for the inner person. What effect does this kind of admiration have on that person? What is meant by the "inner person"?

Possible Answer--Such admiration creates conceit, vanity and total self-involvement. Modern psychologists and sociologists have also noted that such people have excessive concern for success and prestige, crave attention and admiration, and express a deep fear of losing all these. Out of their anxiety they may also tend to become temperamental, ruthless, and calculating. They frequently manipulate and use other people in order to heighten their own importance and achieve their goals. The "inner person" refers to intelligence, sensitivity, imagination, empathy (understanding others) and sympathy (sharing the feelings of others).

FOLLOW-UP ACTIVITIES

1. There are companies which call themselves dating services whose business it is to bring lonely people together for companionship. Make up a suitable name for such a company. Design a questionnaire to be filled out by the clients who are interested in these services. Describe yourself on this questionnaire which is to be fed into a computer to "match" people according to interest and life-styles. Describe your physical characteristics and then your internal qualities which cannot be seen, such as personality and intelligence.

2. Write the following quotes on the board. Add to them any other expressions you can remember having to do with beauty, handsomeness or other external characteristics. Work out the meaning of each.
   a. Beauty is only skin deep.
   b. Handsome is as handsome does.
   c. Beauty is in the eye of the beholder.
   d. What is beautiful is invisible to the eye.
   e. You can't tell a book by its cover.

3. Research the scientific reason for the sound of an echo. Find the definition in the dictionary. Can you describe the conditions under which an echo will be heard? Echo chambers are used in pop music recordings. Explain what they do to enhance the music.

4. Start a booklet in class to which each member of the room will contribute, including the teacher. Title it "BEAUTY IS...." For example, Beauty is:
   a. carnival lights sparkling at the edge of my town.
   b. a 10-speed bike on Christmas morning.
   c. a closed school building during summer vacation.
   d. the winter beach looking like a moonscape.
   e. a plump juicy hot dog crackling over hot charcoal.
   Whatever you consider to be beautiful is acceptable.

5. Imagine that you lived in the woods where Narcissus came by on his hunting trips. The pool where he saw his reflection is on your property, and you observed his strange obsession with the reflection in the water. Write a letter to a good friend of yours describing these peculiar events.

ECHO VALLEY FRIENDSHIP CLUB

ROLE PLAY

Statement: The story of Echo and Narcissus defines the nature of narcissism and its possible effects on interpersonal relationships. Narcissus is the archetype or model because he bears *all* the traits that a Narcissist can have. Some of these traits, in less concentrated form, are observable in almost all people.

The Scene: A gathering at the Echo Valley Friendship Club where a planning meeting takes place and the personality prototypes are identifiable. The leader says to the gathered club members, "We are meeting today to plan a party to introduce new members. How do you feel about it, what are your suggestions and how should we proceed?"

Cast of Characters: Call for six to ten volunteers to demonstrate personality types to be identified by the class. Assign prominent numbers to be worn by each for easy identification, for discussion and reference. Provide strong clues for the actors upon which they may base their performance and dialogue.

A Clotheshorse: Only interested in what will be worn, whether the party will be formal or informal, talks about apparel nonstop and criticizes the tastes of others.

Always Bored: Yawns a lot, looks at watch, inattentive, noncontributing, could not care less.

A Braggart: Constantly keeps comparing what is presently happening to better times, better events, and more impressive experiences in times past, "When I belonged to the Acme Social Group we had a gala fireworks show that was covered by every newspaper in the state..."

Very Cooperative: Comes up with all kinds of ideas, offers to make calls, runs errands, helps with decorations and almost anything that will help.

Bossy but Organized: Has the whole plan worked out for the party, has figured out the committees, who is to do each job, how much money can be spent, etc.

Undecided about Everything: Agrees completely with every suggestion that comes up even when it contradicts with another!

Objective: To demonstrate that traces of narcissism can be seen in different types of people.

Discuss the Skit:
1. Use a word or a phrase to describe each person.
2. Who had attractive or positive qualities?
3. Who had undesirable or negative qualities?
4. Did you recognize any self-centered behavior?
5. Why might you and your friend react differently to the same person?

Write your feelings about the class role-play experience and discussion.

VIII. DANGER! DON'T PROVE IT TO YOUR FRIENDS-- PHAETHON

CAST OF CHARACTERS

PHAETHON (FAY e thon):   A young schoolboy, son of Apollo

APOLLO (uh POL oh):   God of the sun, patron of music, archery, mathematics and medicine. Son of Zeus and Leto (a mortal woman). A twin to Artemis, goddess of the moon.

CLYMENE (CLIME uh nee):   Mother to Phaethon; a sea nymph who attended Poseidon, god of the sea.

Some young schoolboys were seen one day after their lessons sitting around, talking and exchanging stories about their adventures and generally boasting about their exploits. One of the boys by the name of Phaethon hung back but listened to the others brag extravagantly about how accomplished and important their fathers were. Phaethon, however, was left out of this boastful contest because sadly he had never met his father. His mother Clymene had told him many times that he indeed was the true son of Apollo, god of the sun, who resided in the golden palace of the East. She helped him envision the glory of his father, Apollo, who rode his brilliant chariot pulled by stallions with manes of fire in an aura of blinding light. She told how they careened across the morning sky seizing the sun and pulling it higher and higher, finally to rise in the blue eastern sky where it would burst on the horizon and bring dawn to the world. The boy was enthralled as he listened to this story and needed desperately to let his friends know that none of them had a parent as important to the entire world as he. Reassured by his mother and no longer able to contain the information about his father, he declared openly to his friends:

"I am the son of the greatest god of all--Apollo the giver of sacred sun and source of all life, the most stunning of the gods in the Pantheon. You can't match that--not a single one of you!"

The more his disbelieving friends laughed, the more Phaethon boasted. But there was no end to their tormenting.

"Of course you are Apollo's son. We are all the mortal sons of gods. Prove that you are so big and better than all of us if you can. But you can't really, can you? How will you show us your father is Apollo? Well.....do something!"

Their laughter and teasing bit into his flesh and his anger was doubled because he did not know, in truth, how he could prove anything to the whole pack of them. Goaded beyond endurance, the golden-haired Phaethon was determined to make them all look like fools.

Humbled and unsure, Phaethon set out on a journey to find Apollo's Eastern palace in the Land of the Sunrise, with very little hope that he would ever arrive. In the way of the gods, Apollo knew his son was coming and magically assisted his arrival. Miraculously, Phaethon found himself in the audience of his imperial father, a towering handsome figure with a crown of dazzling sunbeams which flashed around his head. He sat on a throne of gold whose spires were replete with amber and topaz. The glare was blinding and exalting. Somehow, Phaethon found courage in himself and asked directly,

"Am I, Phaethon, truly your son?"

The answer he had always dreamed of came quickly with warmth and affection. "Yes, you are my son and I am prepared to prove it to you by granting you any wish you may desire."

It was for Phaethon the moment he had longed for. He extracted the promise from his father that anything he wished for would be his. Apollo swore with a solemn oath by the sacred river Styx that it was so.

Without a moment's hesitation, the boy, thus assured, blurted out, "I want to ride the golden chariot across the sky and make the sun rise and set just as you do."

A gasp of dismay escaped from Apollo upon hearing this shocking request. Never did he think the boy would ask for this unthinkable wish. He pleaded with his son not to hold him to such a favor which would surely mean the death of the youth. He tried to impress his son with the responsibility of this grand design which he alone assumed as lord of the sun. He told Phaethon about the slow, labored drive up along the narrow paths between the constellations to pull the sun into its morning ascendancy; about the unbridled power of the horses which only he in the entire universe could control; about the frightening dive into the ocean stream which pulled down the final shade of night. He tried to explain his exhaustion at sea when he would enbark upon his regal ferryboat and sail back to his Eastern palace serenely gratified that he had performed his godly feat.

But the boy was not to be deprived of this chance to impress his friends and silence their taunting at last. He did not listen, nor did he take it seriously when his father said:

"Should you fail, this would mean not only your death, but the devastation of the world."

But Phaethon would only say, "You promised." And indeed Apollo had promised by the sacred river Styx which held him to his word. "You promised"--haunted the father's peace of mind and he yielded.

As he took his place, the boy was puny and insignificant in the massive grandeur of the golden chariot. The white horses were each the size of mountains with golden hoofs and flowing yellow manes which swept the sky. Smoke shot from their nostrils as they neighed, impatient to be harnessed and on their way.

Apollo spoke to Phaethon, but he was not listening. You do not have the strength to drive these horses which have the power to sear heaven and Earth. But if you must do this thing, listen carefully while I tell you that you must keep to the middle sky. If you drive too close to Earth, the world will be scorched to a blackened wasteland by the heat of the chariot. If you soar to the highest reaches of the sky, the world will freeze under a cruel and impenetrable cover of ice. I enjoin you to heed me if you value the safety of the earth and all its creatures.

The four horses (Pyroeis, Eous, Aethon, Phlegon) ascended the steep incline of the sky instantly aware that they were led by weak and unskilled hands. They kept to the middle trail but only for awhile, for Phaethon, lulled by the ease of the flight, wanted to descend just barely close enough to the ground so that his friends might see him in all his noble brilliance. He wanted to experience the sweetness of his victory as the true child of the sun god and put an end to their taunting which had gnawed at him so cruelly. But as he directed the horses to plunge toward Earth, the heat of the brilliant chariot set everything aflame, burning fields and scorching all living things in a smoldering, charred foresaken waste. Terrified by these consequences, Phaethon strained to the limits of his endurance to control the reins. But they were like hot blistering ropes which demanded the strength of a giant. He failed, as he must, while the wild steeds whinnied angrily and arced into the farthest reaches of the sky, leaving the furnace below--up, up, up until the earth was chilled to death, leaving Arctic peaks of frigid, bone-chilling wasteland and a sombre frozen mask of extinction.

Beyond the clutch of terror and nightmare, Phaethon helplessly realized that the horses were once again descending toward Earth to bring heat, melting ice and floods to the tormented survivors. A great wave of sorrow, anguished weeping and despair rolled out from the grieving of the people, which reached the ears of the almighty Zeus. He reacted swiftly and with outrage to save the world. He hurled his mightiest thunderbolts at the boy Phaethon and, as a last desperate measure, set him afire. Pitifully his frail, fiery body was wrenched from the chariot, dropped through space like a falling star and became a charred and dying ember as his remains plummeted silently into the water below. He was mourned by his mother and his sisters who wept human tears until Zeus, out of compassion, turned them into poplar trees which now stand on the banks of the water and weep amber tears for their departed younger brother. The earth still shows signs of that fateful ride which left behind frigid and tropical zones, ice-capped mountains, volcanoes with underground chambers of steam, deserts, and darkskinned people who were deeply browned when the sun came too close to the earth.

Alas, there was no way of knowing if Phaethon's friends finally realized the real truth of his stories or even cared in the least. But the tragedy remains that the poor headstrong boy died painfully for his foolishness.

INSIGHTS FOR THE TEACHER

Few Greek myths are used so blatantly to explain natural phenomena as this one. The tale claims to establish the origins of volcanoes, frigid and tropical zones, deserts and darkskinned races. But, like most myths, it has social and psychological nuances just beneath the surface. Most obvious are the perennial issues or peer pressure and foolhardy boasting, but there are others as well.

Phaethon may have felt lonely as an outsider and tried to become a part of the in-group. Yet he went about this by insisting that he was even further isolated, that is, superior to his peers by virtue of his parentage. Once again, competition seems to be the general rule of life even among friends: these boys mirror Western adult society as they relate to each other in contestual, or antagonistic ways. Community feelings are strained when each member tries to assert individual superiority. A secondary point here is that Phaethon is without a father (like most Greek boys whose fathers avoided the household) and without friends. He is not only lonely, but anxious, worried about his image and his identity.

Phaethon is goaded into insisting on an absolutely unreasonable favor. His father, who unwisely makes a blank promise, cannot refuse, or perhaps does not care to, since he has shown no genuine affection for Phaethon until this point. The question here is why has Apollo neglected his son? The Greeks did not find this unusual; indeed, it was the norm for father-son relationships. If Phaethon, a headstrong youngster, is irrational for asking to drive the chariot, his father is doubly senseless for allowing the adventure to proceed. It is not so clear that the responsibility for the tragedy lies totally or even primarily with Phaethon. Just as Phaethon cannot control the horses, he cannot control his own passions, and Apollo cannot control his son.

Probably the most contemporary issue in the story is Phaethon's boasting to impress his peers. It proves dangerous and even deadly. Phaethon might have recognized the meanness of his comrades and ignored them, he might have asked for a more humble favor, he might have tried to gain respect on his own, but instead, the boy turned to outside help, lost his temper and reason, did not think, and lost his life.

REFLECTIVE QUESTIONS

1. What is the resemblance between Apollo's chariot and Phaethon and today's family car? How is the car the source of controversy in the modern household?

   Possible Answer--Although Apollo's chariot is exclusively his (and not his family's), the analogy is appropriate. Young adults often see the family car as a way to demonstrate coming of age to their contemporaries. Although they may be physically capable of driving, important decisions on how and why to use a car, which can be a deadly machine, need more experienced minds. Thus, worried parents may struggle to withhold the car from an aspiring child, and the child may resent a lack of trust. What is further involved, again, is the awareness that other young people are already driving, and *not* to drive can be a sign of social inferiority.

2. Apollo wisely resisted Phaethon's rash request, feeling this could and should not be done. Often people will resist a new idea or activity by saying that it can't be done. Under what circumstances do you think this attitude would be *unwise*?

   Possible Answer--The pioneer spirit begins with a refusal to accept taboos like this one. So, too, do intellectuals, pioneers, scientists, reformers, etc., believe in themselves and have the confidence to go ahead despite resistance from traditional wisdom or authority. Unlike Phaethon, however, their projects are usually, but not always, more than personally motivated.

3. Phaethon was mourned by some for his bravery because he dared to try. Others mourned him for his foolishness. Did Phaethon act out of loneliness? Explain.

Possible Answer--If Phaethon is considered a hero, it is because he sought to scale the heights of achievement and failed in a noble effort at greatness. More temperate views may judge his behavior as audacious or foolish because it *clearly* was beyond his abilities or social position (in this case, a mortal trying to do what only an immortal can). If he was lonely, the attempt was to achieve attention and recognition from his friends, make a name for himself, gain his identity through this single heroic action. He is an outcast, ridiculed and alone. That might explain his desperation and his outrageous demand.

4.   Peer pressure may be a trap which forces you to prove something to your friends. What is peer pressure? How do young people try to win acceptance from their friends? Faced with taunting schoolmates, Phaethon had to "show them." What might have been an alternative for him in such a situation?

Possible Answer--Peer pressure is the need to conform to group demands and patterns of behavior among your contemporaries. The story of Phaethon implies that while the specifics change, the pattern of conformity remains in Western culture. Modern children may try to conform, to earn acceptance, in some of the following ways: fashion (wearing certain styles or brands of clothes), driving, drinking, drug abuse, rudeness, even deliberately doing poorly in school. Most of these are or may be negative. There are positive ways to win acceptance: excelling in sports or academics, participation in extracurricular activities, helping others, cooperating, etc. Suggestions for alternative behavior for Phaethon should come from the students and may include: he could have ignored his schoolmates; he could have chosen to challenge one or more of them to a personal contest; he could have endeared himself to them as an interesting person who is cooperative and friendly; he could have asked his father for a more reasonable favor.

5.   Apollo made a promise to Phaethon to prove his love for him as a son. When he heard what the boy wanted, he was shocked. Phaethon would not release him from his promise. Under what circumstances should a promise be broken? Are there times when someone has broken a promise to you? What was your attitude?

Possible Answer--It is conceivable that a promise might be broken because circumstances change. What may have seemed reasonable at the time, may for many reasons now be impractical, dangerous, or simply not a good idea. The promise may have been made in haste--and people ideally should always have the right to analyze and reconsider their commitments.

FOLLOW-UP ACTIVITIES

1. Phaethon and his schoolmates were caught in the contest of bragging. The trouble with lies is that they sometimes start to grow out of control. In folk literature these lies were called tall tales and were wild fun to listen to. Organize "A Tall Tales Event." Ask for volunteer storytellers from your class. The tellers may write their own stories or find some in literature, for example, Paul Bunyan, John Henry, Mike Fink, Pecos Bill, Captain Stormalong.

2. Organize a bulletin board with the heading, "They Said It Couldn't Be Done" or "That's Impossible!" List pioneers in all fields of endeavor who challenged what was accepted to be absolutely true or impossible, in their lifetime. For example: Albert Einstein determined that the prevailing view of the universe was not suitable for modern physics, and so he said he would invent a new explanation.

3. Phaethon's experience involved a terrifying journey across the sky to prove a point to his friends. Create a story entitled "My Desperate Ride." *First,* describe your conflict with friends or others which inspired you to embark on this dangerous flight. *Second,* describe your own heartstopping adventure.

4. Phaethon was the name of a buggy and later became the name of a grand touring car. Design your own Phaethon vehicle from an historical period (from a chariot to a futuristic energy transporter). Draw it, name it and describe it in a newspaper ad for interested buyers.

5. Discuss what the world would be like without the sun. Would there even be a world?

6. Mythology and folklore of all cultures share a common interest in the power of the sun as the giver of life and an object of worship. The charted course of Apollo in his fiery sun chariot is the ancient Greek explanation of how the sun rises and sets. Find an account of this natural phenomenon from other nature myths (Nordic, Celtic, American Indian, Eskimo, African, etc.). Explain to the class how some of these are different from each other.

ROLE PLAY

Statement: Phaethon deals with the consequences of a foolhardy response to peer pressure.

The Scene: On the main street of town after an auto accident.

Characters:

Older Citizen: Does not understand what happened. Heard something about playing "chicken" and wants someone to explain what this means in terms of the car crash. "Why do kids do this sort of thing?"

Other Students: (Assume these roles and volunteer opinions.)

1. Explain why some kids will take a challenge.
2. Explain why everyone wants to be accepted by the group.
3. Explain that kids do things because of pressure every day, but the results are not always as drastic as a car accident.
4. Explain that your friends are important and sometimes you might do dumb things, but adults do foolish things socially, too.
5. Explain the things you might do in response to a dare that would avoid a similar tragedy.

Objective: To explore the nature of peer pressure and how everyone is affected by it.

Discuss the Skit: Teacher's choice (Depending upon the drama which unfolds, other questions may be more relevant.)

1. What point does this role play make about human nature and our relationships to our friends?
2. What could make you act very coolly even if you were afraid and were with your friends?
3. Did you ever do something in a group that you would never do if you were alone? What makes the difference?
4. If you did something and nobody knew about it, could there still be consequences for you? Give examples.
5. Are there some things which you would have said in this skit which were not said by the participants? What were they?

Write your feelings about the class role-play experience and discussion.

IX. THE VOICE OF EXPERIENCE-- DAEDALUS AND ICARUS

IX. THE VOICE OF EXPERIENCE--
DAEDALUS AND ICARUS

CAST OF CHARACTERS

DAEDALUS (DED uh lus): The greatest inventor and problem solver of ancient times. A favorite of the goddess Athena who taught him mechanical principles.

MINOS (MY nos): King of Crete; son of Zeus and Europa

ICARUS (ICK uh rus): Son of Daedalus; a boy whose imagination exceeded his power

THESEUS (THEE see us): One of the great heroes of Greece who became King of Athens

MINOTAUR (MIN uh tor): A monster who was half man and half bull, imprisoned in the labyrinth built by Daedalus

Daedalus was a remarkable architect and inventor who made countless improvements in handicrafts and the arts. He loved the wonders of complicated mechanical things, and he thought about every problem as a challenging puzzle that could be solved no matter how impossible it seemed to others. His reputation was known far and wide as a man with a creative and fascinating mind.

Minos, the king of Crete, had heard about the clever inventor, and he decided to call upon Daedalus to help him solve a horrible problem. It was hard to believe, but this king owned, of all things, a monster called a minotaur. It was a huge, savage beast that was half bull and half human, and it could not be contained like any ordinary animal because of its size and strength. The minotaur was fierce and cruel, even more hideous, it ate humans alive--crunching them like tender flailing straws as they screamed and fought for their lives. Still, the king refused to destroy the frightening beast, for he had other plans for him, but somehow the ugly creature had to be kept confined in a place from which there was no escape. Everyone knew there was only one person who could find such a solution, so the king, as expected, turned to Daedalus.

The inventor considered this strange assignment carefully and then designed and built a maze that was a marvel of confusion. One convoluted path led into another and another and another--with dead ends, false exits, and endless turns. Once inside this labyrinth, there was no way out. Daedalus guaranteed that the minotaur or anyone else could never escape.

King Minos was ruthless and had little regard for human life. Once, after he had defeated Athens in a war, he demanded as a punishment the annual delivery of twelve of the most beautiful young people in tribute to him. He sacrificed them all to the minotaur. Forced to walk into the labyrinth, they were never seen again. But the king's plans were foiled when he sent a young man named Theseus into the maze to meet certain death, for Daedalus, out of kindness, arranged for the young man's escape. The king was furious to have lost his prisoner. He decided upon a suitable and twisted punishment. Ironically, he imprisoned Daedalus and his son Icarus in the very maze which Daedalus had invented. He was sure that the great man would soon be dead. But the imaginative mind of the inventor was always active, and he told his son that, though they could not escape by land or water, they could escape into the air. Icarus, relieved and joyous that they would soon be free, was full of wonder at his old father's wisdom.

Daedalus, with his son's help, cleverly fashioned two sets of wings made of wax and feathers which rivaled those of nature. He carefully attached the amazing wings to their arms and across their backs. Prepared for their escape flight, the father looked intensely into his son's eyes and warned him,

"Listen carefully, Icarus. Do not watch the wondrous birds in the sky, but keep me in your sight on a straight and unswerving path always. Do not fly too low because the sea will wet your wings and make them heavy. Most important, you must not fly too close to the sun, for the heat will melt the wax which holds your wings. Follow me, Icarus, and do not be deceived by the ease of flight though the smallest creatures of the sky glide past you."

Daedalus was sure his son would listen and obey him. The two flew heavenward, high into the clouds, at last free of the labyrinth which imprisoned them. The sensation of flight filled the young Icarus with enchantment as he flew and coasted on the air like a strong, unfettered young bird. But soon the foolish boy became too confident. He forgot his father's warnings and soared up toward the beckoning sun. Immediately the wings of Icarus warmed in the fearsome heat and the wax melted all too quickly. He felt it running down his skin in hot little rivulets, scalding his flesh, announcing his doom. Icarus began to cry out, "Father, father, help me. I am falling!" But Daedalus was helpless as he watched his only son drop like a lifeless weight into the sea to disappear beneath engulfing waves. Filled with grief, he swooped low over the water weeping and wailing as he recovered the drowned body of Icarus. He carried his dead son to an island, now known as Icaria in tender memory of the boy. Daedalus deeply mourned his child who, intoxicated with his first flight of freedom, was not heedful of the words of experience imparted by his father and never lived into adulthood.

"Why didn't you listen, Icarus? Why couldn't you listen?"

INSIGHTS FOR THE TEACHER

The story of Daedalus poses questions about parental authority, the youthful quest for knowledge and experience, and the adventure and lure of the unknown.

Out of his experience and wisdom, Daedalus knew what the consequences of flying too high or too low would be. But, as is often the case with parents and children, the son Icarus did not listen and so met his destruction on melted wings as his father had promised. It is not enough for Icarus to understand that his father knows about the dangers of flight. The boy must find out for himself--sometimes an admirable idea, but in this case tragic. Or perhaps the need or the drive to search for our own experience is too overwhelming to resist however foolhardy our impulse may seem. Obviously there are times when we fail to listen and choose to take chances. One can imagine the excitement and joy of flight, the thrill of soaring toward the sun, carried away by the freedom from human limitations. But, as in so many Greek myths, this hero carries his feeling too far, to excess. (See Achilles, Narcissus, Phaethon.)

Having given Icarus wings with which to fly, how could Daedalus have expected him to limit his flight? On the other hand, wise Daedalus naturally assumed his son would obey him. It is a difficult human dilemma, or at least a Western one. In many cultures, disobeying one's own father would be unthinkable. Perhaps the issue here is parental giving of the means to be independent and the almost inevitable problem of youthful ardor and impatience misusing those means.

REFLECTIVE QUESTIONS

1. Why didn't Icarus listen to his father? What reasons can you think of?

    Possible Answer--It is possible that Icarus, like many young people, refused to impute any special wisdom to his elders. But it is also possible that his joy, feelings and emotions about his new freedom overcame his reasons and he simply forgot his father's warning. This makes the tale a tragedy: unavoidable and no one's fault.

2. What kinds of activities have you experienced in which you became so involved or absorbed that you genuinely forgot the advice of parents or older friends?

    Possible Answer--Elicit answers from the students which reflect a range of experiences. They might have something to do with swimming in deep water and going too far out; riding a bike down steep hills in a neighborhood where the presence of cars compounds the danger; walking on a beautiful summer evening much too late at night; using a power saw in a basement workshop where you were invited to do some fun carpentry, etc.

3. Obviously we can't learn everything in life by personal experience. What are other ways that you can learn?

Possible Answer--There are insights to be gained from reading fictional books where you actually get inside the heads and hearts of characters and know what they are thinking and feeling; or, of course, we learn from nonfiction which is instructive. One may also learn from friends, parents, and teachers (the point of the Daedalus story); from the media (television, radio, movies). Generally, one may learn by reading, listening to others, exploring or thinking or through discussion. One can assimilate much of this to learn from the past or use logic to understand the present and face the future.

4. What are some of the warnings and teachings or advice you could give younger friends or brothers and sisters that would help them if they would only listen?

Possible Answer--Elicit answers from the students which demonstrate their experiential background which they would be willing to share with friends and siblings. Emphasize that this casts them in the role of teacher in a very authentic sense. The shared knowledge of humans historically provides the building blocks for others in their growth and development. We may be grateful for this sharing of experience, be it personal, scientific, technical or artistic. Because of this, each individual need not reinvent the wheel.

5. Can you describe a situation in which you had to learn from your own experience and all the advice you received was of no help?

Possible Answer--Once again the answers will be of a personal and unique nature--learning to ride a bike or drive a car, learning to swim, bake bread, diagnose the mechanical problem of a car or some machine, extending your sympathy to someone who lost a loved one, giving a speech to a group or performing in front of an audience. In many of these, one may listen to directions and read information about the mastery of a particular act, but only the actual "doing" and the real involvement enhances genuine understanding and appreciation for everything related to that experience. In other words, in many cases, only experience teaches.

FOLLOW-UP ACTIVITIES

1. Since the beginning of recorded history, humans have wanted to fly like the birds. Paintings on cave walls depict men with wings, primitive myths of all cultures describe men in flight; Leonardo da Vinci, during the Italian Renaissance of the early sixteenth century, sketched a man in a flying machine with a parachute; and scientists through the ages have dreamt of ways to achieve flight. Research some of the early flight pioneers, their successes and failures. Share an interesting anecdote with the class. Don't forget gliders, whirlybirds, hydroplanes, dirigibles, balloons, spacecraft, etc. (and bumblebees, who aerodynamically should not be able to fly)!

2. Daedalus was a master inventor. Think of all the inventions which we take for granted in our daily lives which make ours a technological society. Select one great invention, past or present, which fascinates you and make a study of it. Brainstorm these inventions on the board or keep adding to a bulletin board as more of them come to mind. The list can be infinitely long!

    plumbing   printing press
    incandescent light   television
    camera--still or moving pictures   word processor
    telephone   computer
    automobile   submarine
    telescope   spaceship
    microscope   atomic bomb
    gas engine   radio
    electricity   sewing machine

3. When a person invents something, it is often patented. On many objects we may see the words "patented" or "patent pending" or "copyright." What does this mean and what is the purpose of a patent or copyright? How does one go about securing a patent? Research this information in the library.

4. Inventors are problem solvers, which is a skill that *can* be learned. Once Daedalus was approached with the problem of how to pull a thread through the complicated windings of a conch shell. He tied a silken thread to an ant, started the ant off at the opening of the shell and placed a few drops of very aromatic honey at the other end. Ants love honey, and this ant was no exception. He smelled its sweet bouquet and crawled diligently round and round the convolutions of the shell, pulling the thread behind him. Eureka! He came out the other end and had threaded the shell from start to finish. Develop a voice-of-experience column to solve problems for people in the class. Solicit anonymous problems to which every student is invited to write a responsive letter with a solution. Read these aloud and discuss them. Name your column "Advice from Daniel Daedalus" or "The Sky's the Limit."

5. How many expressions or figures of speech can you think of that have something to do with the sky, flying, etc.? Work with a partner and see how many you can come up with. Compare with the rest of the class. For example:

   a. the sky's the limit
   b. go fly a kite
   c. up, up, and away
   d. he's a space cadet

   e. pie in the sky
   f. a bolt from the blue
   g. greased lightning

6. Pretend that Icarus survived his trip even though he didn't listen to his father. Rewrite the end of the myth, but change your title to "The Incredible Journey of Iggy Icarus" or some other title which indicates success.

CAMP ICARUS
FUN UNDER THE SUN

ROLE PLAY

Statement: The story of Daedalus and Icarus demonstrates the possible cost of indifference to the voice of experience and the personal dilemma of learning on your own.

The Scene: Camp Icarus--Fun Under the Sun. Around the campfire with young people discussing what occurred. A rescue party brought Nick out of the woods where he had been lost for a period of time--long enough to frighten the boy and everyone else.

Characters:

Nick Karus (the lost boy): Went on a camping trip with other kids and a camp counselor. Feels survival is a matter of common sense and ENJOYS ADVENTURE. Was tired of listening to all the rules and regulations and do's and don't's. He recounts them all with some irritation:

a. Always put out a campfire--it is liable to spread.
b. Always carry drinking water.
c. Wear a life jacket when you're boating no matter how well you swim. In rough water you may turn over and get hit on the head. Coast Guard approved jackets will hold your head above water.

and on and on and on.....

Other Campers:

Joe: Wants to know what happened to "common sense" since Nick obviously got into trouble, was hopelessly lost and confused.

Cindy: Remembers the rule that you must never leave a marked path without carrying a map and compass. If you stray without informing anyone, it takes just a moment to lose your bearings. On a cloudy day you can't tell in which direction you're going. Moss grows on all sides of a tree, not just on the north.

Steve: Supports Nick's point of view. There are some things you have to learn for yourself. If you had to depend on everyone else's experience, you probably wouldn't do anything.

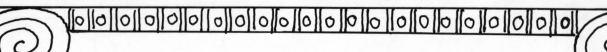

Debra: Believes it depends upon what kind of experience you are talking about. When someone says you can get electrocuted by touching high tension wires, you don't test it out for yourself.

Objective: To demonstrate the relative merits of learning through others' or one's own personal experience.

Discuss the Skit: Teacher's choice (Depending upon the drama which unfolds, other questions may be more relevant.)

1. Were you sympathetic to Nick's reasons for not listening to the rules?
2. When is it possible that too many rules would be a turnoff for people? What message does this hold?
3. With all the rules that bombarded Nick, were some more important than others (*priorities*)? What were they?
4. Whose argument impressed you the most? Why?

Write your feelings about the class role-play experience and discussion.

X. DUMB BUT STRONG--HERACLES

X. DUMB BUT STRONG--HERACLES

CAST OF CHARACTERS

HERACLES (HAIR uh kleez):	The strongest man in the universe, Son of Zeus
ALCMENE (alk MEE nee):	Mother of Heracles, Princess of Argos
IPHICLES (IF uh kleez):	Brother of Heracles
MAGAERA (muh JEE ruh):	First wife of Heracles, Princess of Thebes
EURYSTHEUS (you RIS thee us):	Cowardly king of Mycenae in charge of Heracles' twelve labors
ATLAS (AT lus):	One of the old Titans who fought against Zeus
DEIANEIRA (dee uh NIE ruh):	Second wife of Heracles who was used to kill him
IOLE (EYE oh lee):	A princess with whom Heracles fell in love. His affection for her led to his death.
NESSUS (NESS us):	A centaur whose blood bore the venom of the deadly serpent, the Hydra
MEDUSA (muh DOO zuh):	A female monster, one of the hideous Gorgons

From the time Heracles was an infant, it was strangely evident that this endearing little boy was stronger than ordinary men. One evening, his mother Alcmene gently tucked Heracles and his stepbrother, Iphicles, into the softness of their crib, rocking and crooning them into a tender sleep. At midnight when the house was dark and silent, Queen Hera jealously sent two huge snakes into the nursery. They slithered across the floor slowly and with an unerring instinct found their helpless prey asleep in the crib. The serpents' heads weaved, their tongues flickered, and they hissed as they began to coil themselves around the bodies of the infants in a deadly embrace.

Iphicles awoke screaming in fright, but Heracles, who was not yet a year old, grabbed the snakes, pulling at their treacherous scaly coils. He choked them--and he squeezed them, one in each hand, until the struggling creatures had no more life in them. The babies were discovered by their mother who found Heracles laughing as he held the enormous limp remains of the serpents for everyone to see. It was certain at that very moment that Heracles would nave nothing to fear for the rest of his life--except, perhaps, the wrath of Hera.

Now, it is important to know that Hera, the queen, hated her stepson, Heracles, even before he was born. She was jealous of Zeus's other loves, especially Alcmene, the mother of Heracles. Hera, forever spiteful, was determined to make Heracles' life miserable. He was given a special name by Zeus which meant "Glory of Hera" but though she knew he would bring her glory in his manhood, none of this softened her heart toward him. She had been tricked by Zeus into giving Heracles her mother's milk which made him immortal; but no matter, for she would attend to his torment faithfully to the last of his days.

Unfortunately, there was a problem with Heracles from the time he was a young boy, for he always used his muscle and superior strength before thinking or listening. Later, he would always have cause to regret his sudden temper and the harm it would bring. Heracles was slow at learning. Indeed, it was dangerous to try to teach him something he did not enjoy or tell him something he did not wish to hear. Once, he became angry with his music teacher, Linus by name, and struck the poor, patient man a blow on the head which killed him instantly. It was the first of a long line of violent events which marked the savage career of this uncontrolled man.

The list of his offenses was very long! Once, when he was angered by some messengers asking for taxes, he cut off their ears, hands, and noses and hung them around their necks. Defeated in a fair fight, he lay in wait for the twins Moliones and slaughtered them without mercy or warning. When a cupbearer spilled water on him, he struck him so hard he caved in the poor man's chest. Another time, without troubling to examine the evidence, Heracles wrongly accused Iphitus of stealing his horses, seized the innocent man and hurled him off a cliff. Though he loved the princess Iole, when her brother came to offer his support, Heracles promptly crushed his skull. But still, in spite of these excesses, he was everyone's darling and the favorite of the most intelligent of men, for Heracles embodied what the Greeks worshipped--the strength of the winner and the elegance of the human body.

Heracles never really meant to do harm to people and was always desperately sorry for his deeds, but his apologies later never undid his violence. As he grew, he realized that without a doubt he was the strongest man on Earth. In his vanity, he became arrogant and boastful, behaving outrageously. Once, when the heat of the day became too much for him, he was known to have put an arrow in his bow and threatened to wound the sun. Another time, as he tossed in a boat on the sea, he became seasick and shouted a warning to the waves that he would punish them if they would not be calm.

The great god Zeus was his father and he knew that only magic could destroy him, so he continued on about his wild ways with no one to stop him! There was, nevertheless, much kindness in this powerful man, and he performed heroic deeds for which the people were almost always grateful. The trouble was that Heracles never gained wisdom from his experience and could never be trusted to do the intelligent thing. Early in his life he was married to Princess Megaera who was given to him as a gift for his bravery. He had three sons whom he loved dearly. But one day, in a fit of anger, Hera caused Heracles to go mad and he killed his family. When his senses returned, he realized that this was the greatest and most destructive tragedy of his life. Though others were willing to forgive their hero, he could not forgive himself. Hera, in her hatred, would surely not forgive him and the fates in their zeal to see an offender punished would not have it any other way. They would torment him until he paid for his crimes.

Heracles wanted sincerely to pay for his harsh and insane acts. He talked to a priestess at Delphi who told him that in order to be purified for his sins, he must go to his cousin Eurystheus, the King of Mycenae, who would devise a suitable punishment. The king, who was not fond of the boastful and headstrong Heracles, gave him twelve tasks to perform, each of which seemed impossible to accomplish. These were called "the labors of Heracles." During these labors, Heracles killed monsters that were threatening the lives of people, wrestled giants who were destroying cities, drove away plagues of birds that had taken human lives, and journeyed to many places, including Hades, the lower world of the sea. With each labor, King Eurystheus profited immensely and gave a slave's portion of the booty to Heracles, insulting and humiliating him. And with each of his accomplishments, the fame and glory of his stepmother, Hera, rose to the heavens as her name echoed the world over in praise of her stepson.

Heracles' sixth labor was something of a relief to him because it did not involve violence, but rather required that he solve a problem and use his strength after careful thought. He was commanded to clean the famous Augean Stables in only one day--just 24 short and fleeting hours! These stables were owned by King Augeas of Elis, who had the most disgusting habits one could imagine, for he owned 3000 magnificent oxen which he neglected irresponsibly. Almost impossible to describe, the stables had not been cleaned in thirty long years. His cattle were a gift of the gods and they never died, but they did create filth as ordinary animals do, and the stench and foulness could kill a person with a weak constitution. It seemed a hopeless, insuperably difficult task to be performed and would have remained undone, dooming Heracles to failure but for the suggestions of two wise advisors of Heracles and his enormous strength. He cleverly diverted the courses of two rivers, the Alpheus and Peneus, by lifting them from their natural beds and heaving them into the barns where the water rushed through the stables in a great tumbling, roaring flood of power and white foam, washing and cleansing everything in its relentless path!

The eleventh labor was a visit to Atlas, the Titan, to bring back the Golden Apples of the Hesperides. Atlas was the gardener where these enchanted apples grew. The tree was Hera's special one and she had it protected by Ladon, a hundred-headed serpent whose massive body was wrapped lovingly around its trunk. Atlas, too, protected the orchard, since Zeus had condemned him, as a punishment of war, to stand forever upholding the burden of the heavens with his immense shoulders and hands. Heracles bid Atlas kindly to pluck the apples for him. But Atlas trembled at the thought of an encounter with the hundred-headed monster. Heracles, without hesitation, always fearless and sure, slew the serpent in the blink of an eye. Once done, he pressed his cause again but this time offered to hold up the heavens if Atlas would do him the favor of fetching the apples. Atlas agreed with a quickening of interest. He lifted the heavenly universe and transferred its weight to his visitor. How he stretched his tired muscles; how he flexed his arms and legs; how he delighted at last to be relieved of his burden. Most certainly, he did not intend to take back the weight of the world, and he thanked the fates for having sent this stupid young man who gave him his blessed relief. Heracles, of course, suspected these ends and innocently asked Atlas to take back the heavens for just the very briefest moment so that he might find pads for his irritated shoulders. When Atlas resumed his burden, he was deeply vexed to find that he had been tricked like a simple-witted fool as he watched Heracles walk away free and unencumbered. Later stories say that Atlas was eventually punished (or some say relieved) by the hero Perseus who returned to the garden and showed Atlas the hideous head of Medusa the Gorgon. She was the youngest of the three beastly sisters. Her hair was entwined with vipers, twisting and hissing through their fangs, and when she threw back her foul wings, she revealed treacherous claws and red, protruding eyes. One look at the grotesque monster and Atlas, in shock, froze into stone. This huge stone is now called the Atlas Mountains in Africa where it has withstood the inroads of time for centuries.

Heracles, after his labors were through, continued to enjoy life and play many a noble game. He decided to marry again and herein lay the seeds of his destruction. His choice was Deianeira, a princess who drove a chariot, wore armor, and practiced war. His courtship of this woman took him into high adventure when she was stolen from him by Nessus, the centaur. Now the centaur was wicked and dangerous and belonged to that race of people from Thessaly in northern Greece. He had the head, arms and chest of a powerful man connected to the sleek body of a horse. Like most of his kind, he was wild, fleet of foot, lawless and took what he wanted--and on one fateful day he wanted Deianeira. When Heracles heard her screams, he went forward to save his bride. He reached for his bow and slew the centaur before the man-horse could gallop like a whirlwind and escape. As Nessus lay dying, he offered the innocent Deianeira a gift which he claimed was a sign of his repentance for having wronged her beloved Heracles. He whispered as his strength waned.

"Take the blood from my wound and mix it with the oil of olives. It will make a love potion which will bind Heracles to you forever. And if in time he should ever wander from you or desire another woman, rub the lotion into his tunic and his love for you will never falter."

The princess of course did not tell Heracles. It was to be her own precious secret to hold his love which she cherished! Little did Deianeira know that the centaur's blood contained the venom of the Hydra, the poisonous serpent and pet of Hera. The venom made Nessus' blood more lethal than any weapon, for when exposed to heat, its vitriol would burn even immortal flesh. It could turn fertile soil into red dust and reduce stone to ashes. Unhappily, it came about that Heracles in time longed for a young woman from his past by the name of Princess Iole. When he brought her home, Deianeira was in a jealous rage. She remembered the potion Nesses had given her. Desperately she soaked Heracles' favorite shirt in the lotion. When Heracles put on the deadly garment, the heat from his body activated the vile poison. In blinding pain and agony he struck out and killed his friend Lichas, who had come to his aid and tried to save him. He felt as if he were bitten by one thousand serpents as the venom began to corrode his flesh, eating away at his bones and boiling his blood. In this horrifying way Heracles, who could not be killed by mortal men, was consumed by a mystical fire as his friends watched from a distance in utter horror. Deianeira, anguished, finally understood how she had been used by the centaur to realize his revenge. She hung herself even as her husband was in his death throes, for her grief and guilt were more than she could bear.

Thus ended the life of Greece's strongest and greatest hero, victim of a serpent's venom, of his own appetites, of violence and vengeful Hera. Zeus so loved him that he formed Heracles into a heavenly spirit, allowing him to live on Olympus where Hera finally accepted him as her true son and he was honored by the gods. But alas, his mortal part was sent to Hades, where it stalked madly back and forth in eternal suffering over his transgressions.

INSIGHTS FOR THE TEACHER

Historians sometimes interpret the career of Heracles as reflecting Greek history. After invasions of barbaric, violent and wild Dorian tribes from the North, Greece evolved into the most civilized of classical cultures.

Heracles seems to also progress from the random violence of a brute to a productive force that aids the building of civilization. For example, he washes the Augean stables, bringing order and civilized cleanliness; he rids the world of such monsters and bandits as the Hydra, the Ladon and Nessus. Yet he is *not* civilized. He is the force that could bring civilized culture, but remains wild, unrestrained and murderous. Civilization often accidentally arises from such blind ambition as Heracles has; and when it does, the force, unless rigidly controlled, perhaps by law (as with police), must be banished. So Heracles wanders, banished again and again for his rages.

Heracles is compulsively violent. The list of arbitrary murders and slaughters is lengthy, and it becomes clear he remains a brute without self-control. All he enjoys are these destructive victories, and he seems to take no pleasure in life. He is driven--by himself and his stepmother Hera--to achieve glory, which means conquest and overcoming obstacles. He cannot tolerate being slighted or defeated: thus his anger at the Moliones (the twins), his strange, violent outbursts against his teachers and friends and family. A chronic laborer, he takes no time or interest in his achievements after they are completed.

There was a shrine in Greece dedicated to "Heracles the Hater of Women." From the beginning of his life Heracles is seen in antagonistic relationships with women: Hera hates him and defeats her envoys, the two snakes; he wounds her as she suckles him and deepens her anger and jealously; Zeus lavishes honors on his son and Hera resents it; Heracles' troubles derive from Hera's choice of Eurystheus--a weak, vindictive and avaricious king who insults, humiliates, and takes advantage of Heracles. She, his stepmother, drives him mad, and in his violent fit, he destroys the other mother figure in the myth, his wife, Princess Magaera. In a word, Hera despises him. Yet he brings glory to her name--literally and figuratively. He is, by the way, frequently helped by Athena in his labors--she is responsible for craftily convincing Hera to nurse the baby, thus immortalizing him. Deianeira resembles Athena in interests and form.

Heracles can be seen as a sufferer, a tragic figure forced to sacrifice all he loves for the sake of others in the tradition of Prometheus. He may, however, unlike Prometheus, be seen as stupidly brutish, dumb but strong; hot-tempered, unthinking, and deserving his fate for his appetites. Finally, he is boastful, narcissistic, misogynous, athletic, leery of involvement, quarrelsome and glory-seeking. One commentator has pointed out that Heracles exhibits all the characteristics of modern, preadolescent boys. The apotheosis of Heracles symbolizes his split personality. His immortal part in Olympus opposes hunters of helpless creatures, is nonviolent except to advocate eliminating wolves, lions and other harmful wild beasts. Yet his mortal spirit in Hades is still violent, swinging a club or brandishing a spear, decorated with scenes of slaughter.

Heracles stands as one of the most popular culture-heroes the Greeks had. There are more stories of Heracles than any other Greek mythological (or historical) character. His ambivalent relationships with his mother, his anger, industry and glory, all seemed to attract the Western imagination.

REFLECTIVE QUESTIONS

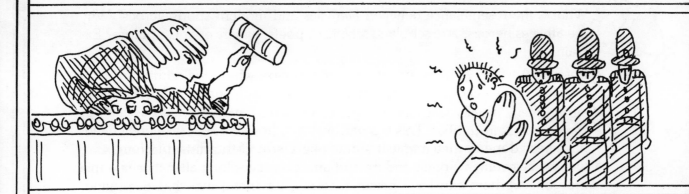

1. Heracles committed a great many violent acts and hurt many people throughout his career. He was almost always forgiven by people with intelligence or those in high places. Ordinary citizens would have been severely punished for doing the same things. Why are some people like Heracles less accountable in our society than others? Is everyone equal before the law?

    Possible Answer--In the case of Heracles, everyone feared his angry outbursts and strength so no one dared punish him. He has power--physical power--and power often seems to grant immunity from prosecution because people are often awed and/or afraid of it. In theory, everyone is equal before the law, but in practice it is not always so. Money may buy one out of trouble; a well-known name may gain favors. Like Heracles, special favors are granted to people who have power, political or social influence, money or a prestigious family name. It is conceivable that those who administer the law may bestow preferential treatment on such people.

2. "Might makes right." What does that statement mean and what is your opinion of it?

    Possible Answer--The statement means that no one will question the strongest, or that victory decides what is right. Thus, the winners of wars dictate to losers what they consider wrongs done in the course of the conflict. The murder of a single person, if the killer is powerful, might be justified by the criminal and go unchallenged. In modern legal cases, law breakers with much money can afford dazzling defenses and often rationalize their crimes or escape punishment. So Heracles determines what is right and wrong by virtue of his massive strength and high social position as the son of Zeus.

3.	What is the resemblance between Heracles and modern sports heroes? Why are athletes heroes? Are scholars, scientists, poets, writers or artists heroes? Explain.

Possible Answer--A hero (or heroine) is a person whom we admire for their nobility, great deeds or exceptional qualities. Traditionally, this has meant strong men, usually warriors or competitors who have won high acclaim by their prowess in combat. This is a narrow view, however, because great deeds have been done by men *and* women, thinkers, scientists, artists, teachers, etc., whose achievements often endure and affect our lives long after those people are gone. A hero can be a personal relative or friend who has been kind, helpful or just present when needed. Heracles resembles the athlete in physical stature and competitive drive. Athletes become heroes because they embody what the culture values, in this case, strength, victory, competitiveness, glory, fame and individuality. It is clear that writers, poets, etc., are usually not culture heroes (at least in the West). The discussion here should focus on the relative values placed on violent, competitive activities and more passive, intellectual ones. This should not obscure the idea of combining the two, presumably the Greek ideal and ours. It would seem that the *combination* of intellectual and athletic qualities occurs infrequently.

4.	Heracles is always sorry for his destructive acts. He apologizes and is willing to put himself at the service of others to pay for his crimes. When a person does something harmful, or habitually brings grief to others, what does an apology do? Are apologies always enough to offset the harm done?

Possible Answer--"Apology" in Greek means "defense." So an apology may be considered a defense against accusation. In classical Greece it was rarely so easy to assuage one's conscience or get off the hook with an "apology" because defense was difficult. But the idea of saying one is sorry has carried over to modern definitions. Often an apology helps no one but the offender when it clears the conscience. If, as in the case of Heracles, a person offers to do more than apologize, it sometimes does offset the hurt, but not always. Heracles, for example, is willing to serve, yet this is no real hardship for him and never brings back the lives of those he has slain.

5.	Can small people be giants and large people be dwarves? What is a deeper meaning of strength in humans beyond physical strength?

Possible Answer--The word giant is often used as a figure of speech to denote qualities of greatness which have nothing to do with size: giant of intellect, of goodness, of spiritual strength, etc. Conversely, when we speak of someone being "small," it may have nothing to do with size but rather is a description of a pinched, mean, and ungenerous spirit, a narrow view of life, and a selfish attitude toward others.

FOLLOW-UP ACTIVITIES

1. Heracles encountered Atlas, a powerful Titan being punished on the far western margin of the horizon where he stood holding the world on his shoulders for centuries. The picture of Atlas and his burden is familiar in commercials which suggest a powerful feat. Make a partnership arrangement between Atlas and Heracles in which they enter into a business. Will they sell goods or services? Describe their enterprise in detail, complete with advertising, a business name and logo.

2. Heracles had twelve labors to perform in order to do penance for his crimes. Now! You think up the "13th Labor of Heracles." Describe in writing the job to be done and the reason the task is important.

3. Like Heracles we are often ruled by emotion. We may say or do something we regret very much afterwards. Write a brief account of such an experience in your life entitled, "If I Could Do It Again," or "If I Had a Second Chance."

4. Imagine Heracles as a participating athlete in a sporting event--baseball, football, basketball, hockey, tennis, etc. You are a sports writer for the local paper and have been assigned by your editor to cover the event. Write your sports story of this astonishing afternoon for the morning edition of *The Herald*. Read the sports section of your paper for a sense of style and the use of colorful and hard-hitting verbs and adjectives.

5. What is the name for a bound collection of maps in book form? (An atlas.) Why does it have that name? Look through an atlas very carefully and make a list of the different kinds of information it provides the reader. Find your own city or town in the index and record some interesting information about it.

ROLE PLAY

Statement: The story of Heracles raises the issue of the admiration given heroic figures for their physical strength without any consideration of intelligence, responsibility, kindness, self-control, or other qualities.

The Scene: A committee of students in school is trying to make a decision. They are to select a student for a school award for special merit. This person is to represent the school in a large state-wide conference, as the most exemplary student of the year.

Characters:

Josh: Wants to select the school's outstanding athlete, Harry Eckles. His most significant contribution has always been his incredible performance on the tennis court. He has never been too bright, but the community adores him.

Amy: Wants to select the school's outstanding scholar, Kathy Lenter, whose intelligence and brilliance has been an inspiration to a great many students.

Susan: Believes that the school should award the person who best represents the values of the school and community. She agrees that Kathy, the bright student, would be a good choice but is afraid her brains may put people off. She wants a candidate who has both athletic prowess and is very smart.

Eric: Is in favor of a candidate whose name is Joe Goodfellow. He has none of the qualities of the other candidates. He is not good looking, he is not athletic, and he is not an exceptional scholar, but he *is* a person who cares sincerely about the general welfare of the school and others in the community. Everyone loves him and goes to him to discuss problems because he really listens. He is empathetic, sympathetic, and a supportive person who knows how to make people feel good about themselves.

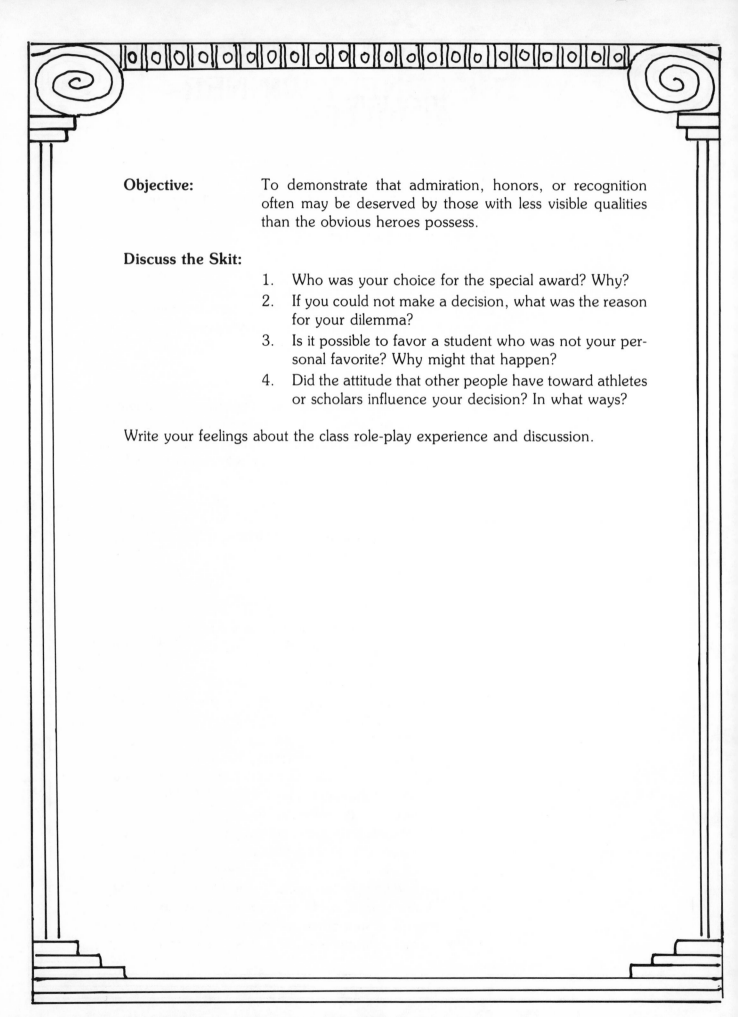

Objective: To demonstrate that admiration, honors, or recognition often may be deserved by those with less visible qualities than the obvious heroes possess.

Discuss the Skit:

1. Who was your choice for the special award? Why?
2. If you could not make a decision, what was the reason for your dilemma?
3. Is it possible to favor a student who was not your personal favorite? Why might that happen?
4. Did the attitude that other people have toward athletes or scholars influence your decision? In what ways?

Write your feelings about the class role-play experience and discussion.

XI. THE LONELY WINNER--ACHILLES

XI. THE LONELY WINNER--ACHILLES

CAST OF CHARACTERS

ACHILLES (uh KILL eez):	Greatest Greek warrior
THETIS (THEE tus):	A sea goddess, mother of Achilles
PELEUS (PEA lee us):	King of Phthia, brave and great warrior, favorite of Zeus and father of Achilles
ERIS (AIR is):	Goddess of discord
PATROCLUS (pa TRO clus):	Achilles' closest and dearest friend, a brave warrior
AGAMEMNON (ag uh MEM non):	King of Argos, leader of the collective Greek forces at Troy
HECTOR (HEK tor):	Bravest Trojan warrior, son of Priam
PRIAM (PRY am):	King of Troy
CHRYSEIS (cry SEE us):	Priestess of Apollo, taken as a prize by Agamemnon
BRISEIS (bry SEE us):	Beautiful woman taken as a prize by Achilles
ODYSSEUS (oh DIS ee us):	Most intelligent and persuasive of the Greeks

Thetis, a sea goddess, was a most graceful and desirable creature with emerald green eyes the color of the waves and flaxen ringlets entwined with the exotic flora of the ocean. At one time both Poseidon and Zeus wanted to marry her but were frightened off by a prophecy they knew would come to pass. The chilling prediction was that a son born to Thetis would be greater by far than his father. The gods, quite clearly, took no pleasure in being bested by mortals, by other gods, or by their own children least of all. Since it was unwise to take her for his own, Zeus, in his infinite wisdom, decided that she must marry a mortal man. Thetis then, against her will, was given in marriage to the splendid King Peleus, who was a great warrior and a favorite hero of his time. Thetis was wretchedly unhappy, as could be expected, since she was not consulted in this transaction which traded off her life at the whim of Zeus.

The wedding festivities were magnificent and everyone of importance, gods and mortals alike, were invited to this majestic triumph of the social scene--everyone that is except Eris, the goddess of discord who spent her days creating blood feuds, arguments, and hatred wherever she could.

It was because of Eris's anger over this social slight that the seeds of the ghastly Trojan War were planted on that very day when Thetis and Peleus were united as man and wife. Not only did the wedding produce the war, it produced, too, Achilles, the son of Thetis and Peleus. This young hero would finally end that terrible conflict and be responsible at the same time for the total annihilation of that once magnificent city, Troy.

Because she had been forced to marry a mortal, the union of Thetis and Peleus was an unhappy one. Thetis believed that the only valuable part of her marriage was her son in whom she placed the highest hopes. She wanted to make certain that her precious child Achilles would live forever. With that goal in mind, she took him on a journey to the river Styx. The magic river coursed through the wilds of southern Greece where it raced over a sheer precipice and dropped soundlessly into the sombre darkness of Hades, the land of the dead. Here Thetis bathed the naked infant in the magic rushing waters to assure him of everlasting life. She held fast to his heel as she immersed him in the greatest, most sacred black river of Tartarus. But as she dipped and washed him, her husband Peleus came upon her and thought she was drowning his son. He had been suspicious of her actions as she prepared for the journey and mistakenly assumed that her resentment for him would be vented upon his son. Peleus shrieked in horror and broke the spell before Thetis could complete the ritual. Thus, this untimely interruption stopped the ceremony before its purpose was fully realized. Achilles had been made immortal everywhere except on his heel, where his mother had held him tightly with encircled fingers, and the water had not yet touched. It was the only vulnerable, weak, mortal place on his entire body, and because of it, he knew as a young boy that he would not live forever.

His mother Thetis told him that he alone could make a life choice for himself: he could have a long, quiet existence with good health, children, and a home--serene and content; or he could have a short, brilliant, and glorious life as a warrior to be remembered forever. Achilles chose the short life. He would make himself famous, he said, and his mother, too! Thetis was pleased. He would fight harder, run faster, wield weapons of war with stunning grace, and make men quake on the field of battle. He would make frightened sheep of all other mortals, and he would cheat death by making a name for himself that would live forever--long after he was gone. Thetis would get recognition through his deeds because all men would know that her contribution to the world had been her son. Thetis aspired to live in the shadow of her son's greatness, for no woman in ancient Greece, not even a goddess, could ever claim glory in her own right.

His ambition was fully realized for he knew everyone was powerless to hurt him. His skin was like a tough hide--he was a frightening adversary, and his mere presence in a battle terrified the enemy so desperately that they would be rendered helpless and refuse to fight. Thetis, in her way, had indeed achieved her ambition for her son. The fulfillment of Achilles' destiny was to be played out at last in the ten-year Trojan War at the expense of thousands of human beings--a cost too staggering to contemplate.

In the ninth year of the Trojan War, Achilles quarreled with his commander, King Agamemnon, over a matter of pride. Each of them had been given a captive maiden from a neighboring city they had sacked. The women were prizes of honor and indicated how prominently each warrior had figured in the violence. Chryseis, tall with flaming red hair, was for Agamemnon and the petite raven-haired Briseis for Achilles. When Chryseis was presented to Agamemnon, it was revealed that she was the daughter of a priest of Apollo. The seizure of such a holy gift was forbidden by Apollo, and so the Greek camp was duly punished as the god brought a miserable devastating plague upon the men. Achilles persuaded the other Greek leaders to force Agamemnon to give Chryseis, his prize of war, in order to appease the sun god Apollo. But Agamemnon was angry and humiliated. He insisted petulantly that now Achilles must give up his prize, the maiden Briseis. Both men were blinded by their pride and position. Achilles was forced to give in to his commander-in-chief, but not without anger, for he stormed off and determinedly refused to fight in the war any longer. Like a little boy deprived of his belongings, he went directly to his mother, Thetis, raging with fury and frustration, weeping that he was being robbed of his rightful glory. His mother, as always, set things right as she appealed to Zeus, who had promised fame everlasting to her son.

Without Achilles, their strongest warrior, the Greeks began to lose even more badly, but he was determined to make his friends and allies plead with him to save them. This was how he would humiliate and humble Agamemnon. Hundreds of men died needlessly day after day. Odysseus, the wily one, tried to persuade Achilles--but he stubbornly refused. All the warriors tried to bribe him--but he stood fast, sullen and insulted, sulking in his tent and waiting until they had all but lost so he alone would receive credit for conquering Troy. His teachers, elders, friends, all implored him but could not lure him back. He constantly reminded them of his past, of his fate, and of his inescapable future. Finally, his dearest boyhood friend, Patroclus, whom Achilles loved more than any other person, could stand the slaughter of their compatriots no more. He persuaded Achilles to give him his armor whose very appearance would deceive and terrify the Trojans into retreat, thereby giving the Greeks time to gather their forces. It worked for only a short while until Hector, the great defender of Troy, struck down the valiant Patroclus. When the word of Patroclus' death reached Achilles, he was filled with remorse. He fell weeping to the ground at the loss of his childhood friend. He was disconsolate and out of control, moaning that he was responsible for the tragedy. His mother heard his grieving and came to him. "You wanted to bring the Greek army to the humbling edge of defeat and you have done so." Achilles, overcome with misery, made his decision. Now was the time. He made his peace with Agamemnon and then returned to the war to avenge the death of his beloved friend. The great hero was utterly alone now, responsible for the deaths of his friends and enemies alike. He knew his fate and went to meet it: he would kill Hector, the bravest Trojan of them all, and die soon after.

At first Hector fled from Achilles, fully aware of his end should he fight this man. But Athena disguised herself as Hector's chariot driver and convinced him he could kill Achilles. Too late Hector realized the trick of the goddess (who loved Achilles like a sister) and he was enticed into the greatest single combat in all history. Their swords rang out, great shields locked together. The weapons of death refracted prisms of light between the sweaty, muscled warriors, and all other fighting ceased as if everyone knew the fate of both armies was to be decided by these two lion hearts. Finally, Achilles' spear found its murderous mark as he drove the thin, keen blade through Hector's throat. He watched as each pulse beat emptied out the life blood of his valiant enemy in rhythmic waste upon the sand. Achilles was the victor! Still crazed with fury, he refused to give the body of Hector to the family for a proper burial and the ritual to which all men were entitled. Instead, he committed a ghastly deed. He tied the feet of the body of Hector with a rope which he fastened to his chariot, and to the horror of all, he defiled the dead man, driving his horses hard and pulling his dead burden round and round through the foul dirt of the battlefield for all Troy to see. Over the distraught moaning and lamentation, the old father of Hector, King Priam, approached Achilles and beseeched the warrior to give up the body of his son for burial-- out of respect for the laws of gods and traditions of men. Then, in an act of mortifying and crushing humbleness, the old man, Priam, fell to his knees and kissed the hands of the man who murdered his son while he pleaded with Achilles to relinquish the body.

Troy wept; and Achilles, too, wept for his lost friend Patroclus, for old Priam, for his own father, Peleus, whom he would never see again, and for himself. Together they cried, this old man and this doomed young one, lonely and lost in their mourning.

Soon after the funeral of Hector, Paris, guided by the hand of Apollo, shot an arrow during the continuing, dreary battle and hit Achilles in the heel. The arrow tore the tendon severing the band of tissue on the single and only mortal spot on his body. Achilles died, knowing his name would live forever, but sad that he would never see his home again, never be a father to children, and sorry, finally, that he had chosen a short life of glory. He was grieved, too, in those last moments, that Priam had lost a great son and would now lose his city and all of its inhabitants. Achilles, the most luminous of warriors, wondered, in the end, whether wars had any meaning.

From the myth of the death of Achilles comes the expression "Achilles' heel," which describes a person's particular weakness or vulnerable spot. It is this very weakness of which both friends and enemies may know about and some day take advantage.

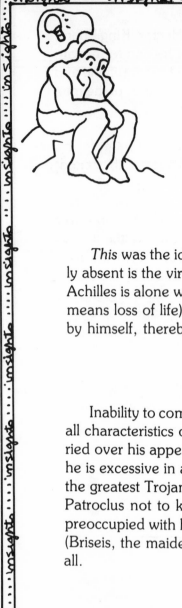

INSIGHTS FOR THE TEACHER

Achilles became the archetypal hero for the Greeks. He is strong, brave, determined, glorious, and faces his fate with little remorse, or at least chooses his own life-style. He controls his own fate as much as any mortal can. Courageous and mighty, Achilles sought to achieve glory through victory, foresaking a long, dull, mediocre life with family at home.

This was the ideal, the model for Greek children and adults alike. What is conspicuously absent is the virtue of cooperation, of "team spirit," of love of family, hearth and home. Achilles is alone with his glory; he pouts at any insult; he prays that all the Greeks lose (this means loss of life) so that his importance is acknowledged; he fantasizes conquering Troy by himself, thereby attaining *all* the glory.

Inability to compromise, intolerance, fear of loss of self-esteem, and dreams of glory are all characteristics of a narcissistic personality, someone excessively self-centered and worried over his appearance and reputation. He craves the envy of his former comrades, and he is excessive in all that he does--even mistreating Hector's body. The murder of Hector, the greatest Trojan, can only be accomplished by the greatest Greek. Thus Achilles warns Patroclus not to kill Hector lest he usurp Achilles' fame. Achilles seems single-mindedly preoccupied with his own valor and reputation. He has no friends (save Patroclus), no love (Briseis, the maiden, is his "prize"), no sense of loyalty to anyone but himself. Winning is all.

All this changes as Achilles confronts Hector's father, Priam. Surprisingly, Achilles shows compassion, mercy and sympathy. Or so it seems. It is the thought of his own father and his own death, however, that touches off his uncharacteristic caring. In short, this may be yet another narcissistic expression--the sympathetic wound to Achilles' own immortality. It is not sorrow or remorse for his murder of Hector or the death of Patroclus that makes Achilles weep with the old man, but the recognition that he, too, will die soon. In *The Odyssey*, Odysseus finds Achilles in the underworld and he (Achilles) laments his choice of a short life. Like Prometheus or Heracles, Achilles embodies the lonely striver; driven to compete or become Number One, he rejects or loses friends, family, and love in order to reach his goal. In the end, he is a tragic hero only because he abandons human beings, and ultimately his alienation makes him not the winner of the Trojan War, but the loser of his humanity.

REFLECTIVE QUESTIONS

1. Why is it so hard to win with a person like Achilles on your side even though he's so great?

   Possible Answer--Although he seems to fight for the team, personal glory means more to Achilles than the safety or victory of his comrades. He hates to lose and accuses others of mistakes and weaknesses, thereby causing tension among the ranks. Driven by ambition, he is willing to expose himself to physical danger and perhaps put others in jeopardy. The fact that he is a "mama's boy" and rushes to her with his distress does not suggest maturity or generate confidence among the others. When the leading hero is aloof, and contemptuous, immature and undependable, the morale of the team will be severely undermined.

2. Why do so many people let others get away with bad behavior?

   Possible Answer--It is often the case that, although some actions are seen as bad or damaging, no one dares oppose the person who possesses power or authority (see Heracles). Some may not perceive arrogance as offensive or improper, but may wish they had the status or power to behave the same way (the victim identifying with the aggressor). Just as no one stops Achilles from desecrating the body of Hector, for example, so in modern times people frequently refuse to become involved to stop an unethical act. Nor will they speak out or take more direct action.

3. How do we feel when someone tries to belittle us or make us insignificant or unimportant? This may be an experience which is our first encounter with the difference between physical and emotional hurt.

Possible Answer--This question is subject to personal interpretation with some common themes. One may feel that the rest of the world knows about our weaknesses, as we are exposed or diminished. Such personal confrontations may cause one to feel vulnerable or open to attack. Or perhaps one feels humiliated and a target for further assault. People often become conscious that deep inside they have secret fears and worries about self-image that must be defended at all costs. One may also feel bewildered by the extent of psychological wounds, puzzled at not understanding the experience intellectually while feeling it emotionally.

4. Why is Achilles called the "Lonely Winner" in this story? Are there such people in modern times?

    Possible Answer--In the eyes of the crowd, Achilles is the victor, the winner. But, in order to achieve this status, he has let no other human considerations stand in his way. He has used people and events for the single-minded purpose of coming out on top. For him, the end justifies the means by which he achieved glory. Inevitably he destroyed all warmth, love and human ties along the way. Like many successful men, for the sake of winning and glory, he has chosen to give up family, home and community. He left behind a great name, but no descendants, no friends and no fond memories because he was not a beloved comrade.

5. What are some of the bad things created by competition? Some of the good things?

    Possible Answer--Each person stands alone in the desire to win or come out ahead. Therefore, everyone else may be perceived as an enemy, trying for the same prize, whatever it may be. There is envy, jealousy and bad feeling generated between winners and losers, or between competitors who are even on the same side. Competition may not be good for personal relationships because it can force people to work against each other for personal success. The notion of cooperation for the good of the group becomes a problem because the glory of the individual is more important than the greater good. Such an atmosphere can create anxiety in children and adults alike. Some regard competition as a way of inspiring excellence. Each person strives to do the very best to come out ahead, and the system of rewards provides ample incentive for better performance and productivity. The quality of the community might then be enhanced with everyone striving hard to be successful and increasing production for the benefit of the society. Everyone is energized and highly motivated, and competition is envisioned as conducive to innovation and vitality.

FOLLOW-UP ACTIVITIES

1. Like Superman, but not as endearing, Achilles was almost impossible to defeat. Develop a comic strip or a movie script which captures the incredible event when "Achilles meets ___" (insert any superhero). Remember that Achilles and his super opponent have much in common: they are both blessed with extraordinary power and strength (Achilles has a hide that is stronger than armor and even the gods are afraid to face him in battle). Will this be a friendly, interesting meeting or will it be hostile?

2. Achilles was brought down as a warrior when he was shot in his heel--his only vulnerable spot. From this comes the popular figure of speech which refers to a person's weakest point as an "Achilles' Heel." Working with a partner, how many figures of speech can you list that use parts of the body for emphasis or effect? Some examples: "He's the apple of my *eye*"; "I broke my *neck* to be on time!"; "You're breaking my *heart.*"

3. Many people with genuine handicaps (handicappers) have neither magic nor mythic powers to help them through life as Achilles did. We have all read about great people who have, by themselves, overcome physical handicaps and achieved a different kind of heroism because of their accomplishments. Research this topic with the help of your librarian. Look in bibliographies under HANDICAPS. Find a story on this topic which you think is exceptional and share it with the class.

4. Even in ancient times the ritual of marriage was observed as in the very elaborate wedding of Achilles' parents, Thetis and Peleus. Eris, the goddess of discord, was furious because she was not invited and did not get over these hard feelings easily. This is still true today with the problem of party invitations and slighted friends or relatives. Drawing from family or personal experience, write a fictional modern version about the one who wasn't invited-- Aunt Emma, Uncle Harry, Cousin Cedrik, or *you.*

5. Make a list or a chart of the Greek heroes (Heracles, Narcissus, Phaethon, Prometheus, etc.). Use Achilles as the first personality. List their qualities to see which traits they have in common. Are there any traits they all share? Can you think of modern heroes or personalities who share these qualities (good and bad)? Add them to your list.

ROLE PLAY

Statement: The story of Achilles deals with the need for social acclaim and public recognition at all costs. Friends, relationships and every other consideration are secondary.

The Scene: The locker room of Athens High before the last play-off game of the soccer tournament. It is the critical game against perennial rival Sparta High.

Characters:

Coach Augie Mennon: Is not feeling well and can't make the important game. He wants Al, the team's star forward, to take his place as coach for the evening and not play in this big game. Al is the only one on the team who can fill in and do this really important job for everyone's sake!

Al Chilles: He is a big star and he doesn't want to act as coach at this important point in his career. All the sports editors have predicted that this evening has to be Al's stellar performance. He knows it's true and feels it in his bones. His fans are waiting to see him on the field. He really rebels and won't participate in the game in any capacity. He is firm in his refusal.

Assorted Team Members:
Pat, Les, Perry, etc. Some try to convince Al that they need him; others argue among themselves about what position he should play (coach or forward); some plead with him--regardless of which position, he's needed *somewhere*; some get angry with his stubbornness.

Objective: To explore the dilemma of sacrifice for the team versus achievement of personal glory.

Discuss the Skit: Teacher's choice (Depending upon the drama which unfolds, other questions may be more relevant.)

1. Is it fair or unfair to expect that Al should give up his big chance just because the team needs him? Why?

2. Considering what was said today, how do Al's teammates *really* feel about him?

3. How could the wisdom of an older person have saved this situation? What kinds of things might that person have said?

4. Would Al rather have friends or prizes? How do you know? Is this attitude right or wrong?

5. Which is more important, the individual or the team? Support your opinion with reasons.

Write your feelings about the class role-play experience and discussion.

XII. THE TROJAN WAR

XII. HISTORY AND MYTH COME TOGETHER-- THE TROJAN WAR

CAST OF CHARACTERS

PARIS (PAIR us): Son of King Priam of Troy

ACHILLES (uh KILL eez): The greatest Greek warrior

HELEN (HEL un): Queen of Sparta, wife of Menelaus, most beautiful mortal woman in the world

MENELAUS (men uh LAY us): King of Sparta, brother of Agamemnon

AGAMEMNON (ag uh MEM non): King of Argos, organizer of the Greek expedition against Troy

ODYSSEUS (oh DIS ee us): King of Ithaca, cleverest and most cunning of the Greek leaders, favorite of Athena because of his intelligence and skill

LAOCOON (lay OCK oh on): Son of Priam, priest who warned against the Trojan Horse

CASSANDRA (ka SAN dra): Daughter of Priam, priestess of Apollo; she could foretell the future but was never believed

HECTOR (HEK tor): Son of Priam, the most valiant and strongest warrior of Troy

The story of the Trojan and Achilles' destiny are bound together. Both begin at the same moment--the life and death of one man, Achilles, and of one city, Troy, are inseparable. Stepping back in history, we recall that the only one not invited to the regal marriage ceremony of Achilles' mother, Thetis, and his father, Peleus, was Eris, the goddess of discord. Despised and feared by all, she was angry beyond forgiving as she listened to the laughter and gaiety of the celebrants. Fomenting trouble was her glorious specialty and she plotted her intricate revenge savagely. Determined to make them all regret this slight, she made a swift trip to Hephaestus, the smith god, and asked him to design a golden apple of compelling beauty. It was to be engraved with the simple message, "To The Fairest." As soon as this was done, she swooped down to the elegant party and placed this Apple of Discord on a table in front of the three goddesses--Athena, Hera and Aphrodite. A hush fell. Everything stopped at that moment in dreaded expectation. The talking died away-- the festivities halted--the laughter ceased as the cunning evil of the plan began to weave its sinister effect. Attention was riveted on the table of honor when each of the three goddesses at once reached for the apple--each perceiving herself as the fairest and claiming the coveted prize. The quarrel began! Who was the fairest? Who was the fairest? Who was the fairest?

No one who cared for his safety would dare answer the question and the goddesses were tireless in praise of their own beauty. The three hands clutched the apple in an unyielding iron grip. No one would let go. There was no way this argument could be permitted to continue, surely until the end of time. So Zeus in monumental exasperation decided to find a mediator, a mortal hero, whose honesty and integrity could be depended upon. He chose Paris, son of King Priam of Troy, a shepherd known as a judge among men. The level-headed Paris was to judge this heavenly beauty contest with infinite care trying earnestly to be fair and impartial. But then something unexpected happened as each goddess, feverish to win, began to bribe him with offers of gifts. His integrity began to weaken as, awestruck, he listened to these extravagant promises. Hera offered him great power over man; Athena offered him the benefits of wisdom; but, at the last, Aphrodite offered him the most irresistible gift of all. If he judged her to be the winner of this contest, she would grant him the present of the most beautiful woman in the world, whom all knew was Helen, Queen of Sparta. And so it was that Paris surrendered his honor and awarded Aphrodite, goddess of love, the prize of the golden apple. She would be acclaimed the fairest!

Now Aphrodite had no right to offer Helen as a prize, for this divine woman was already married to Menelaus, the King of Sparta. But such trivial considerations did not matter to gods and goddesses who were accustomed to doing whatever they pleased. That such a choice would hurt someone was never a serious consideration. For truly the effects of this act were to reverberate down through history.

Aphrodite quickly made arrangements for Helen to be shot by Eros with the arrow of love. Paris in expectation went directly to Sparta to steal Helen away. He was welcomed as a guest in the palace of King Menelaus who did not suspect the motives of the visitor. Paris wasted no time in capturing Helen away, for she was indeed the most exquisite woman his eyes had ever beheld. The love arrow had hit its mark and she went most willingly. She left her husband without hesitation and accompanied Paris on the romantic journey to Troy. The reception of the Trojan citizens was overwhelming as they greeted their beloved Paris and the most beautiful of all women, claiming her forevermore as Helen of Troy. She knew she belonged to them as they shouted praises to her comeliness.

Helen's husband Menelaus was not to take this outrage lightly. He raced to his older brother, King Agamemnon of Argos for help. Agamemnon, agreeing that Helen must be recovered, travelled all over Greece recruiting kings, princes and heroes as warriors to take part in this gigantic expedition against the greatest of cities, the wealthiest city in the world, Troy. The brothers, Menelaus and Agamemnon, for their part saw an opportunity to destroy the city and take its wealth; and their allies were willing to risk much for a share of the booty. Odysseus, Ajax, Diomedes, Nestor and many more warriors heartily joined the two monarchs in their lust for the spoils of war. The last thread was picked up in this long and fearful story when a prophet told Agamemnon that Troy would never be defeated unless Achilles the great warrior was with them. The Greeks set sail for Troy in a fleet of 1152 ships which is why Helen was known later in history as "The face that launched a thousand ships."* The war lasted ten interminable years as the Greek and Trojan armies clashed and washed the land in blood. The capricious gods watched and took sides, intervening to deepen the senseless misery of all.

The Greek armies lived off the surrounding countryside all that time. They attacked villages, islands and neighboring cities for miles around the walls of Troy, bringing havoc and death to peaceful communities of farmers, shepherds and townspeople. They stole food and riches and took women as slaves and prizes. Fighting Troy and risking their lives in battle seemed to be a small price to pay for all the plunder they were collecting. The people of Troy and those areas around that fateful city were made miserable by those long years of madness stretched by suffering hardship. Families were separated, children and old people were killed, starvation stalked the land, sickness and poverty came to a once healthy and prosperous people. And Troy fought for its life, led by Hector, bravest of Priam's fifty sons.

Hector's death at the hands of Achilles seemed to turn the tide against Troy. But Achilles died soon after, and the Greeks despaired of ever winning victory. It was only by cleverness and cunning that they defeated the endurance and bravery of the Trojans.

Shortly after Paris slew Achilles, the dispirited Greeks, weary and sick to the bone, pretended to leave for home. But crafty Odysseus, King of Ithaca, the wisest Greek strategist of the Trojan War, devised an incredibly ingenious plan. The Greeks left behind a strange, towering wooden horse, splashed with brilliant colors. Engraved on the shoulder was an inscription dedicating it as a gift to the Trojans in honor of their valor. It seemed to mean the Greeks had finally given up and gone home, resigned to defeat and humility. Puzzled but admiring, the Trojans pulled their prize into the gates of the city as they rejoiced with their apparent victory. They had defeated the Greeks, the largest and most powerful force ever amassed in one place, or so they thought. And this wooden memorial was to be a trophy of war--a prize that would tell the world of their triumph. Only one cautious voice, belonging to the priest Laocoon, cried out at first: "Beware of Greeks bearing gifts!" He was laughed at in the passion of the celebration--and who could blame the exhausted Trojans after so long and bitter a fight? Cassandra, a daughter of Priam and priestess of Apollo, also warned against the gift. But Cassandra was ignored, as always, for she was cursed by Apollo who had given her the ability to see into the future but made certain she would never ever be believed by anyone.

*Christopher Marlowe

As the exhausted citizens slept, late that night, Greek warriors climbed out of the deep belly of the hollow horse, swung open the gates of the city and let in the waiting hordes of soldiers who destroyed everything in their path. They sacked, murdered and burned the great city to the ground forever, leaving its magnificence in a pile of filth and rubble bathed in the blood of its inhabitants. The once proud metropolis was transformed into a graveyard, with bodies strewn everywhere amidst the ruins.

It was a tragic war. Many Greeks were slaughtered. All the great heroes either lost their own lives or saw their friends killed. While they were far away from home, their families pined for them and many of their parents and children died without ever seeing them again. All the Trojans were killed or enslaved--young men and old, women and children alike were butchered as the half-mad Greeks ran through the streets of Troy burning and looting. Agamemnon, the commander, returned home to Argos only to be murdered by his angry wife. Cassandra, who had become Agamemnon's slave and prize, was also killed. Odysseus was lost at sea and made to wander for another ten years and every single one of his brave men was killed. Many Greek heroes who survived finally met with some bitter and tragic end after the war. And what of Helen of Troy? She submissively returned to her husband Menelaus, King of Sparta--trailing her sodden gown through the desolation of a once majestic city.

Achilles, the strongest and most ferocious warrior of all time, who brought so much death and destruction, did not live to see the fall of Troy, but before he died, he asked, "What is the point of war?" He could not find nor was he given a satisfactory answer.

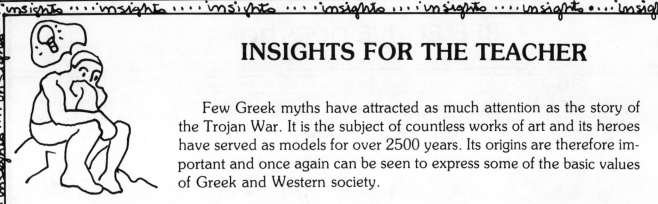

INSIGHTS FOR THE TEACHER

Few Greek myths have attracted as much attention as the story of the Trojan War. It is the subject of countless works of art and its heroes have served as models for over 2500 years. Its origins are therefore important and once again can be seen to express some of the basic values of Greek and Western society.

Troy was an ancient city in Asia Minor. Its wealth was legendary (and historical) and represented oriental opulence to the Greeks. The citadel overlooked the Hellespont, a key waterway between the Aegean and Black Seas. For these essentially economic reasons it was often attacked, destroyed and rebuilt. In short, there were several Trojan Wars and the Greek myth here joins with Greek history, condensing many events into one protracted one. Should there be questions about the reality of the war, a glance at the map ought to help. (Troy was in what is now modern Turkey.) As a political tale, then, Greek city-states looked back on the war as West vs. East, democracy (modified) vs. Oriental despotism, or even as independent, civilized states vs. a barbaric empire. Later, in the early 5th century B.C., the Persian Wars were seen as continuing sequels to the Trojan War.

The heart of the myth, however, is not political but social. Here is Zeus's fear of being bested by a son, just as his own father and grandfather had opposed their sons. To avoid the contest, he forcibly marries off Thetis to Peleus. Once again women are seen as threats, as objects to be bargained for, and as pawns. Eris, too, is representative of the Greek view of femininity, in this case jealousy and divisiveness. This theme is continued in the argument among the three goddesses. But the initial blameworthy character is devious Aphrodite. She seduces Paris, bribes him to give her the prize, no matter the consequences. And the results of her trickery are the slaughter of thousands of men, then women and children as Troy finally falls.

Homer, the main (but not the only) poet of the war, blames Paris for his lust, although Paris argues that one cannot turn down or insult a goddess. Subsequent authors (Aeschylus, Euripides, Sophocles) blame Helen--the arch-seductress and villainess. Hector, the great Trojan hero, defends hearth and home, weeps for his child and his wife, knowing the boy will be killed and the woman enslaved. These are foreign values to the Greeks and are more Oriental, perhaps. Surely the invaders do not seem in any hurry to get home--or if they do long for home, it is a secondary need; first comes victory.

Victory means booty, pride, a name, and that explains in part why all the Greeks participate. It would seem that Menelaus ought to have challenged Paris, his wife's abductor, by himself. (Strangely, this is never considered until the final year of the war and then Aphrodite saves Paris from death.) Since family and home are relatively unimportant, especially compared to pride and fame, all the Greeks are either eager to go to war or are shamed into it. That wives, children, parents will be left alone, some to die while waiting, others to fall prey to an array of disasters, matters very little. Here, then, with the continuing theme of misogyny, are Greek values in all their glory.

REFLECTIVE QUESTIONS

1. The title of this section is "History and Myth Come Together--The Trojan War." If the Trojan War is mythical, then what does the title mean? How are make-believe wars and real wars alike? What do all wars have in common?

   Possible Answer--Wars, mythic and real, are among the great tragedies of humankind. Warfare destroys families when young men go off to fight, perhaps never to return. Women and children are left homeless and often suffer physically from the weapons of war, even though they are not combat soldiers. The land is scorched, cities are devastated, and the men who fight face death and injury, the effects of which they may have to endure to the end of their lives. All war deforms the souls of human beings and leaves scars which disfigure although they may not be seen. Real wars often become mythical over a period of time as they are glorified, dramatized, and romanticized. Wars are transformed by movies, by books, and by memory and the popular culture in ways that reduce and conceal their horror. The Trojan War was an historical event--a murderous conflict that destroyed a civilization. It became a myth with the addition of gods and goddesses, embroidered by the creative imaginations of poets like Homer.

2. Who suffers from war? What are the losses?

   Possible Answer--Let the class members respond from different levels of sophistication in their own ways. Losers and winners both suffer. If the war is fought in one's own country, the physical displacement and harm can be irreparable. Soldiers from both sides who return from war may suffer physical and/or psychological damage because of what they have seen or done. War, in the end, brings destruction to people and civilization by threatening to reduce human beings to animals (dehumanizing them).

3. Why do men wage wars? What alternatives are there to solving problems?

    Possible Answer--Wars may be fought for a variety of reasons, among them territory, profit, prestige, glory, resources, racism, freedom, honor, defense, pride, fear. It is often the case that the reasons given by participants in a war are not the *real* motives. (For example, in World War I all sides claimed they were fighting a defensive war; the Spanish American War was presumably fought because of provocation but in fact had other, more devious motives; and the Trojan War itself was fought for reasons that are not always clear. Troy may have held Helen, but it also held untold riches and a strategic position that would prove profitable to whoever controlled it.) Some obvious alternatives to combat are talking, compromise, mediation, and first and last, peace.

4. There were several women involved in the Trojan War. How is the Greek attitude toward women characterized in the story? Can you think of women in other myths who share similar traits?

    Possible Answer--Eris, the goddess of discord is vengeful because she was not invited to the wedding of Peleus and Thetis and carries out a malicious plan. The goddesses Athena, Aphrodite and Hera are so excessively vain that they will offer any bribe to Paris to be honored as the most beautiful. Helen the Queen of Sparta willingly leaves home and goes with Paris for even greater glory as she is hailed as the most beautiful woman in the world by the Trojans. Thus, the women in this story conform to the stereotypes. They are vain, fickle, devious, dangerous, and bring only misery to men. Women in other myths who share these traits are Echo, Athena, Pandora....

5. Who do you think was responsible for the Trojan War?

    Possible Answer--Trying to place the blame for the Trojan War ensnares us in a web whose interlocking threads lead into a complicated network of factors, characters, and motives impossible to untangle. The key to the question is the Greek word "eris" which is "discord." Eris is responsible for the war. But who or what causes discord? Some possibilities (after the goddess Eris): Zeus, with his cavalier attitude about Thetis, forcing the wedding upon an unwilling woman, may be perceived as the originator of the war; the three goddesses of the contest are each jealous and ambitious, and they begin the hostilities; Paris succumbs to Aphrodite's bribe; Agamemnon sees a chance to gain glory and riches while recovering family pride; Helen traditionally has been seen as the fickle source of the war, abandoning husband and home for a fling; she, however, fell into this role as a pawn of scheming Aphrodite. The responsibility lies in the circumstances and the feelings of the players. An inescapable situation arises because of social and individual attitudes of jealousy, envy, ambition, greed and passion.

FOLLOW-UP ACTIVITIES

1. Throughout history, in every country, in every war there has been a call to arms in the form of recruitment posters. The ancient Greeks needed new men to replace fallen warriors. In modern times we recall signs which say, "Uncle Sam Needs You," or "Join the Navy and See the World." At the same time there are also antiwar posters which make strong statements such as, "Make Love not War!" or "What if Somebody Made a War and Nobody Came?" Design a recruitment poster or an antiwar poster. Create a catchy slogan and an illustration as an attention getter. Use an ancient or modern theme for buttons, bumper stickers or T-shirts.

2. Divide the class into groups and write persuasive editorials either for or against the Trojan War. Read the editorial pages of your local newspaper in order to copy the style. Follow up with letters to the editor expressing your approval or disapproval.

3. Find a bibliography of war books for children or young adults with the help of your librarian. Select one or more of these stories from any period in history--the Revolutionary War, Civil War, World War I or II, the Korean War or the Vietnam War. Try to interest your classmates in the experience of war from a young person's point of view as expressed by the character in the book. Present a story which made the strongest impression upon you.

4. Select a team of newspaper reporters to interview the leaders of the Trojan War. Everyone in the class may participate in whichever role he/she chooses. Compare notes and interviews by making oral news reports. Title your newspaper article with something catchy like: "Is Achilles Really a Heel?" or "Paris in the Spring" or "A Horse of a Different Color."

5. All through Greek mythology one reads of giving women to men as gifts. Pandora was a gift to Epimetheus, Princess Megaera a gift to Heracles, Briseis a gift to Achilles, Chryseis a gift to Agamemnon, and on and on, as one would give away personal property or slaves. In a democratic society the notion of humans as objects to sell or own runs counter to our notion of freedom. Can you imagine a gift catalogue designed to sell humans as presents? How would it read? Imagine yourself being sold as a workhorse, companion, clown, builder, nurse to young children, etc. Write out an ad with the details for a potential buyer.

6. To better understand the depth of the Trojan War, look up and explain what each of the following has to do with the Trojan War:
   a. Homer (the *first* poet of Western civilization; blind storyteller of the heroic events of the Trojan War).
   b. *The Illiad* (the "story of Ilium" which is Troy. *The Iliad* is Homer's classic account of the war. It was recited annually and is the origin of Western literature and values, reputed to be the first epic poem of the Western world.)
   c. *The Odyssey* (believed to be Homer's second work and is "the adventures of Odysseus" in his ten-year perilous journey homeward as he was punished by the gods after the Trojan War. Odysseus returned home, finally, with Athena's help.)

After your research, design a *mural* which illustrates the importance of these three.

TROJAN BROADCASTING COMPANY

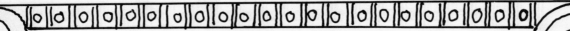

ROLE PLAY

Statement: The Trojan War raises the issue of inevitable tragic consequences of war, regardless of the justice or injustice of the cause.

The Scene: A TV talk show in the studio of the Trojan Broadcasting Company

Characters: (Whole class participation)

Moderator: Keeps control and respects each person's right to be heard within time limits. Introduces the problem and the reason for the panel discussion: "Good morning. This is TBC, presenting 'Hawks and Doves' for your listening pleasure. As you know, the matter of gravest concern for us today is the action of the country of Bellum which is holding ten of our citizens as hostages. This emergency calls for cool heads, strategies and discussion. We are here to ask the question, What do you suggest? The panelists will identify themselves and their occupations (politician, student, general, scientist, businessperson, concerned citizen, a survivor of a past war, etc.)."

Characters with Following Points of View: (More opinions can be added at the teacher's discretion.)

a. Eager to wage a war against Bellum to save the hostages, our national honor and our place in the world as a super power. We must protect our prestige.

b. In favor of negotiating with the Bellumites to release the hostages on any terms. Wants peace talks.

c. Opposed to war--expressing concern about the loss of lives and sacrificing thousands of civilians and soldiers.

d. Eager to wage war to show the Bellumites and other enemies, by example, that they cannot get away with such terrorist acts.

e. A scientific view, opposed to war, expressing concern about escalation and the implications of atomic warfare, the contamination of the entire world, atomic afterlife, and the destruction of the whole human race. Feels there can be no winners in this war. The Bellumites also have the atom bomb.

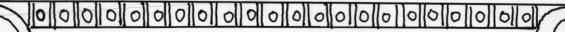

f.   Wants to ignore the whole thing. Regards the hostages as soldiers who are expendable. Refuses to give in to "blackmail." Feels this will show the Bellumites that their tactics will not pay off.

g.   In favor of a rescue mission.

h.   Opposed to the war as a war veteran.

i.   In favor of the war as a war hero.

j.   Horrified at the prospect of war--a mother who lost children in a past war.

Objective: To examine different perceptions of the issues and conflicting opinions in a democratic society. To present reasons for and against waging war in modern times.

Discuss the Skit:

1.   Sort out, as best you can, the reasons for and against this war as expressed by the characters.

2.   Whose reasons make the most sense? The least sense? Explain.

3.   How does age, experience or self-interest affect the opinions of the players?

4.   How would you evaluate the patriotism of the characters? Can people who consider themselves patriotic disagree on a course of action?

5.   What suggestions were made which would offer alternative solutions to war?

6.   If war were declared, who or what would you consider responsible? If this is difficult to decide, why is it difficult?

Write your feelings about the role-play experience and discussion.

FROM MYTHS TO ENGLISH

Here is a special starter list of English words which have their sources in Greek mythology. Many of these we recognize as terms we read, write or speak. Can you find more?*

ambrosia--from ambrosia, the food and drink of the gods

calliope--from Calliope, the muse of epic poetry

cereal--Roman name for Demeter was Ceres, goddess of harvest

chronology--from Kronos, father of Zeus

cloth--from Clotho, one of the fates who spins the thread of life

erotic--from Eros, the archer of love

hypnosis--from Hypnos, the god of sleep

misogyny--from "mis" meaning hatred and "gynos" meaning women

narcissistic--from Narcissus, the vain youth who fell in love with his own reflection

olympic--from Olympus, dwelling place of the gods of "Olympiad" meaning games dedicated to the gods

panic--from Pan, god of shepherds and goatherds

psychology--from Psyche, mortal wife of Eros

tantalize--from Tantalus, disobedient son of Zeus

Titanic--from Titans, the race of giants

Uranus the planet--from Uranus, King of the Sky

*See *Words from the Myths* by Isaac Asimov. © 1961, Houghton Mifflin.

ΕΙΝΑΙ ΕΛΛΗΝΙΚΑ ΓΙΑ ΜΕΝΑ

IT'S GREEK TO ME! A GUESSING GAME

Read the following statements and match the clues to the mythical Greek characters which they suggest. (Design your own guessing game to challenge your classmates.) Some statements may fit more than one character. Be able to prove your point from your reading.

1. Surprise Gift Box Company--When you care enough to give the best. (Pandora)
2. Work at the Macho Athletic Club--Only the strongest need apply. (Heracles or Achilles or Atlas)
3. Use Reflecto Dishwasher Detergent and see your face in your dishes. (Narcissus)
4. Flights leaving daily for anywhere under the sun! (Icarus or Phaethon)
5. Fool Mother Nature--use margarine, not real butter. (Demeter)
6. Hotshot handyman: will clean barns, offices and flooded basements. (Heracles)
7. I'm hardhearted because I eat stones. (Kronos)
8. I always hated liver anyway. (Prometheus)
9. She runs the Exquisite Knit Shop. (Athena or Arachne)
10. Forget the thermostat--it doesn't mean a thing here. (Hades)
11. He carries big troubles on his shoulders. He needs a soothing liniment. (Atlas)
12. He's selling gas stoves now for the Consumer Power Co. (Prometheus)
13. Talk him out of going into the archery business. (Achilles or Paris)
14. The post office hired him for special delivery letters. (Hermes)
15. With a voice like that, she doesn't need a microphone. (Echo)
16. The guy with the beard is our weatherman. He's always predicting thundershowers with lots of lightning. (Zeus)
17. She tells fortunes from tea leaves at the restaurant--but don't believe her! (Cassandra)
18. You can't collect bus fares like that anymore. You make all the customers gag. (Charon the Ferryman)
19. Do you sell dog leashes with three collars? (Cerberus)
20. Who said pet spiders don't have names? (Arachne)
21. Sometimes horsies aren't just cute toys. (Trojan Horse)
22. The neighbors were reporting this stench to the Sanitation Department. (Augean Stables)
23. This shirt is killing me. (Heracles)
24. I'm using snake oil to unknot my hair. (Medusa)
25. If you want a smart lawyer who wins cases, give him a call. (Apollo)

AFTERWORD

As we conclude this book, it may be helpful to evaluate some of the links between the past and the present that thoughtful study of Greek mythology might evoke. Just as sociologists today often disagree on the nature of American culture, historians also continue to dispute the nature of Greek culture. We have argued here that the two share fundamental and essential qualities. Modern society's frequent stereotyping of women, what feminists and discerning people have opposed for centuries, has its roots in Greek culture. Western family structures that assume women must raise children without paternal help began there. Social theorists have shown that such patterns produce frustrated people--mothers and children alike. Women tend to pour their hopes and ambitions into their children and treat them as vicarious extensions of themselves. Children, perhaps feeling the pressure of that burden, grow angry at mothers and then at women in general; they grow angry, too, at absent fathers who, in turn, intuitively fear their sons (and wives). All this produces vulnerable self-images, narcissism, high levels of perilous competition, and low levels of trust and love.

Most of these themes are in Greek myths. Thetis and Hera openly exhort their sons to bring them glory. Fathers like Zeus or Apollo, Agamemnon or Heracles, are rarely there to raise their children. The stereotypes of women are present in Pandora, Aphrodite, Helen, even in Gaea and Athena. And narcissistic children who worry about themselves and who are angry with parents can be seen in the stories of Zeus, Achilles, Phaethon, Heracles, Icarus, etc. These are serious and immediate problems, and they are more clearly highlighted in Greek myths than in our own culture's corresponding creations (movies, books, TV programs, etc.).

Finally, the Greeks virtually invented the genre of tragedy. Tragedy was more than a literary form to them, a play in which circumstances conspire to trap characters and make catastrophe inevitable. That was their view of life itself, as can be seen in epic poems of Homer, histories of Thucydides and Herodotus, philosophies of Plato and Aristotle. Life was a trap, with a disastrous fall lurking around each corner. Happiness was not a primary goal, but glory, victory, some form of achievement mattered most because life was bound to be tragic. From this premise the Greeks proceeded to reason that with the appropriate behavior one could produce deeds and products-- none of which guaranteed happiness, but *did* guarantee what was achievable: fame. These achievements and the prizes they carried were within human control--*that* much of fate could be manipulated.

The other aspect of tragedy that continually appears in the myths is the issue of responsibility. From Pandora or Prometheus to the Trojan War, a main theme is the victimization of human beings because of circumstances. Responsibility is always diffuse. Fate wins and fate, we recall, means death. This is--in spite of the play of gods and goddesses, monsters and fantastic heroes--quintessentially human. If this pessimistic view sounds unbearable to live with, it is responsible for much of what was great in Greek culture and in our own which is built upon those foundations.

What the Greeks have given us, too, are these myths. We see not only *their* culture in them, but ours and often ourselves. In a real sense, the heroes achieved, through these stories, the immortality they and historical Greeks sought. As we read about Heracles, Achilles and Athena, we keep them alive after 3000 years of the history of civilization.

PRONUNCIATION INDEX

Achilles (uh KILL eez)

Agamemnon (ag uh MEM non)

Alcmene (alk MEE nee)

Aphrodite (af ro DY tee)

Apollo (uh POL oh)

Arachne (uh RACK nee)

Ares (AIR eez)

Artemis (ART uh mis)

Athena (uh THEE nuh)

Atlas (AT lus)

Atropos (AT ro pos)

Briseis (bry SEE us)

Cassandra (ka SAN dra)

Cerberus (SIR ber us)

Charon (CARE un)

Chryseis (cry SEE us)

Clotho (CLO thoh)

Clymene (CLIME uh nee)

Clytemnestra (kly tum NESS truh)

Daedalus (DED uh lus)

Deianeira (dee uh NIE ruh)

Demeter (DEM uh ter)

Dionysus (die uh NI sus)

Echo (ECK oh)

Epimetheus (ep uh ME thee us)

Erinyes (AIR in eez)

Eris (AIR is)

Eros (AIR ose)

Eurystheus (you RIS thee us)

Gaea (JEE uh)

Hades (HAY deez)

Hecate (HEK uh tee)

Hector (HEK tor)

Hephaestus (huh FES tus)

Hera (HAIR uh)

Heracles (HAIR uh kleez)

Hermes (HER meez)

Icarus (ICK uh rus)

Iole (EYE oh lee)

Iphicles (IF uh kleez)

Kronos (KRO nus)

Lachesis (luh KEE sis)

Laocoon (lay OCK oh on)

Medusa (muh DOO zuh)

Megaera (muh JEE ruh)

Menelaus (men uh LAY us)

Metis (ME tis)

Minos (MY nos)

Minotaur (MIN uh tor)

Moirai (MOY rye)

Narcissus (nar SISS us)

Nemesis (NEM uh sis)

Nessus (NESS us)

Odysseus (oh DIS ee us)

Orestes (o RES teez)

Pandora (pan DOR uh)

Paris (PAIR us)

Patroclus (pa TRO clus)

Peleus (PEA lee us)

Persephone (per SEF uh nee)

Perseus (PER seus)

Phaethon (FAY e thon)

Poseidon (po SY dun)

Priam (PRY am)

Prometheus (pro ME thee us)

Rhea (REE uh)

Styx River (STICKS)

Theseus (THEE see us)

Thetis (THEE tus)

Uranus (you RAY nus)

Zeus (ZOOS)